Immersion and Participation in Punchdrunk's Theatrical Worlds

CARINA E. I. WESTLING

methuen | drama
LONDON • NEW YORK • OXFORD • NEW DELHI • SYDNEY

METHUEN DRAMA
Bloomsbury Publishing Plc
50 Bedford Square, London, WC1B 3DP, UK
1385 Broadway, New York, NY 10018, USA

BLOOMSBURY, METHUEN DRAMA and the Methuen Drama logo are trademarks of Bloomsbury Publishing Plc

First published in Great Britain 2020

Copyright © Carina E. I. Westling, 2020

Carina E. I. Westling has asserted her right under the Copyright, Designs and Patents Act, 1988, to be identified as Author of this work.

Series design by Burge Agency
Cover photograph: *The Drowned Man*, 2013 © Julian Abrams

All rights reserved. No part of this publication may be reproduced or transmitted in any form or by any means, electronic or mechanical, including photocopying, recording, or any information storage or retrieval system, without prior permission in writing from the publishers.

Bloomsbury Publishing Plc does not have any control over, or responsibility for, any third-party websites referred to or in this book. All internet addresses given in this book were correct at the time of going to press. The author and publisher regret any inconvenience caused if addresses have changed or sites have ceased to exist, but can accept no responsibility for any such changes.

A catalogue record for this book is available from the British Library.

Library of Congress Control Number: 2020934533

ISBN: HB: 978-1-3501-0195-1
PB: 978-1-3501-0194-4
ePDF: 978-1-3501-0197-5
eBook: 978-1-3501-0196-8

Series: Performance and Design

Typeset by Deanta Global Publishing Services, Chennai, India

To find out more about our authors and books visit www.bloomsbury.com and sign up for our newsletters.

Immersion and Participation in Punchdrunk's Theatrical Worlds

Performance + Design is a series of monographs and essay collections that explore understandings of performance design and scenography, examining the potential of the visual, spatial, material and environmental to shape performative encounters and to offer sites for imaginative exchange. This series focuses on design both for and as performance in a variety of contexts including theatre, art installations, museum displays, mega-events, site-specific and community-based performance, street theatre, design of public space, festivals, protests and state-sanctioned spectacle.

Performance + Design takes as its starting point the growth of scenography and the expansion from theatre or stage design to a wider notion of scenography as a spatial practice. As such, it recognizes the recent accompanying interest from a number of converging scholarly disciplines (theatre, performance, art, architecture, design) and examines twenty-first-century practices of performance design in the context of debates about post-dramatic theatre, aesthetic representation, visual and material culture, spectatorship, participation and co-authorship.

Series Editors
Stephen Di Benedetto, Joslin McKinney and Scott Palmer

Contemporary Scenography: Practices and Aesthetics in German Theatre, Arts and Design
Birgit Wiens
978-1-3500-6447-8

The History and Theory of Environmental Scenography: Second Edition
Arnold Aronson
978-1-4742-8396-0

Scenography Expanded: An Introduction to Contemporary Performance Design
Edited by Joslin McKinney and Scott Palmer
978-1-4742-4439-8

The Model as Performance: Staging Space in Theatre and Architecture
Thea Brejzek and Lawrence Wallen
978-1-4742-7138-7

Sound Effect: The Theatre We Hear
Ross Brown
978-1-3500-4590-3

Forthcoming titles
Consuming Scenography: The Theatricality of the Shopping Mall
Nebojša Tabački
978-1-3501-1089-2

Digital Scenography: 30 Years of Experimentation and Innovation in Performance and Interactive Media
Neill O'Dwyer
978-1-3501-0731-1

Sites of Transformation: Applied and Socially Engaged Scenography in Rural Landscapes
Louise Ann Wilson
978-1-3501-0444-0

Contents

List of Figures vii

Introduction 1
    Immersion and the sublime 4
    The technological gaze in interactive systems 5
    Designing for agency, not agents 7

1 Immersion in Punchdrunk's Theatre 13
    Working with Punchdrunk: sensing, making and thinking 19
    Scaling up: space, time, audiences 26
    Audience immersion on- and offline 31
    Theatres of action 36

2 A Genealogy of the Immersive Aesthetic 43
    Key influences on the immersive aesthetic 45
    Anti-realist modernism in experimental theatre 48
    Complicity and participation 57
    Blended spaces and the vertigo of transformation 63
    Punchdrunk's emerging aesthetic 67

3 Punchdrunk's Interactive Systems 73
    The shadow choreography and structure of Punchdrunk's worlds 79
    Emergence and order 85
    Art-work and algorithmic audiences 91

4 Behind the Interface – Making Punchdrunk's Storyworlds 97
    Building storyworlds 101
    Devising and performing 106

5   Audience Experience and Participation 119

    Analysing Punchdrunk audiences 120
    Active immersion 124
    The effects of anonymity 126
    Delinquent system aesthetics 130

6   The Shape of Agency in Interactive Storyworlds 141

    Perspectives on agency in interactive systems 142
    Scenography as experience infrastructure in physical and virtual worlds 150
    The postdigital sublime: beyond the digital mythos 154

7   Impure Futures 161

    Condemned to change 164
    The sublime versus efficiency 166
    Harnessing the un-modern 173

Appendix 183
    Analysis of interview data 183
    Social media data 188
References 190
Index 197

Figures

1.1   Empty space   20
1.2   Basement build   21
3.1   Spreadsheet   77
3.2   Red Moon desert   84
4.1   Design studio TDM   99
4.2   The store   102
4.3   Props composition   105
4.4   Straw men in desert   106
5.1   Room detail   123
5.2   Character models   125

Introduction

This volume explores the design of performances events that centre on the audience as participants and relates this to the design of digital experiences. Theatrical events, experienced live in purpose-built structures or spaces temporarily transformed into theatres, are increasingly extended in time and space by virtual spaces and digital technologies. The latter is a broadening category and spans virtual reality (VR), blended (XR) or augmented reality (AR), as well as platforms designed for services rather than entertainment, such as social media. The blurring of boundaries between the physical and virtual space of performance and the incorporation of live and mediated audiences therein raise questions for scenography, particularly with regard to terms of engagement. To create the desired aesthetic effect within the frame of the performance, these terms of engagement may or even must be less explicit than the invitation and solicitation to participate. The aesthetics of immersive theatre are rooted in scenographic processes that facilitate the sensation of being subsumed in a theatrical storyworld, which is often achieved through a multi-sensory experiential engagement with the performance environment, and apparent or actual complicity in unfolding events. With knowing and naïve audiences interacting and 'performing' in virtual scenographies that mesh with the physical and social world, critical analysis of representation in theatre help us understand how their role is shaped by design.

Important links, theories and ways of thinking about audiences not only as central but also as a living material in the production of narrative need critical and creative attention. The philosopher Elizabeth Grosz highlights the critical importance of embodiment and the potential of the living body as the root of innovative expressions and responses:

> The living body is itself the ongoing provocation for inventive practice, for inventing and elaborating widely varying practices, for using organs and activities in unexpected and potentially expansive ways, for making art out of the body's capacities and actions. (Grosz 2011: 20)

The physicality of audiences and the immanent consequences of audience actions are more acutely present to designers of live performance than to those who design exclusively for digital platforms. In addition, digital representation of audiences for computer games and social media occludes their embodiment to designers of such systems. Thus, digitised audiences are rendered uniquely open to abstraction in the design process, both as online actors and data objects, and the vanishing of consequence is facilitated by the remote relationship between producers and audiences. From the occlusion of embodiment to both the designer and their audiences follows a loss of experience potential that hinges on consequence. The fluidity of form and seeming liberation from the 'weight of reality' conferred by digitisation of participation on virtual platforms tempts dismissal of the old (Rancière 2009: 31), which, in the case of virtual and technologically augmented realities, includes the living body and its un-modern emotions and frames of reference. However, as Grosz reminds us, the living body remains the seat of inventive practice and experience, as well as meaning-making.

Accepting Grosz' proposition, the living body is the seat of sensation and innovation – but it is also the conduit for understanding the limits to the human condition: time, gravity and the bounds of our own agency in relation to that of others. In the digital modern, freedom from these has been celebrated and explored in ways that designers in physical media cannot ignore, for ethical, pragmatic *and* aesthetic reasons. In the postdigital un-modern, we see more clearly that the opaque complexity of embodiment perverts lofty aims contingent on the neat compartmentalisation of different types of participation and experience. The ethics, pragmatism and aesthetics of live performance can, and arguably need to enrich perspectives on experience design in digital technologies. As this volume will show, Punchdrunk create immersive theatrical worlds that expand scenography to not just envelop but *include* the living bodies of their audiences, and scenographic representation in their work affords a formal analysis of participation that applies across digital and physical media.

This book differs significantly from previous books that have focused on Punchdrunk's work, and contributes to the discourses of theatre and media with an empirical study of making and experiencing immersive performance together with a structured analysis of immersion as self-capture, building on the work of Chow (2012) and Bishop (2012). Both are informed by Artaud's vision of a Theatre of Cruelty, which Machon also draws explicitly on in her discussion of the phenomenology of immersion in Punchdrunk's work (2013). However, the key to the importance of Artaud for analysis of virtual and physical scenographies in both isolation and comparison is found in Deleuze's discussion of Artaud's work in *Difference and Repetition* (2014: 209–10). In this analysis, Deleuze articulates the influence on conditions of possibility by transcendent versus immanent subject–event relationships via Artaud's destabilisation of the auditorium in his Theatre of Cruelty. Challenging the subject position of the spectator brings the critique of representation to the self in ways that Brecht's notion of *Verfremdungseffekt* and its associated critique of representation do not. This analysis, together with de Certeau's theory of space and place (1988) combine in this book with critical posthumanism to a critique of physical, virtual and blended immersive scenographies. The resulting theoretical framework accommodates different ways and reasons to read this book: as an ethnography and empirical study of Punchdrunk's pioneering work in immersive theatre and virtual scenography; as a genealogy of the immersive aesthetic in scenography and performance; and as a critical framework for understanding immersive design across physical and digital media through analysis of frames, subject positions and perspectives in relation to notions of the sublime. These points of entry are arranged around a grounded and innovative theory of scenography for live performance and digital applications that incorporate audiences as constituent components of an interactive design schema. The latter is a broad category, and spans virtual reality (VR), blended reality (XR) or augmented reality (AR) as well as a plethora of service design platforms, including social media. While the discussion of infrastructures that support interaction is relevant also for service design, the main focus of this book is design where audience experience is central, and intended to be immersive.

A comparison between live audiences in performance events and remote audiences on digital platforms shows profound differences in thinking and practice in the two fields, as well as obvious similarities. Central to their differences are the relationships and directionality of connectivity and exposure. In live performance, audiences are immediately present as a force of motion and emotion. Their cohesion, velocity and direction change with attention, elation and arousal, giving visible form to Pierre Klossowski's argument in *Living Currency* (2017) that mediated passion is the driving force for production and exchange. This is explicit in Punchdrunk's theatrical worlds, where experience is produced in encounters through the extension of agency in embodied interrogation and articulation of space. Exposure is two-way in encounters across the interface, and immersion is regarded here as the voluntary submission to such encounters. Thus, analyses of the cultures that make this exposure desirable are included in the research. The cultivation and extension of agency within coordinating structures characterise the artwork on 'both sides of the interface'. Hundreds of makers are involved in each production with set building, acting and stage management, and the distributed agency that the company extends to each makes possible the creation of deeply layered scenography that resolves in greater detail the closer you look. This wealth of detail opens a possibility space for exploration that expands upon inspection, similar to how *mise-en-abîme* creates the illusion of an endlessly receding space. The illusion of boundless experiential space produces a vertigo of the embodied subject position that is critical to immersive experience, as discussed below.

Immersion and the sublime

The sublime, which is an experience outside of conventional beauty that is made aesthetic by being bounded or 'removed' by frames or distance, tends to be neither in nor out of fashion, yet its relevance to our sense of meaning persists through time. On 15 April 2019, as this book was being completed, the frequently cynical twitterati shared their grief and veneration on social media as the fire at Notre Dame in Paris burned, and Parisians sang liturgical songs in the streets. The exaggerated proportions and deep contrasts between soaring darkness and jewel-coloured light from stained-glass windows in Gothic cathedrals already invoke vertigo and awe; the sudden reminder of how fragile historical artefacts (and, by extension, our lives) are in the face of time and forces of destruction brought people together, remotely, in their hundreds of thousands. They shared photographs of gargoyles and rose windows and discussed the grain and texture of medieval stone- and woodwork while the blaze spurred contemplation of the fragility of civilisation. The vertigo of possible destruction temporarily muted all other debates, demonstrating an important aspect of the sublime experience: its power to put the human illusion of sovereignty in perspective. Jacques Rancière describes this, with regard to Jean-François Lyotard's reformulation of the sublime as one of the two available options in the face of inescapable alienation:

> Either the disaster of the sublime, the recognition of the immemorial dependence of the human mind on the immemorial law of the Other inside it, or the greater disaster of the promise of self-emancipation and its completion in either the overt barbarity of Nazi or Soviet totalitarianism or in the soft totalitarianism, the anaesthesia, of commodity culture. (Rancière 2004: 15)

In Rancière's analysis, Lyotard reverses the Kantian sublime, in particular with regard to reason in relation to the vastness that engenders the sublime feeling. Rancière's comparison of the sublime in Lyotard versus that of Kant aligns with the tension between an immanent perspective ('within' the moment or event; on the same plane) and a transcendent one (from a removed vantage point that allows for the illusion of dominion or comprehension). As is discussed through case studies of Punchdrunk's work in this book, this distinction sheds light on how the relationship between makers, players and audiences in live events creates different conditions of possibility than that between digital makers and players and their remote, digitally mediated audiences.

The technological gaze in interactive systems

The logic of techné comprises language and skill (Sterne 2006), and in interactive systems where audiences play narrative parts that are emergent to a lesser or greater degree, the relationship between system logic, or point-of-view, and the human participants that are its 'moving parts' shapes conditions of possibility. The problem of thinking aesthetically, functionally and ethically about participation as a feature in interaction design must start with an interrogation of this point-of-view, or gaze; the nature of its vantage point and relation to its object, and how this informs, and forms, conditions of possibility for 'self' and 'other'. In Punchdrunk performances the vantage point of gaze is rendered immanent by the temporary suspension of prevailing order/s and collapsing the physical distance between stage and auditorium. Although there is an imbalance in degree of dominion through 'knowingness' in encounters between performers and audiences, it is mitigated by the unusual degree of agency afforded the latter, as well as their identities being masked to the former. The capacity of both to impact on the other is emphasised in the designed encounter. By contrast, the distributed, pervasive gaze or facility for surveillance that is embedded in digital networks and the platforms they support establishes distance and executes power through systematic objectification. Legacy heuristics in software engineering skew towards agent-based modelling; the understanding of audiences as stereotypes with extended characteristics based on past behaviours (Benyon, Innocent and Murray 2014). The digitisation of system users or audiences objectifies them in and through their persistent and ongoing rendering as data objects. In the physical world, objectification occurs through representational and socio-economic processes and transactions that establish distance to confer status and power on the objectifier at the expense of the objectified. Objectification is not effective because the objectified are *less* than human; the transaction is powerful precisely *because* they are human. Incrementally and persistently, digital interactive systems objectify their users; systematically and, through the extension of global networks, at vast scale. The wholesale submission and instrumentalisation of human capacity provides the 'smarts' that power such systems. System users (or participants) submit their human ability to perceive, interpret, process and play and through doing so are reduced to data objects, more narrowly defined with every transaction. Their 'thingification' confers power to the objectifier. The capacity that is embedded within the system to survey, order and objectify constitutes an executive position, exercised through the affordance of placing and holding its object (human system users or participants) within a conceptual frame and form. The systemic rendering of human participants as data objects is thus an expression of power at scale, embedded within digital infrastructures to support delivery of services, mediation of interaction and revenue generation. This particular form of objectification is obscured by naturalisation within the design scheme, but its outline can be traced in its resistant or subversive mirror forms, for example in self-objectification, where a personal brand is raised through system affordances or the generation of so-called bot armies or 'astroturf'; fake identities that can be recruited to mimic popular support for brands or political positions. Such tactics co-opt the distributed and systematised manipulation of identity and boundaries in distributed networked systems. The symbolic and actual power of shape-shifting stands out most clearly when contrasted with control that is exercised through limitation of social and physical mobility, including the instrumentalisation of stereotypes to confine those constructed as minor within their allocated place and form.

In *Unmarked* (1996), Peggy Phelan argues that being visible and framed as a 'lesser other', or indeed as a demographic data object cannot confer empowerment, even when individuals are celebrated in the capacity of fame. Expanding on her argument, Maike Bleeker adds:

> Visibility does not necessarily serve the interests of the one made visible. Representation is almost always on the side of the one who looks and not on the side of the one who is seen. The images of women in films, advertisements, in paintings or on stage, do not so much show women 'as they are', as they are revealing about the subjective point of view from where these women are seen. This point of view is outside the image, yet implied within it, like the vantage point in a perspectival drawing. (Bleeker 2008: 98)

As implied by Phelan's argument in *Unmarked* (1996), power is less about 'being seen', and more being afforded the ability to change your circumstances. In digital and administrative milieus, this includes form and location. Both systemic and narrative aspects of Punchdrunk's work articulate themes of shape-shifting and the relations of power that are associated with it. While captured within the art-work, their audiences are afforded unusual agency; they are masked and at liberty to reconfigure themselves, and to move at will in this capacity. Relevant to a critical comparison with software systems, the identity of Punchdrunk audiences within the performance space is irrelevant at the technical level, and anonymity within the 'system' is not only possible but essential to the aesthetic experience. The temporary suspension of identity and the protection afforded by anonymity are critically conducive to emergent encounters. Masks thus play a complex role in Punchdrunk's work: they confer the power to shape-shift on their audiences and destabilise their identity within the art-work. This allows audiences to explore worlds that issue challenges to persistent play with extended agency that might be described as postidentitarian (Cull 2012).

Designing for agency, not agents

Punchdrunk's work with agency as a critical, dynamic and unstable material in scenography combines broad strokes with deep detail. Their scenography is designed for response capacity to meet and negotiate the curiosity and force of free-roaming audiences in their hundreds, night after night for extended runs. The efficacy of their methods is demonstrated not just by the volume of their audiences, but by the willingness to return up to a hundred times to revisit their experiences, or to explore what they previously missed. First-hand accounts from company and audience members show that the craft and detail at the 'back end' of the interface supports immersion as an active state on the other – not because it fools audiences into believing the illusion, but because it tells them that suspension of disbelief and commitment of agency to the experience will be met and supported. Even in near-darkness, audiences perceive the commitment to and creative investment in the storyworld by the company, and rise to meet it. Even though they are new to the experience they are able to read the social dimension of the material, and it informs their embodied experience of space. Chiming with Grosz' quote at this beginning of this chapter, their living bodies, sensate and social, produce experiential space. The social dimension is central as immersion is a state of voluntary entrapment, reliant on the perception of support in the joint art-work. Acknowledging agency as a force that cannot be controlled but invited, shaped and directed with the active consent of the audience creates immersive conditions of possibility. In Punchdrunk's 'theatre machines', the social is embedded in every detail through care and attention to detail, and is legible to their audiences even in the darkest corners of their scenography. If technological systems are to not reduce but extend the capacity of their human components, technology must yield to the social instead of folding the social into technologies that don't know how to be human. The balance is precarious and easily lost in accelerationist idealism. In response to this challenge, this research turned to empiricism. The skill, or *metis* of Punchdrunk and their making culture is a rich source of grounded knowledge of working with the agency of the living, creative body as a material and a space for experience.

Much skill in the live events and performance fields is dedicated to invoking, expressing, negotiating and managing forms of thought that are not easily articulated in words, but are nevertheless high-level cognitive operations, including embodied and social expressions of intuitive or emergent thought. The consequences of getting this right or wrong are immanent and immediate. One of the aims of this book is to interrogate the embedded knowledge in Punchdrunk of working with the live agency of audiences. The company has worked together since 2000 to produce large, immersive productions and consistently create extraordinary experiences for and with their audiences. *Sleep No More* in New York has run since 2011, *Sleep No More* in Shanghai opened in 2016, and *The Drowned Man: A Hollywood Fable* in London ran for just over a year, playing to audiences of 600 every night. Punchdrunk audiences move freely within the scenography for three hours, interacting with the performance environment and its actors at close range. They move at pace, in intimate proximity to the set, props and the actors, and typically have strong experiences in response to the performance.

In comparison, digitally mediated audiences, which are normally remote, are a less obviously formidable force to designers. Misconceptions of the creative potential of audiences, whether it is in alignment with designed affordances or engaged in the kind of fertile caprice that de Certeau calls 'delinquency' (1988: 129–30) has consequences. Networked and at scale, these are hard to predict and locate but we can see the impact of the present design and business model of social media, interactive digital systems that rely on their audiences to generate and share content on public discourses. These effects are shaped by the way human audiences (who act as 'moving parts' within the design scheme) are conceptualised and defined within such systems. Personalisation is the modelling and programmatic targeting of thin-sliced demographics. It is the mechanism that drives the social media business model, and it relies on rendering human participants as data objects. Through digitisation, human participants are objectified by their representation as stereotypes, or what Alexander Galloway calls 'cybertypes' (2012: 137). This generates intrinsic flaws, reducing and distorting information about the human 'moving parts' of the system. The problem is not confined to poor resolution, however. Modelling human participants in interactive systems as data objects rather than sources of capacity invites an ontological misstep that is amplified as it scales. From an empirical perspective in live events design, crowds are not usefully conceptualised as multiples of individuals, and individuals cannot be faithfully modelled as fractions of a crowd. Assuming that individuals are of a kind with crowds fails to accommodate the dynamic volatility of human components when they form crowds, and the loosening of the compacts that maintain individual social identity. The resulting bleed between hedonic creativity and delinquency is readily observable when designing and managing live events, as are the effects of proximity and scale.

How we conceptualise audiences, whether live or mediated, matters not only to aesthetic and functional design, but also to public discourses. A plurality of voices is essential and most agree that different perspectives and information, relayed from diverse points of view, enrich and constitute a healthy public debate. Social media nominally support plurality, but nuance is easily drowned out by populism in mediated public discourse. Discourse can challenge without polarising its constituents and the mediated present needs discourses that sustain such dynamism. This study explores, among other things, how representation of the human component in interactive systems inflects conditions of possibility. The present moment suggests, as will be explored in this book, that failure to recognise and accommodate the dynamic instability of human agency, while incorporating it as a material in systems relentlessly designed for connectivity, over-incentivises polarisation. To those with experience of live events it is also clear that modelling human 'moving parts' as more or less static, if cumulatively enriched data objects flows from a way of thinking about human participation that is fundamentally ideological, and not based on an empirical understanding of human audiences at scale. How the speaker and the spoken-to relate to each other, and how this is formalised and instrumentalised through the design of their respective roles, is critical.

The history of theatre and performance often focuses on stage representation, but if we look at scenography and performance with the audience in mind we can trace how their role has been configured and negotiated almost as clearly as if it were spoken out loud. Within this book series Aronson describes the spatial-architectural arc within which immersive theatre sits in *The History and Theory of Environmental Scenography* (2018), while McKinney and Palmer's edited volume *Scenography Expanded* (2017) focuses on its technological, socio-political and material legacy. The layouts, plans, materials and technologies of amphitheatre, fêtes, festivals, circuses and theatres show how audiences are thought and configured, with regard to the stage and each other. If we include audiences in the totality of performance and how it is experienced and received the auditorium is, and has always been, a structured and interactive space that affords varying degrees of licence and restriction. In this perspective, we can compare physical and digital scenographies, and how their material cultures inflect the priorities of makers and designers. The immediacy of live performance reminds all who are involved in the production of a play or spectacle that proceedings occur within a space of readiness that is accommodated and supported by the interest and compliance of audiences. Immediacy, with immanent consequences, creates persuasive incentives to be prepared and to have response capacity, in case events do not unfold as planned or desired. It encourages an empirically grounded way of thinking about audiences; what draws their attention, how they respond, and what they might do in the emergent present.

In the absence of the urgency and emergent potential for consequence of live performance situations, digital audiences are more readily conceptualised according to an idea of what they are and how they should behave, as opposed to empirically understood. Through rendering as data objects, the representational form of 'digital audiences' is almost infinitely fluid, endlessly replicable and without a natural end-time. Openness of form and ease of scaling combine with remoteness in framing digitised audiences as performers of defined responses, rather than as co-producers of an unfolding event. Such conditions of possibility reduce the differential and particularity of audience responses in the eye of the designer. 'Seen from afar', only crude features of the object of study stand out, and so the general dominates the particular. Compounding this reductive perspective, crowd behaviours differ from how individuals act and respond. Subdivision of crowd behaviour yields little insight into how constituent individuals might act at a local level. Conversely, the multiplication of information about the actions of individuals at the local level will not yield a particularly useful picture of how a theoretical crowd that they form might act. In this light big data, which is used to model and predict behaviour, produces information that is neither fish nor fowl with regard to knowledge of individuals or crowds. Furthermore, big data is dependent on circular queries, as it is typically gathered on platforms designed to harvest information that is (a) useful to the platform owner and (b) 'harvestable' and 'processable' within the means and affordances offered by the platform. When applied to interaction with remote audiences via the platforms that generated the data, the margin for error in the quality of the information is significant, increased by linear scaling, and unchecked by immanent feedback. While technologically extended and blended storyworlds promise vertiginous possibilities for designers at the interface level, reductive audience modelling within software infrastructures is stultifying both at the technical level and in the sense implied by Rancière (2009: 9–14). This is a concern with regard to the expansion of digital scenographies into everyday life and the public sphere. By contrast, errors that result from overly reductive (i.e. simplified, crude, and lacking in complexity and nuance) understanding and modelling of audiences in live performance will be immediate and evident to those delivering the performance, and producers of live events are thus incentivised to employ an empirical, rather than an ideological understanding and approach to thinking their audiences.

Alternative ways of modelling audiences are possible and viable, as demonstrated by Punchdrunk and other companies that incorporate live audiences in 'theatre machines'. Their practice is rooted in a deep understanding of materials, including the agency of makers and audiences and is articulated in the detail of scenography and designed encounters. Thus embedded, it supports suspension of disbelief and produces narrative space through layered meaning and metaphorical potential. This approach invites close engagement with sensory spaces and fragmentary narratives held within a distributed frame of meaning that requires art-work towards the elusive promise of completion by self-captured audiences. The ambiguity that expands between the defined and the undefined in Punchdrunk's theatrical worlds is a possibility space in which the exposure that is inherent to connectivity is negotiated on an emergent basis. This negotiation, teetering on the fault line of reason, is central not only to the sublime but also to immersion as an active state of suspended disbelief. As human agency meshes with interactive systems, the un-modern invites itself, and the design of such possibility spaces may provide not only buffers against incursion and transgression but also the freeplay that calls on active negotiation and emergence on more level terms in immanent encounters. Working with the idea and the reality of audiences as dynamic and unstable elements within physical and digital scenographies alike therefore furthers creative management of both experience and risk. In addition to bringing this grounded *metis* to experience design where human participants are intrinsic 'moving parts', it also accommodates a possibility space for awe through balancing extension and dissolution, both of which are essential to the encounter.

This book seeks to explore how the conditions of possibility within the encounter are configured and inflected by its infrastructures. As we embrace virtual and blended spaces, this becomes critical to both intimate and distributed moments. The ideas discussed in this volume were carefully explored in the context of Punchdrunk's storyworlds and their extension on virtual and blended platforms and can inform multimedia design for immersive experience and beyond. The remit of the book and the research it is based on is introduced in Chapter 1, followed by a genealogy of the immersive aesthetic. Chapters 3–5 are case studies of Punchdrunk's work across, and from vantage points on, 'both sides of the interface'. The concluding two chapters introduce a critical framework for interrogating immersive scenographies and discuss the ramifications and possibilities for theatrical worlds that span digital and physical materialities. Methods, tables and illustrations are appended to the end of the book and provide further detail which might be of interest to researchers and practitioners. The possible futures for immersive performance across physical and digital materialities that are sketched in the concluding chapter suggest that we might think and model participation through emergence and complicity towards a postdigital sublime that flows from the vertigo of possibility, complicated and enriched by consequence. The un-modern, postdigital perspective that emerges may echo the idea of the world as a stage, but in place of transcendent melancholy with regard to its players, it views the living body in immanence a site of resistance and invention.

1

Immersion in Punchdrunk's Theatre

In the opening of *Difference and Repetition,* Gilles Deleuze frames an otherwise often abstract and challenging philosophical text with a gesture towards a focus of his critique: the occlusion of desire by conflation with reason from the uninterrogated subject position. Implied are the hierarchies that flow from this occlusion, in which the body and its senses take a minor position: 'The head is the organ of exchange, but the heart is the amorous organ of repetition' (Deleuze 2014: 2).

Repetition, as Elizabeth Grosz emphasises, is never possible in the sense of replication (2011: 30), and it refers to the inescapable immanence of practice, which occurs in the emergent present and in response to its conditions of possibility. Repetition is thus always particular; an instantiation of the idea, no matter how much the idea seeks to express the general. Its specificity is essential to liveness, but ordinarily attention to the uniqueness of live experience is focused on the stage, whereas its equally unique experience occurs simultaneously in the auditorium. The citation from *Difference and Repetition* above positions exchange as a transaction throughout which framed orders can remain stable, whereas repetition implies engagement within a shared or even exploded frame: an immanent encounter. The implementation and maintenance of frames is a complex operation that simultaneously expresses or reinforces hierarchies and affords meaning-making on terms determined by gaze, even though the containment of difference or change within the proscenium arch of theatre or any other frame can only be an illusion.

Immanence precludes the illusion or reality of control of the moment, whether through framing, generalisation or distance, all of which are relevant to the practice and critique of representation and narrative in theatre. In *Difference and Repetition*, Gilles Deleuze analyses the work of Antonin Artaud and positions immanence as the subject position from where real or precarious thought flows, dichotomous to the dogmatic image of thought, where the thinker is external to the frame of consequence, and may assume control over the outcomes. In theatre these ideas find concrete form, and Deleuze draws on Artaud's work to illustrate, and arguably evidence, a concept with far broader application. The shifting frames of media environments spurs change in how we see ourselves in the world (Meyrowitz 1985), and the virtual worlds of games and pervasive technologies present new forms of connection and exposure. Starting at the Drama department at the University of Exeter, where students are encouraged to take radical embodied approaches to theatrical space, Felix Barrett's vision for Punchdrunk is famously multi-sensory and based in physical design of extreme depth and detail. He and the other senior members of the company – Peter Higgin, Maxine Doyle and Colin Nightingale – supported by a large and growing team of designers and producers, are expanding their storyworlds and the essential audience component into and across virtual worlds. Punchdrunk's immersive theatrical worlds, which are the object of study in this book, notably incorporate the living, sensate bodies of their audiences as active participants and moving parts within theatre machines, comprising scenography and dramaturgy.[1] Audiences and actors share the frame of the performance, bounded in time and by the perimeter of the performance space. While the experience is intricately structured and designed, its 'living parts' will repeat rather than replicate. Participation thus embodies change or difference, and makes concrete the amalgam of potential extension, exposure to uncertainty, exhilaration and precariousness that is central to immanent encounters.

Audiences describe their experiences in Punchdrunk's theatrical worlds with a powerful desire for more, aware that a return would render them no less hostages to fortune. Uncertainty, as a quality of experience, runs through all audience interviews in this study, enmeshed with awe, frustration and desire. Returning to the quote by Deleuze that opens this chapter, these are also amorous emotions with the object of desire laid bare, as it ultimately is in love, as the potential for difference. By contrast, the remote gaze of exchange affords the illusion of control that underpins instrumentalisation of interaction. Interrogation of the subject position is key to understanding the difference between conditions of possibility that is suggested in the above quote by Deleuze. It is also a point of entry for the application of critiques of representation in theatre and performance to interaction design in other media. Through immanent framing and uncertainty, participation in Punchdrunk confronts the subject with its representation to itself and in relation to the event. Rey Chow describes this as capture (2012), which is relevant to the idea of self-exploitation in performance art (Bishop 2012). The art-work of participation begs comparison with instrumentalised participation on social media and the socio-economic emphasis on 'the event' that is discussed in depth by Geert Lovinck (2016) under the rubric of prosumption. In her discussion of self-exploitation in art, Claire Bishop draws attention to the historical moment that participatory and immersive theatres share with network-based production and affective labour (2012: 277), and highlights the importance of possible failure and consequence to embodied participation. This difference is critical, and informs transitions and connections between physical and digital scenographies without abandoning the immanent and precarious thought that is inherent to embodiment. The similarities between physical worlds and virtual worlds on games and social media platforms are seductive; like a Punchdrunk performance, participation in virtual worlds sate and leave you hungry – but while subtle at source, the differences are profound. The possibility and practice of extension has a different meaning if the consequences of failure are embodied, that is, sensed in and through the body. The implications for design and experience become clearer if thought through gravity and its relation to conditions of possibility. The conditions of possibility in physical and digital storyworlds are framed by the presence or absence of gravity, both in the literal and the metaphorical sense of the word. Gravity and consequence thus insinuate themselves as aesthetic dimensions with deeper relevance to design than the initial exhilaration of limitless possibilities suggests – their occlusion from the experience comes at a cost.

The material practice of making theatre in scenography, acting and sense-making as an ambulatory spectator is the focus of this book, but later sections will discuss how the disconnect with time and gravity in digital media might be compensated for in the design process. For the purpose of this analysis, large-scale Punchdrunk performances are thought of as crucibles of sense-making, where masked audiences numbering in their hundreds seek a mixture of sense and abandon in labyrinthine and almost completely dark spaces. Multiple visits, up to a hundred and more by some spectators, fail to exhaust the number of possible recombinations of all the separate scenographic and choreographic elements that comprise Punchdrunk's 'theatre machines'. Countless opportunities for interaction and experience are tiny and hidden, like hand-drawn flipbooks in the corner of old books, stacked in bookshelves without any indication, or one-to-one performances that play out in spaces that may be unknown even to some who work on the productions. These opportunities are too many, too layered, and too disparate in space for any one spectator to attend them all, producing an excess of experience potential that feels endless; an illusion with ambiguous edges. Punchdrunk productions are designed with a careful balance of structure and emergence that comes to expression in the sense of potential free-fall within an experience that is precisely designed. Emphasising this precarious balance, each performance ends with a mass scene for the entire audience to which all arrive by their own routes and narratives, often without noticing how they are directed to do so.

The experience is visceral, not only because you are on your feet most of the time, walking or running to follow performers between scenes. Lady Macbeth's bedroom scene in *Sleep No More* (2011) serves as a signature Punchdrunk moment: a powerfully dramatic, largely wordless and intensely physical scene that plays with boundaries and proximity, voyeurism and exposure, and where acting merges with athletic dance. I attended one of Tori Sparks' performances in the role; she played Lady Macbeth in the original casts in both Boston and New York. After leaving the bath where she attempts to wash blood off her hands, Lady Macbeth danced in a large, glassed dressing room in the corner of the bedchamber, and the intensity of the performances gave me, on the safe side of the glass, a similar experience of awe to that you might feel when separated only by a fence from a magnificent animal in a zoo. Afterwards, she moved slowly through the audience, drenched in sweat and blood, at close enough range that I felt the heat radiating from her body. While the vicarious thrill of being there with Lady Macbeth but not being seen is part of the appeal, the tacit voyeurism is countered by the power of the performer, who inhabits the encounter more fully than you do. You are already lost, or rather committed to the theatrical world in which you find yourself, having been separated from the company you arrived with and pushed into the performance without knowing where or when you are in the narrative, and the combination of disorientation and curiosity that holds you in a state of suspended disbelief is enhanced and held by the power of the designed environment. The relation between suspense and trust that sustains you throughout the experience is central, as one company member remarked:

> I think you... you never get over your initial Punchdrunk experience, I think. That always stays with you. And so if you're going to work with the company, you need to understand what it's like, and what the feeling is. Because I think everyone that works there has had that; that sense of amazement, or being terrified, that then stayed with you.[2]

Punchdrunk's live masked productions are structured as giant clockwork puzzles of complex exchanges between actors, audiences and scenography, that require connection, processing and completion by audience participants to make sense of the theatrical worlds that they find themselves in. The physical environments constructed by Punchdrunk for the productions *Sleep No More* and *The Drowned Man: A Hollywood Fable* occupy several floors of large buildings containing 100 and 170 separately designed spaces, respectively. *Sleep No More* and *The Drowned Man* were created to accommodate audiences of 400 (*Sleep No More*) and 600 (*The Drowned Man*) per night, with each performance including separate one-to-one encounters designed for one audience member at a time. The diffraction and distribution of the narratives across large performance spaces ensures that audiences will have unique personal experiences, which necessarily challenge perceived expectations. There are too many scenes and potential interactions for any single audience participant to exhaust all possibilities, even after many visits. The experience is designed for each audience member to take responsibility for curating their own experience, with no guarantees that they will do so very well.

Sleep No More and *The Drowned Man* share key aesthetic characteristics; filmic references, chiaroscuro lighting, a dynamic approach to space through scale and labyrinthine passages and series of rooms, intensely physical performances blending largely non-verbal acting with choreographed movement, and richly detailed scenography. The plays and novels on which the productions are based are woven through performance and scenography, with the movements of cast and audience forming a two-part spatial choreography, and much of the text encoded and layered into the set. The two productions are both ambitious in scale but structured differently, particularly with regard to how much of the narrative can be pulled together by one audience member during one visit. *Sleep No More* is based on Shakespeare's *Macbeth* woven through with elements from Hitchcock's *Vertigo* and *Rebecca* and pivots around two key areas: the ballroom, where the slow-motion banquet scene with the entire cast takes place, and Lady Macbeth's bedroom. *The Drowned Man: A Hollywood Fable* has a more complex narrative structure. Based on Georg Büchner's *Woyzeck,* a text that is already fragmented and unfinished, the performance is woven through with elements from two novels: Nathanael West's *The Day of the Locusts* and Ray Bradbury's *Something Wicked This Way Comes*. Mirror stories add complexity; Woyzeck-William is mirrored by Wendy, and Marie-Mary is mirrored by Marshall. The dynamic between them follows the storyline of Büchner's original play but with reversed male/female characters. *Woyzeck* is here reimagined for a different time and place, and set in the fictive film studio complex Temple Pictures, which takes the place of the military environment of Büchner's original play. Temple Pictures and its environment; the trailer park just outside the studio complex, the town of Encino (part of the present-day Los Angeles District), and the nearby Mojave desert landscape are re-created on separate floors of the building and both frame and engulf the smaller stories of love, hope, jealousy, insanity and self-destruction that play out within films produced by the studio and moments glimpsed between the characters. The boundaries between different layers of reality within the narratives collapse into each other as participating audience members perform a 'shadow choreography' as they move through and between the nested sets of Temple Pictures within the scenography. The narratives that were woven together for the production were distilled and encoded in space and detail through the devising and design of the sets,[3] left as hidden text fragments in books and scripts, scribbled on walls, and played out in notes and letter correspondence that could be pieced together by combining finds from different locations within the sets. The fragmented, embedded and nested storylines form theatrical worlds that can be likened to large interactive systems in which audiences are the moving parts and 'spatial operators' that animate and connect the whole, and Chapter 5 discusses how audiences frame this as a positive challenge. Describing Punchdrunk's productions as interactive systems nods to their ambitions to expand live performance to incorporate other platforms, but even their physical productions lend themselves to comparisons with computer games (Judge 2019). Felix Barrett harbours open ambitions to take the company's work from immersive theatre to 'playable shows':

> 'When we were described as a video game I started going back to games to find out more about them, to unpack it, and learn more about game mechanics,' says Barrett. He realised while Punchdrunk wasn't 'ever directly inspired by an open-world game', open worlds give birth to choice, which creates a new way to tell stories – similar to what he was trying to achieve in theatre. (Judge 2019)

As in virtual worlds, the anonymity conferred on audiences by the obligatory masks worn by Punchdrunk audiences suspends social inhibition, but the function of the mask is more complex. It marks the boundary between the interactive system (the 'theatre machine') and the participants (its 'moving parts'). As a framing device, it simultaneously lays bare and makes bearable the failure of the self as a form of representation, inviting the sublime as described by Peter Zima: a threat to 'the very foundations of subjectivity' (2010: 125). The mask-as-trope in Punchdrunk's work sits within a historical arc of carnival, masque and ritual traditions, where it is a device that facilitates the temporary upheaval of one identity, in order to take up or manifest/embody another. Through exploration of scenography, dramaturgy and historical tropes such as masking, practical and theoretical research in theatre and performance has fostered a robust critique of representation, subject position and framing. It is equally relevant to virtual scenographies that incorporate audiences as critical parts, whether they are designed for theatrical and immersive experience or for gaming and mass communication. Arguably, the legacy of thinking through and beyond representation in theatre and performance is perhaps the most articulate and versatile framework we have to guide interrogation of virtual materialities and interactive systems.

Working with Punchdrunk: sensing, making and thinking

When I first contacted Punchdrunk, they were looking for a space in London, and were about to open *Sleep No More* in New York. I finally got the chance to work with them as an academic researcher on the build of two productions: *The House Where Winter Lives* (2012) for young audiences in Stratford, London, and *The Drowned Man: A Hollywood Fable* (2013), which took place in the Old Sorting Offices at Paddington, London. *The Drowned Man* was then, and still is, the largest Punchdrunk production to date. During this research, I recorded the experience of makers both within and outside the company, that is, with those who are directly involved in the creation and maintenance of the productions, and a selection of audience members that had experienced them for the first time, and had immediate experience of 'making sense' of a large Punchdrunk production. While I made it known that I was an academic researcher doing ethnographic research, I gathered these accounts while working alongside designers on builds and participating in the creation of storyworlds, and in conversations with audiences as someone who was enriching my own experience by hearing theirs. I was interested in how those in direct contact with the materials and the interface worked and discussed their work, and selected my interviewees with this in mind.

The aesthetic of Punchdrunk's interactive systems and the facility for what feels like voyeuristic participation combines with sensory intensity to create an almost lurid surface appeal that has often dominated discussions of their work (Kaufman 2011; Billington 2013; Gardner 2013). Here, I want to revisit some of the familiar Punchdrunk tropes; the cinematic detail of the scenography, the masks and the *film noir* themes. Against the background of the failure to reproduce immersion when this surface aesthetic is mediated and expanded across digital platforms, as the researchers on *The Séance* found (Dixon, Rogers and Eggleston 2012), I will investigate what, precisely, produces immersion, and something about the mechanisms behind it. It is clear from conversations, interviews and analyses of lay reviews carried out in the course of this research that immersion is not something that 'happens to' a spectator; it is something that they allow to happen; a state that they consent to entering. Further analyses of Punchdrunk's online fandoms give a background for understanding the structure of immersion and the adjustments that fans make to extend and sustain their experience, on social media and through producing fan art. The outcome of these analyses is a framework for understanding immersion as a mutual process flowing from the encounter: not only in live performance but also in digitally mediated and blended experience

FIGURE 1.1 *Empty space. One corner section of one of the emptied floors after the break-down of* The Drowned Man, *with the windows uncovered to readmit daylight. This photo was taken from the centre of the hall, which extended more or less equally in four directions (Credit: Carina E. I. Westling).*

on and across different platforms, including mobile games, blended and augmented reality.

The richly layered and detailed aesthetic of Punchdrunk's scenography is critical to allowing audiences to immerse themselves in their work, but its function, like the masks, is complex. The realism of their storyworlds has been the subject of much attention, but interviews with audiences in this study show that it is more the attention to detail than realism that is of critical importance to immersion.[4] It is read as a compact between the company and their audiences, and 'holds' the extension of self and possibility within the performance. This compact works together with the masks, another familiar Punchdrunk trope that famously disinhibits audiences, as a frame for the art-work. In live performance, the effects of masking on the sense of yourself as a subject are embodied. Wearing a mask for a length of time alters how you experience yourself in the situation, and how others respond to you. The effect of the temporary liberation from performing 'as yourself' is gradual and perhaps most keenly noticed in one-to-ones, when it is abruptly suspended as the actor removes your mask, however gently he or she does it. The sense of exposure, heightened by the cool air that suddenly hits your skin, is immediate

FIGURE 1.2 *Basement build. Traditional scenography techniques were incorporated in* The Drowned Man *in the Masonic basement with a vanishing point motif, making a statement about illusory spaces in and beyond theatre and framing the theatricality of power and its rituals (Credit: Carina E. I. Westling).*

and almost paralysing. I recall a moment in *The Drowned Man* (2013) where I was taken from a room the size of a closet where I had been told a short story in hushed tones, and led down dark stairs into an even darker basement where the actor pointed a torch towards a seemingly dead, life-size horse. The shock was palpable and not diminished despite having seen the hoof of this (extremely life-like) model of a horse under a blanket during the build phase of the production. The effect was amplified by having worked on-site for many weeks but being unaware, up to that point, of that part of the building and what it contained. You might work on a Punchdrunk production for weeks and still not know its totality.

Emergence is central to both designing and experiencing Punchdrunk performances. The mask confers a subject position that might be described as 'present absence' on participants in live Punchdrunk productions. This unsettles the quotidian sense of self and underscores that negotiation of the performance is emergent. The mask facilitates suspension of social compacts upheld by identity, while the detail of the scenography communicates another compact; one that generates and holds the storyworld and its unknown potential. Meanwhile, the gravity of presence is felt as weighted movement within the expanding storyworld, yielding the kind of meaning to the experience that hinges on the possibility of consequence. Joy is defined by Deleuze as the extension of agency in encounters with bodies or events that we willingly enter into composition with (Deleuze 1970: 28). When such encounters, and the composition that follows our willing extension towards the possibilities they offer are embodied, they are also subject to gravitational forces. Gravity, as a factor in falling and the passage of time, brings consequence and frames pathos, emergence and emergency. It plays a part in the compositions we enter in love and friendship, both in their ascendance and entropy (falling-in/falling-out). Gravity also frames risk-taking and triumph in sports or performance arts: the risk of falling and the possibility of soaring evoke the sublime.

The role of gravity in myth, architecture, sculpture, and performance art can be traced in the aesthetics of resisting or embracing limitation of the human condition. The Icarus myth tells a cautionary tale of flying too close to the sun and the inevitable consequence of hubris. Drawing on Peter Sloterdijk's *Sphären III*, Jacques Rancière discusses gravity as the 'weight of reality'; the difficulty or challenge that brings meaning, and terms modernity anti-gravitational in its aims (Ranciere 2009: 31). Gravity, or rather our resistance to it, frames our concepts of time and death, and forms the backdrop against which our ambitions, desires, enthusiasm, failures and entropy are defined. It also creates the conditions of possibility for the vertigo of the sublime. Jean-François Lyotard, in defining the postmodern sublime, associates the experience of being 'deprived of the threat of being deprived of light, language, life' (Lyotard 1991: 99) with sublime vertigo in art, positioning framing by gaze or physical devices as an occlusion that simultaneously rescues and deprives. Whereas the Kantian sublime relies on reason to frame and contain awe, vertigo and the possibility of dissolution, Lyotard's sublime finds vertigo along the fault line of reason and its proxies (life, light and language), and their failure. In contrast with the Kantian sublime, Lyotard's definition is contingent on the possible failure of frames, bounds and the subject position in relation to the threat of incomprehension. This is inherent to immersion as experienced in Punchdrunk's work. Positioned within the frame, the audience must extend and explore under conditions of possibility that are defined by disorientation, challenge and unknown potential, implicit to which is the risk of failure to compose, create meaning or experience fulfilment.

The relevance of this to digital interaction is evident when we investigate mediated agency: without gravity, the weight of consequence is absent, seemingly diminishing the importance and meaning of our actions. Without immanent, weighted consequences, actions are less consequential. Weight brings to our awareness the possibility of falling and failing and is fundamental also to the embodied realisation of complicity. Embodiment is present in the countless instances of touch and repeated movements that are shared between Punchdrunk and their audiences. The negotiated intimacy of encounters where influences merge or enter into composition, and where connection and exposure find a precarious balance, is invited and sustained by carefully layered detail. The resulting stability of material repetition holds, affords and produces change, as embodied life must differ even as it tries to repeat (Grosz 2011: 30), and the material depth of Punchdrunk's storyworlds and the impossibility of either repeating or completing the experience simultaneously hold and drive immersion.

This analysis is salient to the challenge of extending Punchdrunk's and other physical storyworlds across digital platforms, where embodiment is mediated. To elicit the fullness of consequence that is accessible to live audiences, participation on digital platforms must rely on emotions that are amplified so as to register as consequential without recruiting embodiment directly. As we will see in Punchdrunk's fandom discourses on social media, the intensity of the live experience is reframed as ardent devotion to a storyworld with the potential to transgress and impose on the quotidian. Socially shared submission to this devotion, often professed in a self-mocking tone, is expressed through ritualistic and devotional behaviours that invoke playful delusion and, as described by Lyotard in his analysis of the postmodern sublime, the failure of reason. The sublime, as it is configured in Lyotard's and Zima's analyses, is woven through audience accounts of immersion in Punchdrunk's work in this study. It is described alongside vertigo, awe, disorientation and the unsettling failure to comprehend, grasp or frame the experience in its entirety. The influence of Artaud's *Theatre of Cruelty* on Punchdrunk's work in Josephine Machon's analysis (2013: 30, 38) and its positioning by Deleuze as analogous to precarious or immanent thought (2014: 209–10) fold these possibilities into embodied not-knowing, a leading theme in the audience experience of Punchdrunk's theatrical worlds, when brought to the subject position.

The sublime aesthetic speaks of the possible failure of reason; of falling and immersion in uncertainty, which is sharply contrasted by the anti-gravitational optimism that has dominated functional software and web design. The close relationship between the sublime and immersion, or perhaps the efficacy of the sublime in eliciting immersion, is similarly suggested by the proliferation of design devices built around loss, destruction, vertigo, transgression and disorientation in computer games. Examples of the sublime aesthetic in high-end virtual art and games include Char Davies' *Osmose* (1995) and Chinese Room's *Everybody's Gone to the Rapture* (2016); two works on either side of two critical decades in the design and development of virtual worlds. The persistence of the sublime aesthetic where the quality of experience is at the forefront of design suggests the stickiness of its appeal, and the breadth of this analogy is clearer if thought through embodiment and gravity. Char Davies' early VR work recruited proprioception and breathing in standing navigation through the storyworld of *Osmose*, drawing the 'immersant' (Davies 2012) into awareness of foundational perceptions of embodied being, where the self as a construct of the reasoning mind is secondary. As demonstrated by the disinhibition and vertigo of the extended possibilities beyond the 'self' that are afforded by masked participation, loss-of-self, contained within the frames of the storyworld, can be simultaneously liberating and sublime in the sense discussed by Zima (2010: 127). In *Everybody's Gone to the Rapture*, Chinese Room implemented this 'presence of absence' as the locus of the subject: where the subject would normally be found, there is instead an absence that the participant can assume as their minimally representational form within exquisitely rendered storyworlds. To expand and anchor the experience of aesthetic space, Chinese Room co-founder Jessica Curry's Bafta-winning interactive orchestral score creates a soaring and evocative soundscape that meshes the storyworld with the player's experience by evoking pathos and vista. The Chinese Room's impactful work with soundscapes exemplifies not only how sound informs space but also how immersion is elicited through a synthesis of emotion and the multi-sensory experience of space.

The superabundance of detail in the work of both Chinese Room and Punchdrunk in digital versus physical and blended storyworlds is deliberately and passionately irrational, if viewed from the perspective of the radical efficiency of the lean startup model and steep ratios between authors and audience numbers that have been guiding business models of the digital modern. Narrative is an intrinsic part of the design process in both companies, and is deeply embedded in the infrastructure and scenography of the performance, which falls on audience 'actors' in the case of Chinese Room, and is shared by cast and audiences in Punchdrunk. The games produced by Chinese Room are designed for one player at a time, but like Punchdrunk's interactive systems or theatre machines, they require completion by the participation of their audiences. Both companies prioritise resource-expensive processing over the 'cheaper' data intensity, which contributes to aesthetic value (Bogost 2012). Where data intensity is prioritised in interface and platform design, the act of meaning-making is weighted towards the user, and free-at-the-point-of-use systems that depend on content creation and other interpretative acts by users come to depend on incentivisation beyond aesthetic value, and monetisation beyond subscription or entry fees. The business model of the attention economy thus creates the conditions of possibility for the affective labour we see in the platform economy, including social media. As the efficiency principle and the attention economy converge on monetising the applied senses and cognition of system users in interaction design, eccentric behaviours that we might call delinquent, from Michel de Certeau's discussion of the un-modern and the 'old gods', thrive in the hinterlands of the design schema. Edited out of the narrative of modernity, including the digital modern and our attempts at living within it (1988: 129–30), they are largely left to roam under cover of a blindness rendered strategic by prevailing business models. Abusive interpersonal communication and exploitative practices that undermine the democratic process are thus arguably features, rather than bugs, of the conditions of possibility on social media platforms. Largely unarticulated within the design schema, such behaviours nevertheless drive engagement and generate revenue without immediate consequences at the platform level, which disincentivises change within the industry.

With the expansion of networked technologies into almost every corner of everyday life and the creative industries, these conditions of possibility are no longer bounded or fully containable. Our movements in and through physical and virtual designed environments and the inflections on conditions of possibility by physical and digital scenographies thus invite more urgent critical and cultural analyses. Punchdrunk's work offers a unique opportunity to interrogate such environments as interactive systems and our movements within and between them. Bringing critiques of representation in theatre to a comparative analysis of the scaled effects of shifting boundaries and implicit hierarches in digital and physical interactive suggests ways of thinking and negotiating our postdigital present and future. Theatre is a dynamic practice within a legacy, and scenographic critique in particular offers a framework for interrogating the platform or network effects in software systems. An interdisciplinary critique faces a directly relevant challenge, as we will see below in the analysis of *The Séance*, a collaborative research project between MIT and Punchdrunk that took place shortly after *Sleep No More* opened in New York. The research team from MIT wanted to explore the possibility of scaling and extending the immersion as experienced in the live production of *Sleep No More* to include external participants and mediators, who communicated with the on-site participant via sensor technologies and in-world text-based portals. However, adaptations and additions to the experience of *Sleep No More* that was designed for *The Séance* affected the hierarchies of representation and the subject–event relationship and altered conditions of possibility. The following analyses demonstrate the problem space via case studies: first, an analysis of the research report produced by the interdisciplinary team working on *The Séance*, followed by a study of Punchdrunk audiences as they move between physical storyworlds and mediated communities online, and adapt their own storytelling to extend immersion. The final section in this chapter discusses theoretical approaches to framing concepts of moving-within, participating and expressing agency in interactive systems. Responding to the same challenge outlined by Andersen and Pold in regard of interfaces (2018: 165) but with a focus on the nature of immersion and participation, the key objective is to create a discursive space for creative practitioners around audience agency as a scenographic material. As scenography expands to platforms beyond legacy materials and technologies of theatre design, we must interrogate the representational structures they bring in to understand the effects of mediation and platform effects on conditions of possibility.

Scaling up: space, time, audiences

Punchdrunk's digital and augmented R&D work explores the artistic and logistic potential of new technologies for their broader artistic project. It also offers opportunities for comparative analysis of different materialities in relation to immersive experience, from *The Séance*[5] to Fallow Cross.[6] The researchers on *The Séance* wanted to 'rematerialise the virtual' (Dixon, Rogers and Eggleston 2012: 8), and investigate the possibility for extending the experience of *Sleep No More*. The MIT researchers customised a Punchdrunk mask, instrumenting it with network-connected physiological sensors that connected to networked portals embedded within the scenography, which created mediated links between the on-site (live) and an off-site (online) participant. Their communication was further mediated by operators who delivered the online experience to the off-site (online) participant, based on the information streamed from the mask via the portals. The project largely failed to extend the immersive experience beyond the physical performance space. An unexpected effect was reported, however, between a small number of off-site participants who worked in the UK time zone, and hence were active in the small hours of night. They experienced a degree of immersion in the eeriness of the solitary nocturnal experience they had while connected to the operators that received the communications from the on-site participant and transmitted it to the off-site participant (Dixon, Rogers and Eggleston 2012: 22). The operators and the off-site participants shared, in a distributed sense, a plane of immanence in that they participated on the same level; connected remotely to the physical space and each other via computers. This positioned them as closer or more immanent to each other that they were with the on-site participant. This type of mediated immanence was researched by Paul Sermon in his video installation *Telematic Vision* (1993), where the 'telepresences' of two participant in different locations were compositioned on a third screen where they could see and interact with each other, while simultaneously performing 'being seated together' to an audience.[7] However, this mediated intimacy did not extend to the on-site participant, in relation to whom the remote participants occupied a transcendent, or god's-eye subject position. Effectively, the on-site participant was reduced to an 'event' that off-site participants observed from a removed vantage point, which precluded immanent, and immersive, composition.

This analysis produced by the research team as to why immersion in the on-site experience failed came to a different conclusion, and put the relative failure of *The Séance* project to meaningfully extend the on-site experience to off-site participants down to a lack of ritual preparation. The researchers understood immersion as a state that is both liminal and playful, and with the assumption that it is a liminal state, they posited that it is a product of the right induction, rather than a function of the structure of the experience (Dixon, Rogers and Eggleston 2012). The researchers drew on Victor Turner's definition of liminality as one of ritual, which Richard Schechner further articulates as a scripted experience. In both Turner's and Schechner's interpretation, ritual produces *communitas* (2013: 80) – a group's pleasure in sharing common experiences and a feeling of being attuned to each other and the experience, which the researcher team may have conflated with immersion. Applying a critique of representation, objectification and the subject–event relationship to *communitas*, it is more accurate to say that it may be shared by those who are immanent to each other following ritual, but that this experience is not necessarily any more immersive than going to the pub after a football game, or a congregation staying behind for tea and cake after church service. In *The Séance,* the on-site participant and their experience was positioned as an event or object in relationship to the off-site observer-subjects, which introduced a distance between them that is more typical of ritualised sacrifice or performed battle.

In lieu of a critique of representation and hierarchies of subject position or gaze, the research team suggested that design needs to be carefully balanced between 'putting someone in either a directed or playful mood and the personal freedom that is intrinsic to the experience' (Dixon, Rogers and Eggleston 2012: 5). In light of how Punchdrunk designers and actors discuss and accommodate live audiences as a dynamic force in their design process, this conclusion by *The Séance* research team suggests an unresolved analysis of audience agency – or perhaps a more deeply entrenched conflict between designing for stereotyped agents in one discipline, and designing for the embodied agency of live audiences in another. In this subtle difference we find a problem space that I will return to frequently throughout this volume: how the subject position of the observer (including the designer) in relation to the event impacts on conditions of possibility – 'the event' in this case being what emerges between audiences and the performance space, again and again as it repeats, idiosyncratically, for each new participant. A transcendent subject–event perspective, that is, one where the observer is external to the event (or believe themselves to be), will occlude some realities that are manifest to a subject position that is immanent (within) in relation to the event. Among these realities is the nature of agency as an embodied, emergent phenomenon. As will be revealed in Chapters 3 and 4, Punchdrunk engages throughout the design process, conceptually and practically, with the agency of both their designers and their audiences. Furthermore, the audience perspectives in Chapter 5 show that emergent agency is key to the creation of the sublime experience also from their points of view.

While the research team on *The Séance* concluded from the study that the key objective should be to 'get the experience right, not the technology' (Dixon, Rogers and Eggleston 2012: 6), their top-down perspective on the audience position (a.k.a. the on-site, or in-system, participant) is common to software culture. The interrogating gaze, whether in the software industry or in the academy, is rarely turned on itself, and the abstract nature of its materials occludes the subject position within a rationale deemed neutral by default. The research in this book explicitly incorporates both makers and their audiences, and how each represent the other, via the interface and the encounters it accommodates. As audiences are primarily encountered as data objects by designers of interactive software systems, the full impact and nature of agency as it is experienced immanently is not immediate or intuitive in the way it is to a live performer or event organiser. By contrast, the perspective on audiences in live performance culture is informed by the direct and consequential possibility of failure to engage their agency, which is immanent and keenly experienced, within the bounds of the designed situation.

From a vantage point afforded by disciplinary distance, the consequences of mediation of immersive experience are easily missed, as they mesh with the question of subject–event relationships. Towards a quantitative metric of immersion, *The Séance* research team framed their query within ritual process as the three steps of separation, liminality and reaggregation in ritual (2013: 77) and postulated an arc from first learning about an experience to 'forgetting about it'. But while Turner's model explains the progression of ritual from an anthropological perspective, it doesn't support analysis of the effects of mediation or subject position. Although Artaud included observations of ritualistic performance in *The Theatre and Its Double* (1958),[8] it is the performance, and not the ritualistic part, that informs a cogent analysis of immersion as a challenge of the subject position, as made clear by Deleuze's seminal analysis of Artaud's work in *Difference and Repetition* (2014: 209–10). Interviews with audience members, who had vivid, possibly unforgettable memories of *The Drowned Man* several or many months later, and the recounting of live experiences in Punchdrunk's online fandoms for many months or years, add support to the idea that immersion is a state of emergence that challenges the subject position. What's more, Punchdrunk rely on their reputation being sustained by their fan communities, in that they rarely advertise in the conventional sense. Their shows can be several years apart, and yet it can be extremely difficult to get tickets (e.g. *Kabeiroi* in 2017, a game-like experience staged in the streets of London, for which the few tickets that were released were allocated by lottery). Prior to the extended run of *Sleep No More* in New York they never relied on conventional advertising – instead, word of mouth upholds their mythos on- and offline, and even though they now have two semi-permanent shows (*Sleep No More* in New York and Shanghai), their fans talk about their shows in ephemeral terms as rare events that may occur years apart, and for which you need to be 'in the know'.

The sublime, as defined by Lyotard, depends on a perceived threat to coherence within bounds (Lyotard 1991: 99). In *The Séance*, the on-site (or in-system) participant experience was transmitted to the external participant via additional mediatic layers comprising the physical equipment, representations of the information generated by sensors and other technologies as presented to the intermediate operators, and finally their web-mediated communications with the external participant. The external participants were not close enough, in terms of immanence, to the live experience and its immediate range of consequences to experience the sublime, understood as a twice removed or contained threat ('deprived of being deprived'). However, a degree of immersion was reported by off-site participants in the United Kingdom, who, due to being in a different time zone to the operators in the United States (Dixon, Rogers and Eggleston 2012: 22), interacted with them at night. The mediated intimacy with the operator at night created an eerie intimacy and was, if thought through frames, twice removed: first, by the 'frame' of their computer screen, and second, by the mediation of transmission.

Immersion in a live Punchdrunk experience is contingent, as per the structure of the sublime experience, on the possibility of failure to perform *and* failure of the boundary of self. In *The Séance*, technological mediation by the instrumented mask and the remoteness of the off-site participants to the on-site participant minimised the risk of such failure. If the perceived threat is too far removed by mediation, the immersive experience depends on conjuring the possibility of its imposition on the constructed self to engender the sublime. As such experiences move online or to otherwise mediated spaces, several changes to their structure occur that require compensation to produce immersion. Immanence, thought in contrast to the transcendent subject–event relationship, implies that the present agencies occur on the same plane in relation to each other. The situation created in *The Séance*, which introduced sensors and networked portals that transmitted data from the on-site (in-system) participant on the *Sleep No More* set in New York, altered this relationship, and thus conditions of possibility (Braidotti 2013: 62). The immersion that was reported by the off-site UK participants who interacted with the US operators suggests that the shared plane of immanence and the eeriness of the night created conditions similar to those in Sermon's *Telematic*

Vision, where the two participants shared the same plane, and 'performed' this immediacy in front of an audience, creating a degree of risk. Off-site participants thus failed to experience immersion in the activities of the live participant, but under some conditions experienced mediated composition with the operators delivering the online experience:

> [The] experiment successfully created new connections between the online users and the performance, but not where it expected to. The strongest sense of connection for online users was with the operators delivering the online experience rather than directly with the live storyworld itself. (Dixon, Rogers and Eggleston 2012: 7)

Thus, the issue was not so much technological mediation, as the failure to understand the inflections of the hierarchies of representation and the subject–event relationship on immersion. While the off-site participants shared an immanent plane in the eeriness of the night as 'watchers' of the 'watched', it *prevented* their sense of connection to the on-site participant. Meanwhile, their shared perspective and task allowed them to enter into mediated composition with each other.

Observing that online participants connected more strongly with the operators delivering the online experience than with their in-system live co-participants, the researchers somewhat surprisingly concluded that it was not the quality of the production itself that was the cause of immersion in live Punchdrunk audiences, and suggested instead that the performance was 'merely a climax' of a longer arc:

> The translation of these techniques to an online space requires an understanding of the effect and then the design and creation of appropriate process and techniques whereby an online audience is introduced to a liminal digital experience. Mapping the entire experience from when the audience first hear about it to when they forget it, and planning the entire thing at all these stages, is vitally important. The performance itself is merely a climax of the entire experience journey. However, in this project the online experience failed to deliver this user journey, losing the introductory and re-integration phases. (Dixon, Rogers and Eggleston 2012: 5)

Rather than concluding that the specific quality of the experience, including its structure with regard to hierarchies of representation is key to immersion, and the impact on conditions of possibility by their interventions, the research team came to the conclusion that the designed experience is less important to the audience than its framing by advance information and expectation management, much like how experience is conceptualised in advertising.

The difficulties that *The Séance* research team had in explaining how and where immersion failed or succeeded when mediated this way confirmed the initial premise of the research in this book, further supported by detailed ethnographic audience research on- and offline. The company's reputation (the introduction or 'hearing about it') contributed to bringing interviewed audiences to the performance, but also made them wary of the 'hype': several reported finding themselves immersed in the experience *in spite of*, rather than thanks to, Punchdrunk's reputation. They quite explicitly described the detail and structure of the live experience as that which invited them to suspend disbelief and commit to the experience, directly contradicting the notion that they were passive subjects to which the experience happened.[9] A further complication with the explanation provided in the research report on *The Séance* is that the 're-integration' phase appears to be something that Punchdrunk audiences actively resist following the live performances. Quite the contrary; interviewees typically describe their reluctance to re-join the everyday, and their desire to re-enter the storyworld.[10] As discussed in the next section, Punchdrunk fandoms even reinvent their sense of belonging in their favourite storyworlds as a devotional practice. It allows them to hold on to their role as active 'moving parts' in Punchdrunk's storyworlds and invokes, as described below, make-believe transgression of the frame imposed by their screens – and thus the sublime.

Audience immersion on- and offline

Punchdrunk's 'superfans' self-select as co-creators of an extended narrative played out through their repeat participation in live performance, and in their remediation of live experience online. Their devotion is simultaneously at odds and symbiotic with the storyworlds and aesthetic created by the company. Members of the online fandom extract, map and archive that which Punchdrunk embeds, obscures and disassembles. They share gameplays, hacks and level descriptors, much like computer gamers do, and attend as many times as possible; not just to re-experience the show, but also to uncover all the secrets embedded within the dramaturgy and scenographic environment. Superfans visited *The Drowned Man* up to a hundred times, and many have attended the same production dozens of times. Some of them form the core of the Facebook 'Spoiler' groups, who, like urban explorers, map and share everything they can find out about the show, including archives of fragrances used to create the atmosphere of particular parts of the set, one-to-one interactions, annotated choreography, complete character loops and reproduced floor plans of the set. These archives are kept and shared online using collaborative platforms, primarily blogging platforms (e.g. thedustwitch.com), Facebook and Dropbox. This subset of the Punchdrunk audience seeks the solution of the mystery, while at the same time extending it. They invest meaning into productions that company designers and actors aren't necessarily aware of encoding into the productions through repetitions, reengagement and remediations that, even if intended to map the imagined totality of their passionate obsession, cannot fail to produce difference. Punchdrunk productions are not fixed in the sense that conventionally scripted stage plays are. This, in conjunction with their scale, prohibits comprehensive understanding or 'completion' of their totality. By repetition, iterative changes by both audiences and actors are inevitable, and ambitions to create or comprehend a stable system are stubbornly, and addictively, frustrated.

The company is aware of their superfans and the considerable efforts they invest in mapping and extending the meaning of their object of worship, and some vicariously enjoy following how audiences receive, explore and remediate their work in online fandoms:

> That happened a lot, sort of six-seven weeks in: people knew the show. People would be writing essays and hints and tips on the internet, writing about what time to see this scene, and at some points they knew more than we did. In fact there were some bits the audience knew, like the one-to-ones, they'd describe it in intimate details, where we sort of knew the bare bones of it.[11]

Occasionally, the sense-making practice of superfans go beyond mapping what is, and extends to generating narratives that, to company members directly involved with the design and build of the production, neither exist nor were intended to exist.[12]

The freedom with which superfans expand the meaning of the storyworlds on Facebook and, to some degree, Tumblr, extends to reframing the otherwise embodied and immanent experience in live performances as a mystery cult with the storyworld positioned as a transcendent that insinuates itself into everyday life through omens and devotional practices. Fan activities are discussed in terms suggesting pilgrimages, sacrificial offerings and ritual gatherings. The knowingness with which this make-believe is discussed in fan forums suggests the *mythopoeia* of metamodernism; an aesthetic of informed naïvety and romantic expressions, characterised by oscillation between modernism and postmodernism (Turner 2011) while refusing both. The simultaneity of diametrically opposing positions, for example, the sincerity of modernism and the irony of postmodernism, is accommodated in oscillation: 'attempting to attain some sort of transcendent position, *as if* such a thing were within our grasp' (Turner 2015, original emphasis). Vermeulen and van den Akker's rallying call for metamodernism borrows from Gramsci, declaring a 'pessimism of the intellect and an optimism of the will' that allows its participants to re-instate the transcendent in knowing make-believe (2015: 58, 65–6). Metamodernism may emerge from the conditions of possibility on social media platforms, where the affective labour of users populates hyper-rationalist infrastructures of little or no warmth with personal content. For Punchdrunk's superfans, the metamodernist aesthetic facilitates reframing of their nostalgia for the live storyworlds in a form that invokes the sublime via the possible imposition of a mystical, transcendent presence on everyday life. They are at no point victims of delusion; the invocation of the sublime is a deliberate, communal, ritualistic performance that sustains the sensation of immersion, adapted to the affordances offered by different digital platforms.

Analysis of the posts in the Facebook 'Spoiler' groups that refer directly to experiences relating to *The Drowned Man* and *Sleep No More* reveals that nearly a third were associated with themes around ritualistic and cultic activities, including themed game nights where 'Spoilers' can meet and re-enact the storyworld. Just under a quarter of contributions were associated with sacrificial offerings of time, effort and care through creativity and giving, and through effort, expense and surrender, including body modifications (both temporary, e.g. dressing up as characters from the show, and permanent, i.e. tattoos). Fan art by the 'Spoiler' community includes adaptations of the Cards Against Humanity game and a Minecraft version of Temple Pictures. Just over a fifth of posts reflected on profound longing, loss and persistent preoccupations with sensory recollection and recreation of music and smells from the productions. Nearly 15 per cent of posts were devoted to talismanic practices: purchase, pilfering and collecting of memorabilia associated with the productions. This group typically shared photographs and descriptions of their prised possessions in the 'Spoiler' communities, often displayed in home reliquaries or altars. The smallest group of 'devotional' posts (10 per cent) referred to the storyworld pervading everyday life with signs and omens. The often ironic and self-deprecating tone used by posters suggest that these are play behaviours, extending the primary mode of participation in live performances; the 'Spoiler' community does not confuse the storyworld with real life, even in the case of posts describing omens. Instead, fans demonstrate to their community their devotion to the storyworld through willing sacrifice of 'good sense' and creative effort under themes that are circulated within their community as particularly important and symbolic. Nostalgia for a shared world dominated many of the posts after the show closed, with reminiscences, tips on resources where accounts of the show are collected, music playlists and fragrances that remind them of Temple Pictures being shared. Wistfulness and flashbacks triggered by certain patterns and motifs from the live productions seem to build cultural capital within the fandom, with the associations to things or events, rather than being expressions of delusion, marking the sensitised afficionado. Many were preoccupied with smells from the storyworld, and traded tips on room perfumes that reminded them of particular parts of the performance, for example, thunderstorms and earth. Fragrance contributes to ambience in Punchdrunk productions, primarily from the sheer mass of materials assembled but sometimes, artificial scents are added to objects to enhance specific atmospheres. Threads providing guesses about fragrances worn by different characters, as well as the smell of specific parts of the set, ran throughout the production and beyond a year after its run concluded. Fragrance hunts was the most popular category of fan posts on the Facebook 'Spoiler' fandom, and a fragrance post also gained the most comments in total. Attention to detail appears to be as important to online audiences as it is to live audiences, and was an equally prominent quality in interviews with company members. The pseudo-devotional tone of the Facebook 'Spoiler' fandoms overall describe a lifestyle that allows for living, at least part-time, in storyworlds. Commitment to this ideal is demonstrated through detailed descriptions of 'pilgrimage', recollections, memories and artefacts, and the devotional accumulation of exhaustive knowledge.[13]

The modes and tone of participation are inflected by conditions of possibility on different platforms. On Tumblr, some posters advertise their special status, which is more or less completely absent in the Facebook 'Spoiler' groups. On Facebook, elevation to special status is only done *to* select members *by* other members: it is never self-assigned. In the 'Spoiler' Facebook communities, overt self-promotion is mostly ignored, while communally oriented actions are rewarded. Some Tumblr fan blogs draw focus to the author, and claim an enhanced ability to participate and interpret the productions in a correct fashion, displaying signs of particular closeness to the company or its members as evidence of this status, for example, the Tumblr blogs *Back to Manderley*, '*Blood Will Have Blood, They Say*', *Scrapbook* and *Rotten Wood and Wilted Sunflowers*, who, in borrowing aspects from the production in naming themselves make their raison d'etre clear. Other bloggers on Tumblr take a devotional approach, more similar to the Facebook 'Spoiler' discourses, for example, *All Good Things … All Bad Things …*, *Arfman*, *The Fool's Loop* and *Living Inside a Dream*.[14] In comparison with the communally oriented devotional practices of the Facebook fandom, Tumblr promotes self-proclaimed 'sainthood' and visionary practices that are more individualistic, authorial and hierarchic. Interestingly, some superfans publish on both platforms, and change their voice accordingly. The different tone on Facebook and Tumblr even when written by the same person supports the idea that participation is shaped by the affordances, limitations and infrastructures of different platforms.[15] Crowd situations also alter conditions of possibility, and the people that comprise a crowd in, for example, a Punchdrunk performance or a city carnival, do not behave as they would in their homes, or across the conditions of possibility presented by different types of events. Comparisons of the same people on different platforms, or the same people in individual and domestic versus public mass conditions counter the idea that we can form useful ideas of the subject by way of mass data surveillance, Big Data and crowd analyses based on Markov models and derivative machine learning methods. Even though they are designed to be context-independent, they produce pattern analyses that are flawed for application to human agency in at least two dimensions.[16] On the one hand, data gathered on platforms designed to produce and shape this data for optimal ease of processing is going to be more precisely informative about how users respond to present affordances, rather than 'who these users are'. On the other hand, the results produce profiles of users as data objects that cannot represent agency, only agents – and then in reductive, general form based on enriched stereotypes.

Behaviours on one platform reflect local conditions of possibility, and do not necessarily persist on other platforms. Audiences who participate in such interactive, procedural narratives typically adapt to different conditions and the restrictions and influence they exert on communication, exemplifying how we absorb and process discontinuity, intuitively and without reflection. Alexander Galloway uses play (2012: 29) as a term to explain this ability in human participants to overcome narrative gaps and frictions. Thinking audiences as producers of narrative through interpretative processes resonates with de Certeau's discussion of story as a practice that mediates between place (characterised by mapping and hierarchical orders ascribed from a transcendent point of view) and space (emergent, exploratory, and immanent spatial practices) (Certeau 1988: 115–17). In this light, Punchdrunk's online fan discourses are a form of story-play that traverse the mediatic layers of social media platforms, similarly to how Punchdrunk audiences navigate live productions, producing expressions that are distinct to each platform and always the outcome of negotiation and interpretation. In live performances, the art-work of producing narrative is held and framed, immanently, within the bounds of time and space presented by the performance and scenography. In online story-play, which occurs without such bounds and on networked social platforms with different conditions of possibility, the story is stabilised by the players through an imagined transcendent (the mystical storyworld that insinuates itself into the mediated every day). The suspension of disbelief and devotional practices in the Facebook 'Spoiler' group is not an involuntary delusion, but a 'summoning' of the storyworld into a virtual play zone that can be superimposed on everyday life, and across digital platforms.

Theatres of action

Physical storyworlds present different conditions of possibility compared with digital ones, with consequences for scenography, performance and infrastructures. In physical storyworlds, gravity is one of the key restrictions. As discussed in the introduction to this chapter, gravity and our aesthetic and functional resistance to it are fundamental factors in sculpture, architecture and engineering, and contribute to meaning in art more broadly via the possibility for consequence and the weight of reality. The conditions of possibility of the digital modern have been the subject of interrogation by media and digital humanities scholars, for example Friedrich Kittler (1999), Roger Silverstone (1999), Nick Couldry (2012), Alexander Galloway (2004, 2012), David Berry (2014a, b) and James Smithies (2017), in order to understand how online modes of being, thinking and communicating are inflected by technological mediation. Proposing a systems analysis for the digital humanities, Smithies writes:

> Cyberinfrastructure represents one of the central 'unthought categories' of contemporary humanities research. It is a complex interpretative domain, characterised by a blend of technical cultures and socio-political factors that combine to resist simple elucidation. The complexity derives from the fact that it 'does not grow *de novo* – it wrestles with the inertia of the installed base and inherits strengths and limitations from that base'. (2017: 113–14)

Coding languages and their legacy heuristics, like other systems of representation, are discursively formed over time and reflect dominant structures of thought within digital material culture and the digital modern. In this period, which started in the late 1960s and arguably drew to its close in the mid-2010s, the hiddenness and abstraction of software structures in the eyes of the naïve user and maker gave coders a semi-mystical aura. This was achieved in part through the reframing of computer operation and programming, which had been a primarily female occupation since the 1940s, as a high-level, technocratic and male-dominated professional field (Hicks 2017). However, its reintroduction into the socio-political continuity and its historical context became inescapable as the large-scale effects of increasing pervasion of networked digital technologies on everyday life and democratic processes became apparent.

Transparency and accountability for interdependencies are made more challenging by the opacity of software systems, which reasonably comprise not only coding legacies and heuristics but also the contingent 'complex interpretative domain, characterised by a blend of technical cultures and socio-political factors' (Smithies 2017: 113). The infrastructures of what we can see and do in software are as entangled with the politics and economies of representation as any other field of creativity or engineering, but arguably more resistant to interrogation. Cyberinfrastructure is 'continually in flux' and only exists as 'a relational property; it describes a relationship among technology, people and practices' (Smithies 2017: 114), which is true also of conventional infrastructures, whether hard, such as the fruits of structural engineers or soft, including socio-economic institutions. Theatre is no exception; its 'backstage' structures and relationships shape what can happen and inform the design and use of physical infrastructures, the workings of which are sometimes revealed as part of the scenography. The infrastructures of theatre and scenography, conventional or not, have developed to support and manage the production of emotion, meaning, spectacle and illusion, by way of dramatic storytelling. Whatever technologies have been available and used at different points in the history of theatre their success is measured by naturalisation beyond novelty and successful application in meaningful design. In expanding scenography using digital technologies, theatre's legacy of working artfully with the messiness of human life on stage and in the auditorium encounters a material that is averse, at a fundamental level, to ambiguity, metaphor, difference and the complex opacity of embodiment. But however solipsistic, the technological gaze of the digital modern 'does not rescind existing sociocultural and political complexities' (Smithies 2017: 114). Theatre's legacy of thinking through and beyond representation is perhaps the best guide we have in addressing this problem.

The critique of representation in theatre and performance studies is a valuable framework for interrogating technological systems that are designed for human participation. The critique of subject position or gaze is particularly relevant to machine reason, which stands for good sense within its scheme of representation and, echoing its Platonic lineage, is often conceptualised as pure reason. Thinking and designing for participation from this point of view raises aesthetic, ethical and functional questions. It also begs a comparison with how audiences are conceived by creative practitioners with a grounded experience of working with live events, giving form to the otherwise abstract tension between the promise of liberating discrete thought and the continuity of embodiment and its dependencies (Fazi 2018: 2–3, 9). When live audiences are your key material, obscuring the primacy of embodiment will result in unmanaged exposure to several dimensions – aesthetic, ethical and functional – of this problem. Embodiment is the root of audience experience in theatre, and in immersive theatre it is fully revealed as a functional part. It runs counter to purity and rationality as conceived in the technological modern; even if its physical complexity can be satisfactorily modelled at some point, agency will differ. As technologies are naturalised, they are folded into the 'impurity' of everyday life and its entanglement with material existence. Digital technologies, being oriented towards cognition and the idea of formal logic, are given to favour the mind over the body, and ill-dispositioned to accommodate the complexity of actual human beings and their fecund, embodied idiosyncrasy. And so the image of pure reason, flowing from the Platonic ideal through the Cartesian *Cogito* and its promise of sovereignty of mind over matter, resists the social via digital infrastructures, even as they carry 'social media' into everyday life.

The blind spot of the transcendent technological gaze mirrors Phelan's 'unmarked' (1996), making an already abstract concept even more elusive. However, Punchdrunk's work across large masked shows, intimate encounters, and R&D activities, allows us to give form to the question. We can learn from the flaws of *The Séance*, which simultaneously exposed the on-site participant to external surveillance and denied connection through situating them as the objectified 'event' in relation to the transcendent off-site subject position, and propose that immersion requires immanence, interiority and intimacy. We can observe the behaviours of Punchdrunk's audiences as they move between storyworlds and mediated everyday life and see that they are not unwitting captives of immersion, but complicit in its maintenance and extension. They are also willing and able to adapt and reinvent their experience in response to the affordances offered by digital platforms, so that they better carry invocations and insinuations of the storyworld. And we can challenge the subject position in its presumed neutrality when transcendent, and the contingent construction of the objects of its gaze as stereotypes, which are better understood as 'events' in specific conditions of possibility. Based on these observations, we may seek a more precise understanding of what human 'parts' in theatre machines are, at the ontological level, and how they form the compact of immersion through engagement with the performance environment and emergent articulation of space. In interviews, both company and audience members describe immersion as embodied and exploratory, stimulated by disorientation and the tension between what is (detailed expression as opportunities to engage) and what is not ('simulation gaps' created by diffraction, distillation and differential possibilities of interpretation). In Punchdrunk's work, descriptions of awe and urgency emphasise how audiences perceive the designed environment as simultaneously detailed and supporting, unstable and emergent, and how this affects their responses.[17]

These experiences and the forms of exploration that support them are founded at the infrastructure level. De Certeau (1988: 85) conceptualises spatial operations as stories that modify the local order, and Punchdrunk productions begin with the stories carried around by Felix Barrett, sometimes for years as they await realisation when the right building becomes available.[18] Before mapping the inside of a building, Punchdrunk black out the windows and then walk the space, imagining how it can express and articulate the play and its composite narratives.[19] In de Certeau's terms, this is a *coup* that prepares a 'theatre of action' (1988: 122–6). The story-making is seeded through a spatial operation that occurs between the vision of what will be made and the proposed situation, negotiating the topographies of restrictions and opportunities. The in-between negotiation that unfolds the story is called *metis* by de Certeau;[20] a combination of skill and memory that inflects the vision of what can be made and the manner in which the *coup* is carried out. If we apply the idea of the *coup* to networked computational culture and its enmeshing with the everyday social, the topographies of computational culture are determined not so much by gravity or other physical restrictions and affordances, but by legacy heuristics, infrastructure and business models, all flowing from the images of thought that found representation (Deleuze 2014: 203). The peculiar absence of gravity in combination with the dominion of a certain kind of instrumental reason shape what we might call the foundation myths of computational culture. We see them in computer games about quests, conquests and frontier exploration, but also in software culture, whether professional or aspirational. Foundation myths around such quests are generally told from the point of view of the 'questee', often using romantic images of virgin or unknown territories, upon which a new order is visited. The abstraction of computational language and culture obscures and rationalises these mythical affiliations, and the colonisation motif. The natives of virtual virgin territories need not be othered with narratives of race, species, progress and religion – their representation as data objects already naturalises othering, and the absence of gravity in any projected interaction accelerates the vanishing, through abstraction, of consequence.

If we stay with the image of colonisation, the 'user experience', expectations and control of native populations have historically been managed not only through conquest but also with language, custom, religion, law and technology. Computational culture manages user experience via interface design and personalisation, based on aggregated data from past actions and stereotypes (Kant 2020) – a broad practice Galloway calls cybertyping (2012: 137). A data-intense approach to personalisation forms knowledge that leans towards the static via the circular, as past, generalised actions shape predictive models, with more detail gathered about the participants narrowing, rather than broadening scope. In the live interactive systems produced by Punchdrunk, participation is anonymous and detail observed from participation, and subsequently added through design broadens, rather than narrows scope. The root of these effects lies in how system users are thought and defined; in terms of their identity as it is observed, predicted and represented within the system, or in terms of their agency as it is articulated within the system. As these properties are defined at the infrastructure level of interactive systems, a critical study of infrastructures needs to be part of an exploration of how the legacies of theatre and performance inform experience design. These legacies are embedded within the infrastructures, or 'backstage' operations of interactive systems, and their implementation is a *coup* that founds theatres of action. As interactive technologies pervade the everyday, we are recruited to play our parts in these theatres, with or without our explicit, informed consent. An integrated theory of critical infrastructures and the conditions of possibility that they found is thus of interest beyond immersive theatre.

Connectivity is not neutral; it comes, by default, with exposure. Questions around the accounts, accounting and accountability for the consequences of exposure pervade the history of colonisation by trade, war or technology. At a glance, these questions may seem a concern primarily for those who are colonised, but exposure is only constructed as one-directional by force, and then temporarily. Time, gravity and difference are relentless, and the occlusion of consequence by frames of gaze and comprehension excises meaning and depth from lived experience: the result is a malaise, perhaps not so different from nineteenth-century mal du siècle.[21] The Romantic sublime emerged out of this aesthetic mode as a craving for awe and a sense of existential vertigo that is lost without the depth of time, space and the prospect of our own dissolution in their vastness. Lyotard's postmodern sublime draws on the Romantic but finds vertigo more specifically along the fault line of reason. A postdigital sublime that describes aesthetic encounters within networked systems takes a few more steps along that path, towards the unknowability of agencies both external and internal to oneself. In support of such encounters and the conditions of possibility that invoke them, this book discusses spaces that may inform new digital topographies. Such spaces must accommodate ambiguity and the long-worn, deeply layered wealth of experience that is carried into the interaction by its human participants. I will suggest, based on the research presented and discussed in the chapters that follow, that this needs not a general or totalising understanding of human nature, but a more intent focus on the unfolding moment of interaction. The issue balances on the distinction between generality and the particular, and the recognition that the former must always be reductive while the latter is emergent. Within bounds, such as those defined by a performance environment or storyworld in which audiences participate voluntarily and with the option of exiting at will, an interaction can be sufficiently understood in the moving present through the detail of exchange, given that it is carefully articulated in the moving present. Being clear about what we need to know for the designed system to function, aesthetically and otherwise, allows us to review how participants in interactive systems, which are storyworlds of a sort, are represented and modelled.

The question of thinking audiences in terms of their agency for design purposes is an overarching concern of this book. Punchdrunk's live productions play out in the gravitational, physical world where unplanned actions are consequential; thinking audiences as a dynamic material supports both their experience and the company's design process. De Certeau uses the term 'delinquency' for emergence that is unaligned with plans and grids of modernity and efficiency. I will borrow the term to imply emergent expressions of the un-modern that at times push against the bounds of storyworlds, with the latter regarded as compositions of rules and affordances, place and space. This becomes a useful consideration in light of the sheer physicality and generosity of affordances in Punchdrunk's theatrical worlds. From a pragmatic point of view, their live productions have to accommodate hundreds of people per night over very extended runs. The institutional knowledge and empirical legacy of the company has produced, and continues to produce methods for engaging and negotiating 'delinquent' agency on the edges of what is sustainable and creative within the system, and within the aesthetic of the storyworld. These come to expression in the role of the Black Masks, which is described in detail in Chapter 4 and which might be described as usher, stagehand, stage manager and performer rolled into one, acting as an extension of the scenography. Black Masks operate at once within and without the storyworld, and their methods are designed to preserve the integrity of the storyworld functionally and narratively, articulating and negotiating encounters on its boundaries. A perhaps counter-intuitive effect of their interventions to engage and steer delinquency is enhanced audience experience through a kind of sublime vertigo that we might term postdigital, and which occurs in encounters between system agencies that simultaneously disrupt the subject position and the frame or perspective on the event.[22] These themes will be explored through case studies of Punchdrunk's work across, and on either side of the designed interface in subsequent chapters, following a genealogy of the immersive aesthetic.

Notes

1   Coined by Keith Johnston, theatre director and educator, who founded the Theatre Machine improvisation group in London (touring internationally in the 1960s and early 1970s).
2   COM4.
3   COM2.
4   AUD1, AUD3, AUD5.
5   *The Séance* (2011) was a NESTA/AHRC/ACE-funded collaboration between Punchdrunk, MIT Media Lab in Boston, and researchers from the University of the West of England, Bristol, the University of Dundee and the University of Central Lancashire in New York.

6 Punchdrunk's indoor R&D village in Tottenham, London from 2017 to 2019 (and possibly beyond).
7 A synopsis of Telematic Vision by Paul Sermon (1993) can be seen at http://www.medienkunstnetz.de/works/telematic-vision/.
8 Already familiar with Noh theatre, Artaud attended a performance of Balinese dance theatre at the Exposition Coloniale that was held in the Bois de Vincennes, Paris, in July 1931. This experience directly inspired his description of a Theatre of Cruelty in *The Theater and Its Double*, which was first published in 1938 as *Le Théâtre et Son Double*.
9 AUD1, AUD3, AUD4, AUD5.
10 AUD1, AUD2, AUD5.
11 COM6.
12 COM2.
13 The 'Spoiler' community for *The Drowned Man* on Facebook (closed group; permission to join or access the content can be sought directly from the administrator) was the primary source of this research.
14 See Appendix.
15 See Appendix.
16 Open Markovian models that underpin crowd analyses for the purpose of generating demographic stereotypes for personalised programmatic advertising and content distribution online are employed on the premise of being context-independent (Sauvagnargues 2013: 127–8) – the flawed presumption is that the individual is, too, and that the interactive systems from which the data is gathered are neutral and not rhetorical environments.
17 COM3, COM5, AUD1, AUD5.
18 COM6.
19 COM2.
20 From the Greek μῆτις, describing a combination of wisdom and cunning.
21 An existential state of ennui, disillusionment and melancholy; the 'spiritual sickness' of the Romantic alienated self that seeks unity with a greater reality.
22 AUD1.

2

A Genealogy of the Immersive Aesthetic

This chapter seeks to locate the work of Punchdrunk within a legacy and articulate connections between key movements in European arts practices and contemporary developments in immersive theatre. The perception that immersive experience is a new phenomenon may be encouraged in the context of media products, but a review of historical modes of presentation unearths deep roots and a rich body of skill and critical understanding of the interaction between scenography and spectator. This perspective locates the work of Punchdrunk in relation to other companies making immersive work and within a tradition of experimental theatre that stretches into the past, as explored here, and the future, as discussed in the final chapters of this book. The conclusion of this chapter charts the development of an immersive aesthetic in blended realities across theatre and digital platforms via the human facility for completing, expanding and processing narrative. The particular theoretical frames used here to understand immersion as an experience, within and beyond scenographic mode of presentation, come into their own in analyses of design practices that combine and move between the restrictions and affordances of the theatre form and other immersive mediated experiences.

Artaud's interrogation of the subject position sits within a historical arc of challenging representation through dramaturgy and scenography. Arnold Aronson maps the historicity of the components brought together in a comprehensive vision by Artaud and acknowledges Theatre of Cruelty as a key influence on environmental scenography, that is, theatre that is critically concerned with the place of the spectator within the spatial organisation of the mise en scène (2018: 1, 66–7). Before and after Artaud, Schlemmer and Wilson foregrounded 'the role of scenography in the process of creating' avant-garde environmental theatre (McKinney and Palmer 2017: 125). From the mid-nineteenth century, the avant-garde challenge of representation splintered along two broad lines of enquiry; one that sought to reveal the material world beyond mimesis, and one that sought authenticity of experience. The former came to expression in what is more commonly considered modernist aesthetics, whereas the latter, from Symbolism through Surrealism, developed along anti-realist lines. The disparity is less dichotomous than it first seems. Both are concerned with interrogating representation, in the first instance of the material world; in the second, representation of the subject to itself.

Environmental theatre places the spectator subject within the scenography, and Punchdrunk's immersive theatre plays with the subject position of its audiences in multiple ways, while recruiting them as critical 'moving parts' within the clockwork whole of their productions. Situating their work within the genealogy described here articulates a vision and theory of scenography that expands to include and incorporate interactive systems and their infrastructures. The critical framework introduced in this book aims to support migrations across physical, virtual and blended materialities, whether from a starting point in theatre or in contemporary game design. It is grounded in the history of environmental theatre, with particular attention to Punchdrunk's distinct perspective on audiences and the structure of immersion in their large masked shows. Their body of work and material culture offer rich opportunities for research and critical analysis with a focus on thinking and modelling audiences in immersive experience design.

Borrowing from Schechner's 1971 proposal for environmental design, Aronson describes the historical context of the immersive aesthetic, with a focus on its architectural visions, as environmental scenography (2018: 165). Interfaces, here primarily thought as the surfaces of interactive systems as they are presented to human users, include the constructed environments in which we move physically, with thresholds and openings that present points 'of transition between different mediatic layers within any nested system' and their codes (Galloway 2012: 31–3). At the theoretical level, Galloway's concept encompasses what Christian Ulrik Andersen and Søren Bro Pold call 'metainterfaces'; the designed shape and layout of cities, websites and other logistic structures that are at once infrastructures and cultural expressions in their own right (2018). Galloway's concept of nested systems allows us to frame physical as well as technological interfaces and the agencies at work within them from an immanent perspective, whereas Andersen and Pold look primarily at the transcendent vantage point that informs metainterfaces: models, templates, generalised ideas and maps of systems and their habitats (2018: 35–7). Punchdrunk's physical scenography that audiences are in immediate contact with includes the first-hand experience of how the performance space is planned and subdivided and is therefore discussed as a form of interface, whereas the supporting conceptual, social and physical frameworks are discussed as infrastructure. The interpretative gaps of nested systems and their encoded layers necessitate and afford play both as an expression of freedom of movement within a system and emergent expressions of negotiation and mediation of tensions and frictions. Interactive systems thus present a spatial metaphor for Jacques Derrida's notion of freeplay. Freeplay is at once subordinate to and deviating from the central idea of an interactive system, making its articulation in response to spatial opportunities and challenges a minor tactic (Cull 2012: 20).

Key influences on the immersive aesthetic

Charting the development of the immersive aesthetic reveals its constitutent elements, which is critical to analysis of immersion across theatrical and virtual scenography. In a historical view, Artaud's Theatre of Cruelty stands out as a theory of scenography that articulates with some precision both the phenomenological essence of immersion and its place in critiques of representation. The analyses of Theatre of Cruelty in *Difference and Repetition* (Deleuze 2014: 209–10), and *Writing and Difference* (Derrida 2001: 351–70) confirm its seminal role in theatre and beyond to challenging gaze and the subject position in designed experience, as well as the primacy of embodiment over critical distance. It is along these vectors we see most clearly its structure as an aesthetic in the minor register; that is, one in which the subject position is not flattered as sovereign, inviolable, rational, lofty and stable or persistent.

Laura Cull's discussion of minor theatres draws on Deleuze's critique of representation, which specifically includes the subject position. This is critical to an interrogation of interactive systems, where the authorial subject position is distributed, often hidden and sometimes networked. 'Minor' refers not to relative numbers, but to positions within the Cartesian order that ranks the body as secondary to the mind and the senses as a lower form of cognition than reason. This hierarchical order privileges that or those *defined* by mind, will and origin of gaze over that or those framed, by gaze, as *limited* to their bodies and senses; the gaze that frames imposes the limits, and it emits from a subject position that is defined by this facility. Challenges to established systems of meaning in the minor register often include distortion, discontinuity and distribution of authorship and agency to unsettle established hierarchical relations of gaze and comprehension (Cull 2012: 20), and eschew the comfort of immediate understanding, critical distance and control. Such challenges have informed the trajectory of experimental performance and theatre that confronts, envelops and eventually immerses the audience to impose on their subject position subtractions and incisions, alongside those imposed on material representation. We can trace both in experiments with acentric narratives, disruptive staging and audience provocations from the anti-realist modernism of Symbolism through to Italian and Russian Futurism, Dada and early German Expressionism, with precursors of the immersive aesthetic in Max Reinhardt's 'theatre machines' and early Russian theatre in the round with ambulatory audiences (Aronson 2018: 81–96).

In *One Manifesto Less* on minor theatre, Deleuze discusses the subtractive operations performed by Carmelo Bene in the production of *Richard III* (1979). Subtractive, rather than additive operations in minor theatre cut back or into the representational layers that support established systems of meaning, excising 'elements of power, the elements that make up or represent a system of power, which are subtracted, amputated or neutralized' (1979: 206–7). Representational layers include the structure of narrative, décor, costume and script; the organisation of representational elements, for example, the order or coherence of narrative, the plan and organisation of the performance space; and the processes or facility for organisation and understanding afforded the audience, for example, the transparency and locus of authorship. As means to escape the trappings of representation, Deleuze underscores subtractive methods in theatre that strip and distort narratives, and defines the theatre maker as an operator, who is at once a calculator and surgeon:

> The man of the theatre is no longer an author, actor, or director. He is an operator. By operation, one must understand the activity of subtraction, of amputation, but already masked by another activity which gives birth to and multiplies the unexpected, as in a prosthesis: an amputation of Romeo and immense development of Mercutio, the one within the other. This is a theatre of surgical precision. (Deleuze 1979: 205)

In accord with Deleuze's broader critique of representation, this surgery, precisely executed so as to cure and not kill the 'patient' (the possibility space of Mercutio within the tragic figure of Romeo), must be performed on the subject position and not the body itself. A minor theatre, whether its gestures are small and intimate or sweeping and grandiose, is one of the body and its expression. We see this in the machinic aesthetic of Futurism and early modernist theatre, and in the embodied complicity of audiences as agents and co-producers of meaning in participatory immersive theatre. Aronson (2018) describes this development through the architectures of performance and its audiences, whereas this book focuses on scenography as the conduit system for the 'voluptious emotions' (Klossowski 2017) of audiences as a critical material in experience design. Below and in subsequent chapters, it looks at how 'freeplay' (Derrida 2001) is invited and managed through the design and shape of complicity in audience self-exploitation (Bishop 2012):

the performance of spatial and interpretative acts that complete designed systems (Bogost 2007; Chow 2012; Galloway 2012) and, at the same time, articulate the intimate outline of the performing subject.

The notion of complicity, as discussed by Bishop in *Artificial Hells* (2012), is important to the immersive discourse through questions of agency, distributed authorship and the situated body in avant-garde theatre, performance, ritual, site-specific theatre, happenings, installations and live art. The contemporary immersive aesthetic as developed by companies such as Punchdrunk, Blast Theory, Agency of Coney, and dreamthinkspeak all centre the audience in physical productions with elements of blended reality and pervasive games. Typically, they explore questions of agency and complicity through a first-person, immanent audience perspective within performative interactive systems. The legacy of these features can be traced in the anti-realist modernism of the late nineteenth century, the idea of the *Gesamtkunstwerk*, and the modernist experimental theatres of Futurism (in central Europe as well as Russia), Max Reinhardt, Erwin Piscator, Bauhaus and Nikolay Okhlopkov, and the visions of Frederick John Kiesler and Antonin Artaud. The visions and methods of these theatre-makers in the first decades of the twentieth century mirrored defining cultural, political and technological developments in Europe. Performance responded directly to the popularisation of photography and moving image through the advent of celluloid photographic film to avant-garde politics and the impact of war (and its documentation) and brought several revolutions to the idea of representation in the late nineteenth and early twentieth centuries. Photography and film afforded different ways of seeing and thinking time, movement and form, and the First World War and the Spanish Civil War brought urgent challenges to conventions in theatre and art, renewed in the twenty-first century by internet and virtual technologies through which we both enact and consume war as entertainment, whether the real wars in the Middle East and other regions, or the fictional and proxy wars of games and social media.

Anti-realist modernism, tracing an often somewhat romantic path alongside more positivist expressions of modernism, critiqued the supremacy of the rationalist position, and often looked to internal realities, and the darker aspects of emotion and drive. The Second World War established the postmodern perspective; not simply as a negation of modernism, but as a complementary, problematising and sometimes, but not always, playful position in relation to 'grand' progress narratives. During the historical postmodern period that followed the devastation of two world wars, and which founded the postmodern aesthetic and texture of thinking and feeling, several seminal movements in philosophy, art and performance emerged which are all critical to our understanding of immersive theatre.

The social turn included avant-garde art movements such as the Situationist International and art interventions in the public space (Bishop 2012: 11). The participatory shift, which again sits within a much older European history of fêtes, pageants and processions (Aronson 2018: 25) came to expression in public spectacles as well as intimate happenings in the period outlined here. The scope of such events ranges from the very large to the very small, and finds a reflection in Punchdrunk's masked productions, from the epic scale of *Sleep No More* and *The Drowned Man* to the close-range intimacy of one-to-ones. The avant-garde and celebratory spectacles and art interventions of theatre and performance history that disrupted the quotidian order and cut across mapped and gridded urban landscapes now face other rule-based topographies: those of blended and virtual realities. The final section of this chapter looks at ways we might draw on a rich history of interventions, insinuations and impositions to better accommodate what we are beyond who we think we are in the virtual scenographies that are superimposed on everyday life. For this, we need to look at the nature of the tensions, frictions and narrative gaps in between, which interpretative acts can enter and move within. For virtual scenographies, we might consider an aesthetic of occlusions and absences, and work towards Guillaume Apollinaire's instruction to Serge Férat, his designer for *Parade*: 'The décor [...] will be the air in the theatre' (Brandon 1999: 10).

Anti-realist modernism in experimental theatre

Punchdrunk's theatre can be seen to be the latest in a long tradition of experimental performance with roots in anti-realist modernism. It is important to acknowledge that their approach did not emerge fully formed out of nowhere, but is a development of European traditions in theatre, art and literature. Late-nineteenth-century Symbolism, which came to inspire both Dadaism and Surrealism, was a reaction to realism and countered its rationality constructs with emphasis on subjective experience. It sought to elicit direct experience of the sublime, an aesthetic experience defined as dichotomous to beauty (Holmqvist and Pluciennik 2002):[1] an amalgamate of awe and terror that produces pleasure through suspension or containment of the perceived threat within the vista or artwork. Symbolist poetry and art sought to transgress or collapse the separation of mind and body through the sublime, articulating that which lies beyond normative concepts of beauty, harmony or 'good sense'. Here, the minor aesthetic is expressed through representation of the subject to itself; not mind over body but centring the image of sense and sensation at-sea, with possible loss of control a present possibility. The work of artists and poets Puvis de Chavannes, Odilon Redon,

Edward Munch, Charles Baudelaire, Arthur Rimbaud, Paul Verlaine and Stéphane Mallarmé thus predated abstraction as an expression of anti-realist modernism, albeit through aesthetic spiritualisation and the extension of the Romantic sublime into the 'recesses of the soul'.

The latter half of the nineteenth century and the early twentieth century saw rapid scientific and technological progress, new theories of psychoanalysis and the subconscious (notably by Freud and Jung), social and political unrest, devastating wars and new means of documentation that brought images of the world to the masses with photographic realism. The tension between the promise and terror of progress narratives inflected artistic expressions, many of which were associated with the sublime. Irreverence with regard to conventional representation and the incorporation and of elements from popular culture and new technologies were, and are still key features of twentieth-century experimental theatre and performance art. Companies like Punchdrunk, Coney, Blast Theory and Ontroerend Goed draw on computer games, surveillance and virtual forms of representation, or create work that explores inflections on the social and personal by technology through the collision of intimacy and exposure.[2]

In his manifesto *L'Esprit nouveau et les Poetes* (1918), Guillaume Apollinaire proclaimed a renewal of art and cultural life that embraced modern technology and liberated poetry from the burden of representation and repetition. He was keenly aware of the possibilities created by new technology (cinema, radio, telephone and phonograph) to open the field for a 'synthetic' theatre art, combining poetry, music and movement, and called for artists to eschew aestheticism and formulae, and embrace 'sublime novelty' or be left to the forms of pastiche, satire or lamentation (Apollinaire 1918: 385–96). Apollinaire's friend Alfred Jarry, who also influenced early Surrealism, was embedded in the Parisian Symbolist circles or artists and writers with roots in the humourist groups and artistic cabarets of Montmartre in the 1880s and 1890s (Dubbelboer 2012: 41–5). With *Ubu Roi* (1896), he took their rejection of rationality and the emphasis on subjective exploration of the complexity of sexuality and the nature of existence into absurdist theatre (Bowness 1972: 78–86). The play revelled in crudity, and famously opened with the expletive *merdre!* It was received with uproar from more conventional audience members, and applause from the avant-garde. It had neither a coherent plot nor conventional characters, and satirised the stupidity, vulgarity, cruelty and greed of modern man in concurrent parallel narratives. In its profanity and upheaval of good sense, *Ubu Roi* anticipated Dada and Surrealism. Jarry's infantile assault on the senses and shape of the physical body through profanity, denunciations of beauty and sovereignty ensured that the play was only performed once – after riots closed the night of the premiere, Jarry took the play to a puppet theatre. Jarry and other theatre visionaries of the first decades of the twentieth century were urged by critical and aesthetic visions that spearheaded discourses and critiques of representation that remain salient, but neither the technical cultures nor the socio-political milieu at the time were ready to support their realisation.

The search for expression beyond conventional representation presents a more persistent challenge in theatre than it does in arts that lend themselves more readily to abstraction, as the physical presence of the actor problematises escape from the commodity form, the body and its intransigent connotations (Blau 1992: 4). Processes of abstraction are more easily compromised and made precarious, as the body of the actor is entangled with the hierarchy of visibility and sensibilities around the body as a socio-economic object. Early-twentieth-century experimental theatre and performance challenged the presence and form of the physical body through deliberate lack of technical perfection, alienation of the audience and, later, a machinic aesthetic in costumes and scenography. Jarry's work for theatre inspired Apollinaire, who collaborated with Jean Cocteau, Erik Satie, Pablo Picasso and Léonide Massine (of Diaghilev's Ballets Russes) on the ballet *Parade* (1917), for which Picasso designed the costumes and the curtain, and Apollinaire wrote the programme notes, coining the term 'surréalisme'. *Parade* incorporated influences from popular culture such as movies (which at that point were silent), fairground and music hall motifs, which were already becoming modernist tropes in experimental visual and performance art and explored ways of moving that challenged conventional stage representation. Everyday materials were used to produce costumes (e.g. cardboard) and sound (such as empty bottles and typewriters), forcing the dancers to adopt disrupted and machinic movements in sharp contrast with the conventional ballet form, which emphasises continuity and ethereal lyricism. The controlled and idealised form and expression of the body suggests that its submission to time and gravity can be transcended; the artistic perversion of this ideal reminds of fallacy and submission.

Also inspired by *Ubu Roi*, Filippo Tommaso Marinetti presented *Roi Bombance*, referencing Jarry's earlier work, at Théâtre de l'Oeuvre in 1909, two months after publishing his first Futurist manifesto. The disruptive Futurist vision for theatre, art and society eschewed convention, comfort and continuity and excelled, like Artaud's would later, in manifestos rather than realised productions, but Futurist evening events offered provocative cabaret or variety style theatre that expressed the spirit in which these manifestos were written. Marinetti admired the focus on novelty, in contrast with narrative depth, in variety theatre and preferred the irreverence and proactivity of cabaret audiences. Variety theatre inspired Marinetti to proclaim the purpose of Futurist theatre being to 'destroy the Solemn, the Sacred, the Serious, and the Sublime in Art with a capital A' (Goldberg 2011: 17). Futurist theatre combined atonal sounds, nonsense text and mechanical physical movement in an intentionally alienating machinic performance aesthetic. In an early challenge of the conventional relationship between stage presentation and expected behaviours from audiences, direct provocations were designed to produce extreme responses, often resulting in performance events being rounded off by a barrage of vegetables thrown at the stage and/or arrests (Goldberg 2011: 16–17).

Russian Futurists Vladimir Mayakovski, David Burlyuk, Velemir Khlebnikov, Aleksey Kruchenykh and Vasily Kamensky formed an artists' collective under the name *Hylaea* from 1911 to 1912 around an avant-garde café theatre in Moscow, where they presented tragedies and operas sharing some of the characteristics of the Italian Futurists. In 1913, Kruchenykh composed the Futurist opera *Victory Over the Sun,* and Mayakovski created the tragedy *Vladimir Mayakovski,* with both works combining influences from circus (like variety theatre, a popular or 'low' cultural expression) with a cubist, non-objective aesthetic. Running in tandem, the two productions sought to integrate set, costume, actor and gesture (Goldberg 2011: 34–8) towards the disintegration of the boundary between stage and auditorium through spectator participation that we see in the work of Punchdrunk, Blast Theory and dreamthinkspeak. The members of *Hylaea* soon took their theatre to the streets and beyond the confines of the stage, reflecting influences from the longer history of public spectacles, fêtes and carnivals (Aronson 2018: 25) and heralding promenade theatre. The off-stage activities of *Hylaea* included public appearances in outlandish outfits, poetry readings in the streets, and assaults on members of the public, reflecting the title of their 1912 manifesto *Slap in the Face of Public Taste* (Lawton 1988: 51–2). Vsevolod Meyerhold, who like Jarry began his career as a Symbolist, experimented with circus-like effects on stage and formulated the biomechanical acting method, a departure from Stanislavski's focus on the psychological processes of the actor that emphasised the link between the physiological and the psychological. Frustration with the limitations of the spoken dialogue in comparison with visceral physical expression and experience propelled such experiments, and became increasingly relevant in Punchdrunk's work from 2003, when Barrett invited Maxine Doyle to collaborate on their first rendition of *Sleep No More* (Doyle 2006).

Challenges to representation through the body, its costume and movements on stage were important also in Dada performances, championed by Sophie Taeuber-Arp (an early Laban student). Between 1915 and 1917, Tristan Tzara, Hugo Ball, Taeuber-Arp and Jean Arp staged Dada events at Cabaret Voltaire in Zurich, blending dance, avant-garde costumes, puppeteering, music, poetry and early experiments with transmedial performance. This legacy is continued in performance and theatre artists through experimentation with mixed-media and new technologies and also in the merging of music, dance and circus with theatre. Taeuber-Arp brought choreography, dance and costume design to Dada performance at a time when dance was

> moving from a proscribed repertory and technique into a radically new system concerned with spatial and bodily relations. The dancer would become an object to be manipulated; identity and meaning constructed through gesture. (Belcen 2015)

Like the Russian Futurists, Dadaists took performance outdoor, beyond the cabaret stage (Aronson 2018: 40), culminating in the Dada-Season of 1921 (Bishop 2012: 66). The desire to break down the boundary between stage and auditorium in Futurist and Dadaist cabaret and theatre formed two strands in the 1920s which continue to be relevant for participatory art and performance: one seeking to disrupt and provoke, the other inviting and celebrating collective creativity. Common to both are the desire to emancipate and empower participants, both actors and audiences. In their live shows, Punchdrunk focus on disruption and separate audiences for the main part of the experience in order to unsettle and stimulate exploration from a socially unmoored subject position. Collective spaces feature, however, in their mediated and after-show experiences, for example, the bar through which audiences typically exit performances. The cabaret bar at New York's *Sleep No More,* Gallow Green, regularly features music and other types of performance and has become a venue in its own right.

Provocation, which typically breaks with conventional representation, creates interpretative gaps and tensions that may invite physical or symbolic enactment. Participatory elements challenge authorship as a hierarchic principle and may take a collaborative approach to the creative process and the assumption of collective responsibility. The latter is relevant to the critique of alienation in avant-garde art, for which collective responsibility and collaboratively elaborated meaning, in order to restore the social bond, is regarded as the remedy (Bishop 2006: 11–12). An early example of monumental collective creativity was Nikolai Evreinov's 1920 mass re-enactment *The Storming of the Winter Palace* in Saint Petersburg (or Petrograd, as it was then known), which involved 2,500 performers and military vehicles, and combined disruptive and collective narratives in ritualistic re-enactment of the events between the February Revolution and the storming of the Winter Palace in 1917. Blurring the boundary between performance and celebration, this type of mass spectacle sits within a long European tradition of public pageants, processional performances and carnivals (Aronson 2018: 94–6). They far exceed the scale and ambition of Punchdrunk productions, but face other challenges, including the degree of control that is possible through design. Bishop's distinction between forms of participatory spectacle is relevant to this comparison. Whereas Punchdrunk productions tend to depart from the spatial narrative of the urban settings in which they create their work in order to disrupt and provoke new modes of participation, *The Storming of the Winter Palace* is an example of public participatory performance that celebrates collective creativity – in this case framing and re-enacting a key event of the Bolshevik revolution as such, in dramatised form.

Dada, too, took to the streets with art interventions, which culminated during the Dada-Season of 1921 in Paris, when large outdoors events were programmed to actively engage the public. The St. Julien le Pauvre excursion, which was part of a series of art events that intended to attract visitors to 'places that have no reason to exist', drew over 100 participants. The creation and reframing of spaces for events outside of conventional experience is central to the creative impetus of Punchdrunk, and the company has evolved the capacity to create ambitious alternative realities at sometimes extremely short notice.[3] André Breton coined the phrase 'artificial hells' shortly after to describe the wave of Dada events that had moved from the cabaret stages to the streets. He found the spectators' willingness to participate in the 'Dada game' to be evidence of failure and started rethinking the Dada strategy of provocation through scandal (Bishop 2012: 67–70). Later that year, Breton's ascendance as leader of the Dada movement culminated in the *Barrès Trial*, a mock trial of the Symbolist novelist Auguste-Maurice Barrès. This event marked a shift away from the anarchic Dada provocations towards a more intellectual approach that would develop into the Surrealist movement (Bishop 2012: 73).

Jarry's work continued to influence experimental theatre, and inspired Antonin Artaud to found *Theater Alfred Jarry* in Paris together with Roger Vitrac and Robert Aron in 1926 (Artaud 1976: 610). Artaud's vision of theatre was inspired by Surrealism and Jarry's absurdism and sought to disrupt complacency by collapsing aesthetic distance and inciting chaos (Jamieson 2007: 21–2). Artaud placed the audience in the middle of the spectacle, engulfing them emotionally and physically with incantations, guttural utterances and screams, early electronic instruments (e.g. the *ondes Martinot*, an instrument that made radio waves audible) and pulsating lights (Banes 1993: 115). He wanted to integrate the text and the body in a theatre that compromised conventional representation through direct, unmediated experience with no barrier between audience and actors; a theatre that, according to Derrida, 'summons the totality of existence and no longer tolerates either the incidence of interpretation or the distinction between actor and author' (Derrida 2001: 232–5). Never fully realised by Artaud, his vision was formative to Punchdrunk. The company has come close to consistently realising it within the means of scenography through the integration of space, light, sound and movement, while presenting a compelling theatrical whole that deprioritises the spoken word. Experimental theatre has tended to alter the relationship between the spectator and textual and spatio-temporal narratives, prompting architectural and environmental innovation in scenography and staging technologies (Aronson 2018). In Derrida's perspective on the traditional stage as theological, the 'passive, seated public, a public of spectators, of consumers' was dominated by the words of the author-creator who controls representation (Derrida 2001: 297). New relationships between the spectator and the narrative, and the integration of architectural and technological innovations a well as acting, dancing, singing and multimedia broadened the opportunities for interdisciplinary devising. Derrida called the hybridity and physicality of Artaud's theatre a spatial language that prioritised 'sounds, cries, lights, onomatopoeia' over speech, which emphasised the formative in becoming (Derrida 2001: 303).

By the time Artaud's *Theatre and Its Double* (which contained the two Theatre of Cruelty manifestos) was published in 1938, theatre-makers were already working with nonlinear staging and active parts for audiences in the physical composition of narrative. Nikolay Okhlopkov, who was strongly influenced by Meyerhold, started experimenting with theatre in the round in 1935 at the Realistic Theatre in Moscow, where he was appointed director in 1930 (Roose-Evans 1996: 78). By operating several stages, he was able to cut between scenes and break away from linear presentation; a feature that Punchdrunk developed into the 'Punchdrunk system' that allows the company to distribute and manage performance segments in a cyclic model across twelve performance zones and twelve time slots, repeating hourly.[4] A contemporary account of Okhlopkov's production *The Iron Flood* by André van Gyseghem describes how audiences were invited into an auditorium where the play was already in progress on five-foot-tall, uneven, rocky banks in a long hall; another feature used by Punchdrunk, who start the performance fifteen minutes before audiences arrive. The audience was incorporated in a scene where actors identified them as comrades, presumed lost in hostile country (Roose-Evans 1996: 79–81). The *Gesamtkunstwerk*, which informed also Punchdrunk's vision, calls for expressive theatre infrastructure and the interdisciplinary confluence of skills to produce a total theatre. These visionary elements were systematically explored by Max Reinhardt in the 1911 production of *Das Mirakel*, which built on the Germanic tradition of Volk festivals. Reinhardt produced *Das Mirakel* for arena, rather than proscenium staging (Aronson 2018: 43–8), and, using lighting and sound, transformed London Olympia into a vast cathedral space (Gjefsen 2012: 18). The production, which played before nightly audiences of 8,000, toured Europe and incorporated more than 2,000 actors, singers, dancers and stage technicians, with elaborate stage machinery, music and lighting, but no dramatic dialogue. The ambition of *Das Mirakel* and other works by Reinhardt, for example, *Jedermann* and *Faust* (staged on a Salzburg mountainside in 1933) was to transform stage technology and realise the Wagnerian vision of a total theatre (Roose-Evans 1996: 65). In 1912, the stage production of *Das Mirakel* was followed by two feature films based on the Vollmoeller play; one authorised by Reinhardt that featured the original cast (produced by Joseph Menchen), and one unauthorised version (by Continental-Kunstfilm). Both films were promoted on the back of the success of Reinhardt's production, with the Menchen production marketed as a filmatisation of the original play, allowing audiences to see more of the detail of the performance and making the movie a transmedial development of the theatre play.

The dramatic potential of scenographic infrastructure that we see in Punchdrunk's scenography and the confluence of creative disciplines was revolutionised by Reinhardt's disciple Erwin Piscator, who evolved the idea of the *Gesamtkunstwerk* into Epic Theatre, which emphasised the active audience subject position. Piscator took a transmedial approach to text in scenography through the systematic use of movie projection in front, back, simultaneous and overlapping 'living walls' (Willett 1979: 60, 111, 113), and considered 'a revolutionary theatre without its liveliest element, a revolutionary audience' to be 'nonsense' (Willett 1979: 191). He developed the staging and dramaturgy techniques of Epic Theatre at the *Volksbühne* in Berlin between 1919 and 1927, where he emphasised adaptation and collaboration, and frequently used montage, a Dada technique (Willett 1979: 108). Piscator embraced the technological thrust of the modernist vision in his designs for theatre machines with 'hoists, cranes, practicable traversing platforms with which weights of several tons could be shifted around the stage at the press of a button' (Roose-Evans 1996: 66–7), and introduced theatre machinery that extended hemispheric, rotating stages with lifts, bridges and treadmills (Willett 1979: 88). While Brecht left more of a legacy in the form of writing and disciples, he acknowledged that his own achievements would have been impossible without Piscator (Willett 1979: 186). Both Piscator and Brecht rejected naturalism, and sought to strip back the representative layer of theatre to 'reveal the machine', the narrative and mechanical devices that produce meaning and emotion; a concept that finds new meaning in Punchdrunk's work against the background of affective labour in the early twenty-first century. They worked together in the 1920s on the adaptation of scripts for Piscator productions, but Piscator only staged an original play by Brecht after the playwright's death in 1956. While Piscator invented the *Verfremdungseffekt* as a physical expression in theatre design (Willett 1979), Brecht was to be remembered as the primary theorist of Epic Theatre, as he formalised the concept within a socio-political framework to describe the surprise, discontinuity and distortion of expectations that disrupted of the illusion of representation.

Frederick Kiesler was another visionary of scenographic space. Active in European avant-garde artist circles in the 1920s, Kiesler developed the concept of the space stage to scientific precision, centring the actor within an abstracted theatrical space, almost free of figurative representation, which 'ceased to be a picture' (Aronson 2018: 53–4). The space stage also inspired Oskar Schlemmer, who provided artistic leadership for the Bauhaus collective's experimental theatre in Germany during the same period. Schlemmer worked in a classicist-modernist aesthetic that pointed in its sophistication and formalism towards the much later work of Robert Wilson. The more anarchic experimentation of Dada and Surrealist performance was brought under a coherent vision that still celebrated mechanisation and strived for a synthesis of art and technology, albeit through an expertly executed modernist aesthetic. Schlemmer's students at Bauhaus refined early modernist features, including music, lighting, innovative costumes and sets, as well as acting informed by dance rather than spoken words. Guided by Schlemmer's modernist theory of performance, dramatic devices that were pioneered by the Dadaist and Surrealist movements were incorporated and disciplined within an intellectual framework that emphasised structure and purity of expression. This fed forward to the precise material formalism of Robert Wilson, whose *H.G.* (1995) was seminal to the emergence and development of Barrett's – and Punchdrunk's – aesthetic. Schlemmer referred to the Apollonian and Dionysian to express the tension between control and abandon (Goldberg 2011: 97–103), drawing on Nietzsche's definition of the Apollonian-Dionysian dichotomy where Apollo is the ruler of form, brightness and individuation, and Dionysus the god of rapture, ecstasy and the intoxicated 'obliteration of self' (Nietzsche 1993: 14–27). The unresolved tension between the Dionysian and the Apollonian in Schlemmer's work eventually found some resolution in Allan Kaprow's happenings in the late 1950s and 1960s. Kaprow reengaged with formalism in the installation environments he created, representing universal concepts without invoking the transcendent ideal of formal geometry. Instead, Kaprow used mundane objects that were neutralised by everyday use and symbolised, for example, nourishment or rescue (Trimingham 2010: 88).

Geopolitical events in the 1930s and 1940s shifted visions in European theatre away from spatially expansive modernist ambitions, and towards disillusion with rationalist progress narratives. In 1937, in his German diary, Samuel Beckett wrote of rationalism and its causes against the background of political developments in Europe: 'Rationalism is the last form of animism. Whereas the pure incoherence of times and men and places is at least amusing' (Knowlson 1996: 228). The disenchantment with progress narratives and their failure to prevent two world wars influenced much of post-war European art, including experimental performance art. Artaud's Theatre of Cruelty, a theatre 'beyond words', served as a bridge between European inter-war and post-war experimental theatre, with the post-war Theatre of the Absurd embracing bewilderment, confusion and a distrust of language. The movement was driven by a group of playwrights who were influenced by Jarry, Dada, Artaud, and silent movies: Beckett, Tom Stoppard, Eugène Ionesco, Jean Genet and Harold Pinter. Together with their contemporaries in the Art Informel movement, they articulated the prevailing zeitgeist in the immediate post–Second World War period in European art: existentialist, absurdist, questioning and broken.

Complicity and participation

The historical arc within which Punchdrunk's work sits gathered pace as experimentation with the extension and alteration of the physical performance space became more expansive in the 1960s and 1970s. Theatre-makers including Luca Ronconi, Ariane Mnouchkine and Richard Schechner continued the experimentation with multiple enveloping and shifting stages in participatory modes reflecting the tension between renewed optimism and critique. Like modernist art and theatre of the early decades of the twentieth century, the participatory shift in performance and art juxtaposes the idea of audience agency with the idea of the passively consuming spectator to articulate the potential for emancipating the audience from alienation, consumerism and a totalitarian social order, often through the twin gestures of social impact and alienation (Bishop 2012: 275). Artaud's assault on the bourgeois audience in *Theatre of Cruelty* and the frame play and extended performance spaces of Russian Futurists Dada and Epic Theatre continued to influence avant-garde theatre throughout this period, from Situationist art interventions to blended reality games and superimpositions.

At the heart of scenography beyond the proscenium stage lies a critique of the mind-body dichotomy and the idealised spatial constructs that it is bound up with, including the geometric or Cartesian space. The relationship between the Cartesian space and the proscenium stage can be understood in light of the shift from the socio-magical picture space of pre-renaissance representation to the 'objective' linear and centrally convergent perspective of renaissance art (as seen in, for example, Raphael's *The School of Athens*). The single point-of-view set up by the vanishing point perspective creates the illusion of a window on the picture space that is informed by Renaissance Neoplatonic thought.[5] It positions the audience of the artwork in a transcendent subject–event relationship to the object, mirroring the position of the audience in relation to events presented on the proscenium stage. The transcendent subject position, external to the observed event, makes possible the compact or hierarchy that underwrites claims to a single, rational and objective subject position, as well as separation and indemnity from actions and their consequences on stage.

Avant-garde theatre and performance challenged the single point-of-view from a transcendent subject position and continued to incorporate popular and 'low' forms of media in experimental performance and participatory art during the latter part of the twentieth century. Theatre-makers and designers sought to create new forms of play that rejected central authorship, both on and off stage, through pervasive forms of performance theatre and games. The resulting discursive performance space could be imposed, or superimposed, on its context, rather than being bound by the conventions of the traditional stage. Valie EXPORT's work with 'Expanded Cinema' blended interactivity and technology with performance, and brought focus to what frames and screens afford, incorporate and exclude. The idea of expanded cinema, which we see developed in the present moment by companies such as Secret Cinema, was first explored in 1958 by Svoboda in *Laterna Magika*, but EXPORT turned the idea around to address issues around objectification and gaze. In *Touch Cinema* (1968), she emphasised the voyeuristic relationship to the female body in cinema and wider contemporary mass media culture through public performance. Passers-by were invited to touch her breasts by putting their hands through the curtained 'screen' of the cardboard TV that she was wearing strapped to the front of her torso. The artist called this 'the first genuine women's film', as she was in control of the display of the female body within it (Mueller 1994: 15–18). EXPORT uses reflection on several levels in her work, moving between the mediated and the physical body. In *Ping Pong* (1968), an actor representing the audience performed in front of a screen, equipped with a ping pong bat and ball. The screen displayed dots, appearing and disappearing, as targets for the actor to try and hit (Mueller 1994: 9). While at the time *Ping Pong* was acclaimed as a political statement on the reactive role of the conventional cinema audience, later developments in computer and video games give EXPORT's work renewed relevance as an early critique of, and response to, the limits and affordances of technology-driven interactivity. While the idea of realising 'playable theatre' is coming to the fore in Punchdrunk's work more explicitly only recently (Judge 2019), the similarities, cross-over and inspiration from video games have been a formative influence on the structure of the company's work for some time (Jakob-Hoff 2014). The focus in theatre on the quality and nature of audience experience and subject positions brings important questions regarding the critical differences in methods of production and consumption to digitally mediated interaction design, and innovation by designers with the experience and capacity of Punchdrunk in this arena is of significant interest to the broader field.

The expressive potential of interactivity in theatre was explored by Mnouchkine's Theatre du Soleil in *1789* (1970). The play, which had a fairground atmosphere, lasted two and a half hours without interval and freed the audience to find different vantage points (Aronson 2018: 170–1).

It was presented on a circle of stages that surrounded the spectators with simultaneous scenes from the French Revolution. At the storming of the Bastille, the actors invaded the auditorium, accosting the audience as if they were an actual mob witnessing the event. The production challenged the canonical accounts of the events and outcomes of the historical period as recorded in history books, and, instead of focusing on prominent historical figures sought to show the French Revolution from the perspective of the common people (Roose-Evans 1996: 86). In 1969, Ronconi produced *Orlando Furioso*, a play in which the audience were not allowed a linear narrative or a comprehensive view of the stage, and instead had to move around to piece together the story from a series of isolated scenes played by actors on wooden floats, sometimes collaborating to physically move the platforms on which the fragmented scenes were played out. Ronconi followed this in 1971 with *XX de la rue,* a theatre performance in a two-storey building with twenty rooms, ten on each floor, in which the spectators, divided into two groups, watched fragmented scenes depicting the arrest and interrogation of a revolutionary threatening a fascist regime. Critics at the time accused Ronconi of celebrating fascism, to which he responded that it was more important to 'plunge the spectator [...] into the confusion of all conditions that could, at present, make fascism possible' (Roose-Evans 1996: 81–3). Ronconi combined Schechner's ideas of designing theatre in relation to the body rather than the mind with medieval staging (Aronson 2018: 165, 167), resulting in a theatrical experience that emphasised visceral complicity with a certain instability of representation that foregrounded the precariousness of democratic order. The vertigo of possibility that is contingent on exposure is central to immersive experience such as it is described in the audience case studies in this volume. The sublime dimension of exposure, that is, the absence of guarantee that encounters will be comprehensible, unequivocally benign and safe from moral or manifest falling or failing, is a shared theme shared across audience interviews, and laced through descriptions.

Augusto Boal focused on the potential of theatre as a political training ground for audience agency in *Theatre of the Oppressed* in 1973, which introduced interactive methods intended to turn audiences into 'spect-actors'. Boal developed and expanded his methods since the publication of *Theatre of the Oppressed* to include forum theatre, invisible theatre and legislative theatre, and sought to generate change through enactment of semi-staged conflict: a rehearsal of revolution. Boal wanted the theatre, whether it took place in the political, therapeutic, pedagogic or legislative contexts he worked with through his career to leave a sense of unease through lack of resolution, stimulating the 'spect-actors' to seek resolution in real life: 'I don't want the people to use the theater as a way of not doing in life' (Bishop 2012: 122–5). Boal's work with rituals and masks emphasises the ideological culture of a society that is articulated and maintained by social interaction patterns through cultural rituals, for example, confession according to Catholic rites. By changing vantage points throughout the performance, the actors embody the tension between ritual role and socio-economic status so that the power relationships within society can be experienced directly and at a sensory level in enactment (Wardrip-Fruin and Montfort 2003: 351–2). Building on the frame play of Epic Theatre, Boal brought the 'spect-actor' into the physical and dramatic proceedings of performance, erasing the boundary between stage and auditorium. While Piscator's theatre machines required audiences to 'work' discursively with the narrative, Boal, like Ronconi and Mnouchkine, asked the audience to participate physically and enact parts of the dramatic action in ways that are directly relevant to the way Punchdrunk require their audiences to complete the artwork through exploration, perseverance and recombination in the face of disorientation.

Rey Chow describes the artwork as a trap, the design of which is only fulfilled through the 'abduction' of its audiences (Chow 2012: 41–3). While intended as a metaphor for the co-option or recruitment of cognitive as well as physical participation of audiences in the completion of the art-work, we see experiments with actual (voluntary) abduction in Fiona Templeton's *You – The City* (1988), which took one audience member at a time on a two-hour journey through intimate and public spaces in New York. After they introduced themselves with the words 'I'm looking for you' to the doorman at One Times Square, they were taken on a mystery tour in which they encountered a cast of fifteen in a series of meetings, including one where they were pushed into a cab by the driver (Montola, Stenros and Waern 2009: 59). The spectator's role as a 'client' was made visible within the work through a series of scripted interactions with facilities for the actors to respond and adapt to each client and their surroundings. The erasure of the boundary between performer and audience was articulated in the emergent relationships between the actors, the client and the city and finally, in the play's climax the client was alone with another client, believing the other to be an actor (Templeton and Nelson 1990: 12–17). Punchdrunk employ a similar uncertainty of roles in their productions, with actors blending with audiences and inviting them into one-to-one experiences that seemingly collapse the actor-audience distance.

The social turn in live art from the 1990s onwards drew on Debord, de Certeau, the Situationist International, Deleuze and Guattari, Hakim Bey and others to produce art that tended towards de-centralisation, dematerialisation and anti-market (as a transcendent organising principle of capitalism), with utopian themes around collective desires, turning away from neoliberal individualism and fetishised authorship. While utopian in its aims and collaborative in its methods, theatre and performance art in this vein often hinges on the encounter, which invites confrontation and the possibility of failure within an 'on-the-cusp' aesthetic that actively involves a challenged, even compromised, audience. The possibility of failure to 'perform successfully' as an audience member is a seemingly paradoxical driver of perseverance in Punchdrunk that simultaneously heightens urgency and confronts audiences with their self-exploitation. Exploring the poetic potential of the failure of theatrical representation, Elevator Repair Service and Forced Entertainment invoke Deleuze's minor within de Certeau's dynamic space (Cull 2012: 20). Elevator Repair Service reframe and reinterpret props, scripts and choreography to foreground failure, including ensemble dancing and slapstick inspired by musicals, 1930s movies and cartoons that parodies 'serious' drama (Bailes 2011: 160–1). Their ensemble dance numbers typically express social awkwardness and failed communication, incorporating mundane gestures and movements in an absurdist commentary on theatrical hierarchies in the stage and screen musical tradition (Bailes 2011: 154). In the United Kingdom, Forced Entertainment work with an anti-heroic, broken aesthetic that fails to uphold theatrical continuity (Forced Entertainment 2015), for example, in *200% & Bloody Thirsty*, where three drunk people in wigs and a sea of second-hand clothes seek truth or falsehood through enactment of different versions of the real or imagined death of one of their friends in a staged hybrid of a nativity scene and a very messy party (Forced Entertainment 2015). Phelan places the work of Forced Entertainment, which sits between experimental theatre and live art, in the extended context of the 'collapsed world' of Art Informel: the artistic voice of society-wide existential crisis in the wake of war that could still be felt in 1980s Britain, particularly in northern towns and cities like Sheffield, where the company is located (Bailes 2011: 66). Art Informel embraced chance, eschewed top-down formality, and was imbued with the aesthetic of the encounter. In Punchdrunk's work, this is articulated as self-exposure to chance, uncertainty and lack of control in the face of an undefined, but ever-present possible failure to 'perform' the subject position.

The crisis of meaning that followed two world wars resonated across the Atlantic, connecting and inflecting European and American experimental theatre and performance through emerging social and political contexts in subsequent decades. Artists in the Situationist International movement explored social games and *dérive* as art interventions, and had, together with Fluxus and the New Games movement, an enduring influence on counterculture, participatory art and pervasive game design in subsequent decades. They continued to interrogate conventional representation and incorporate 'low' cultural motifs from cabaret, movies, fairgrounds and circus, complemented from the 1960s onwards with TV and computer games. In a postmodernist mode of questioning modernist progress narratives, they emphasised pluralism, fragmentation representation and the possibility of concurrent unscripted interpretations (Fischer-Lichte 2008: 147–8). In 1958,

Guy Debord published *Theory of the Dérive*, which described the Situationist practice of 'drift', in which the participant adopted ways of moving within the urban landscape that were unrelated to efficiency. As well as building on concepts of difference developed by Deleuze and Derrida, the immanent and emergent practice of *dérive* constitutes a form of blended reality in which being-within, as an alternative embodied discourse, is superimposed on the transcendent order of post-Haussman Paris and other modern city grids. Situationist art interventions exploited the tension between awareness of such orders and actions cut across, negated and inverted their purpose in ways that resonate with Punchdrunk storyworlds, which are nested or embedded within the city landscape. Other Situationist parallels with the Punchdrunk aesthetic include disaffection with language and dialogue-driven narratives. The Situationists International were influenced by Dada and Surrealism via Lettrism, an art movement that disowned conventional meaning; in particular that which is carried by written language. The trajectory from the post-war art movements Lettrism, Art Informel and Theatre of the Absurd, through Situationism to the early 1960s art collective Fluxus describes the persistent influence of Dada on twentieth-century avant-garde art and performance through features that are formative influences on Punchdrunk's practice, including the rejection of conventional meaning in representation, art practice as an alternative politics and a material focus on process.

Fluxus pioneered the idea of intermedia, and included performance artists Wolf Vostell, Joseph Beuys, Al Hansen, Nam June Paik and Yoko Ono. A hybrid of the European and the New York-based avant-garde, Fluxus artists worked in an anti-art, neo-Dada aesthetic that blended live performance, video, spoken word, installation art and music in transmedial happenings throughout the 1960s and 1970s. The intent playfulness of Fluxus found a counterpart in the contemporaneous New Games movement that emerged on the American west coast in the late 1960s. Perhaps a more uniquely American movement than Fluxus, it was a reaction to the Cold War mentality and the Vietnam War, born out of the Californian counter-cultures that formed around Ken Kesey's Merry Pranksters and the Gestalt Practice of the Esalen Institute. Embodied enactment and participation are central to Punchdrunk's work and were also the focus of the New Games Foundation, which developed participatory public games that encouraged non-aggressive and non-competitive behaviours (Montola, Stenros and Waern 2009: 55–6). Their activities included the purchase of a fourteen-acre farm to establish the Games Preserve in 1971, a retreat where participants could study play through practice. Fusing practices from the New Games movement and Fluxus, pervasive games in the United States adopted a transmedial aesthetic from the mid-1960s, when mediated storyworlds were extended through live action role-playing, or LARPing. This form of participatory performance typically overlays or superimposes storyworlds on existing cityscapes or other built environment through enactment, combining environmental scenography with the idea of virtual worlds. The movie *La Decima Vittima* (1965) spawned a trend for live action assassination games on US university campuses that became the subject of an episode of the TV series *The Saint* called *The Death Game*, which popularised the genre and spawned new developments (Montola, Stenros and Waern 2009: 67). From the early 1980s, assassination games were a popular genre in LARP games, and games communities started to perform their characters in the physical world (Montola, Stenros and Waern 2009: 64). The genre remains popular, with LARP communities forming around storyworlds in books or games that are typically enacted as superimposed alternative realities that can play out over several days or weeks (Montola, Stenros and Waern 2009: 36–7). The durational format of LARPs and the commitment to virtual storyworlds are important elements in the conditions of possibility for audiences in Punchdrunk performances, and feature even more strongly in the extended storyworlds enacted and maintained by the 'Spoiler' fandoms, particularly with the greater focus on faithfulness or exactitude in enactment or knowledge that can be seen in the fandoms. More like Punchdrunk performances than the strictly scripted and rule-bound LARPs, the so-called Nordic LARP (or Nordic progressive LARP) typically has unobtrusive rules that accommodate a greater degree of improvisation. Nordic LARP often plays out over an entire weekend, but the genre also has shorter forms, for example, chamber LARPs, black-box LARPs and free-form games. The Nordic form has a particularly strong aesthetic focus, emphasising collective design and creative collaboration on sets, costumes, story and atmosphere (Axner 2012). As a practice, Nordic LARP shares features with not just audience but also design practices in Punchdrunk, as demonstrated by the ways company members discuss their relationships to the storyworlds they contribute to building.[6]

Blended spaces and the vertigo of transformation

Immersive performance places the participant within the work, but crucially also claims their sensory and cognitive involvement as agents. LARP communities, in particular those that emphasise collective responsibility for the creation and maintenance of their storyworlds, see this as fundamental to the form, but more authorial approaches to immersive design also rely on 'self-abduction'. Audience agency is invited to 'entrapment' within immersive storyworlds, realised as physical sets or blended reality narratives that superimpose the storyworld on physical reality. The latter is typically, but not always supported by digital platforms, for example, social media, smartphone apps, or other geolocative devices (Machon 2013: 35–6). A coherent analysis of the immersive aesthetic in the early twenty-first century as a product of expanded scenography and practised space, that is, a form that relies on unscripted participation and 'self-abduction' within built or blended designed environments needs to span physical and digital design with keen awareness of the material conditions of possibility created by the specific material cultures of both.

Ilya Kabakov and Char Davies were among the first to use the term 'immersive' to describe 'the totality of audience experience' (Machon 2013: 28). Like Max Reinhardt's *Gesamtkunstwerk* a hundred years prior, the immersive aesthetic comprises architecture, sound, lighting, projection, digital technologies, choreography and installation art. This interdisciplinarity can be seen in Ilya Kabakov's walk-through installations from 1987, when he emigrated from the Soviet Union to Europe, and subsequently to the United States. Persisting across the abstract through to the concrete, the artist then began realising his 'domestic theatre' as physical art installations in gallery settings. Kabakov's domestic theatre; narratives around fictional, lonely characters on the margins of society, were created when he still lived in the Soviet Union, and were documented in the illustrated *Albums* (1972–75) series (Bishop 2012: 153). These characters remained at the centre of his work in their absence, even as their settings were fully realised. Spectators (termed 'actors' by the artist) move through Kabakov's installations, only encountering them as voids left behind. Canadian artist Char Davies combined influences from her fine art practice and her love for scuba diving in the virtual reality installations *Osmose* (1995) and *Ephémère* (1998). Participants, or 'immersants' (as Davies called her audiences), navigated within these virtual reality worlds through controlled breathing and leaning; rising by breathing in, and controlling their direction of travel through leaning. The visual aesthetic was painterly and influenced by natural forms, with translucent shapes through which the immersant could move, sufficiently abstract to suggest shifts between micro and macro perspectives. A 3D soundtrack composed of human voice samples and electronic sounds added spatial depth to the experience and mirrored the combination of organic elements and abstraction (Davies 2012).

The pervasion or collapse of safe distance is key to the immersive aesthetic, making Chow's discussion of the artwork as a trap relevant (Chow 2012: 43). The postmodern sublime unsettles subjectivity: 'the shared purpose of art "which was to illustrate the glory of a name, divine or human" is put into "disarray" by the sublime' (Bamford 2012: 126). The sublime experience traces the boundary between reason and no-sense and can be engendered by the failure of play frames to contain the game, the failure of systems of meaning, or the failure of the participant within such systems. 'The unifying beautiful' and the 'sublime which destroys unity' are dichotomous; one is totalising, while the other disrupts the centre. Herein lies the sublime vertigo that 'threatens the very foundations of subjectivity'; it is other to 'the beautiful [that] contributes, by virtue of its harmony and its universal validity, to the constitution of the subject' (Zima 2010: 125–7). We can draw parallels with the effect of desire on the cohesion of Klossowski's *suppot* or subject, which is drained by the creation of the *simulacrum*, a metaphor for how voluptuous emotion or the *phantasm* drives commodification. Klossowski's somewhat cryptic critique in *Living Currency* (2017) is exemplified by social media, which are sustained by cognitive labour or monetised affect and transgression, in turn driven by the obsessive focus of voluptuous emotion (Klossowski 2017: 24). In Klossowski's perspective, this is a logical destination of industrialisation and modernisation, which pervade on the *suppot* via transaction until the *phantasm* is commodified, rendering us 'living currency'.

Here, a reminder of the difference between transaction and repetition is timely.[7] Repetition, which occurs outside of the order imposed by transaction, implies engagement within a shared or even exploded frame: an immanent encounter. Deleuze's model of joy as a function of extending oneself into composition with an-other that empowers indicates the importance of examining the precise nature and conditions of encounters, in and through design and scenography, whether digital or physical. Thinking and modelling audiences through the general, rather than the particular – and thus seeking to control or limit difference (Deleuze 2014: 2–3) – will shift an interaction towards transaction. This is where physical scenography for live audiences differs most markedly from digital scenography for mediated participation, and where theatre-makers have a pressing task that they are, perhaps, the best equipped to meet.

The immersive aesthetic invites the sublime experience at the edge of reason through subtractions and capture. Its departure from totalising narratives in favour of pluralities of interpretation, and our entanglement with their unfolding, reflects familiar questions asked in avant-garde theatre and art. Boal stressed theatre as a space for rehearsing new ways of acting in relation to, and within, power structures. Applied to digital infrastructures and their inflection of conditions of possibility, this proposition asks us to pay attention to the quality of our interactions as we move in and out of physical and digital designed spaces, which has been a concern of Blast Theory since 1998, when they produced *Desert Rain*. *Desert Rain*, a critically acclaimed game and installation that fused virtual reality and performance, was created in collaboration with University of Nottingham's Mixed Reality Lab. It was nominated for the Interactive Arts BAFTA in 2000 and won the Nam June Paik Art Center Prize in 2016. Superimpositions and blending of mediated and physical storyworld are central to the work of Blast Theory, and a key aspect of their performances is the instantiation, by audiences, of the opportunities and tensions created within their pieces. Since then, Blast Theory has produced technology-aided augmented reality artworks *Can You See Me Now?* (2001), a chase game taking place in the streets using handheld computers; *Rider Spoke* (2007), a street game for cyclists using handlebar-mounted computers; *A Machine To See With* (2010), in which the players receive a series of instructions by mobile phone and eventually perform in a run on a bank; and *Karen* (2015), a piece for smartphones presented as an app, through which you form an intimate, even intrusive, relationship with your life coach Karen via a branching video narrative, supported by the messaging functions of the phone. The work reflected the unfolding discourse around digital culture, as Karen gathers personal information about you during the unfolding of the story with increasing urgency, driven by push notifications and the nature of her questions. With *Karen*, Blast Theory shifted the performance space from the shared urban space to the instrumentalised intimacy of smartphones (Blast Theory 2015). *Operation Black Antler* (2016) was a participatory performance that did not rely on technology. Addressing reemergence of right-wing populism, it asked participants to go undercover and gather intelligence on a fictive right-wing organisation during an event at a local pub. The success of your mission, which was undertaken in small teams, depended on gaining the trust of members that you first had to identify and gather information about, without blowing your cover. You could not succeed without engaging with the task, and as all your interactions were immediate and close up, there was a heightened and escalating sense of risk that was only resolved some time after you were called to evacuate the pub, and realised the performance was over.

The emotional impact of mediation was explored methodically by the makers of *Façade* (2005), an augmented reality game with an interactive narrative, driven by software that reproduced conversation artificially. In the game, you entered the domestic setting of the main characters (Trip and Grace), in the middle of a tense exchange, with several possible outcomes. Depending on how you interacted with the characters, and what you said to them, you could find yourself thrown out of the apartment at the end of the game or witnessing a relationship breakdown. *Façade* was published for three platforms: the immersive AR version of the game where the player interacted with the game space using natural body movements and spoken dialogue, a desktop version with voice interaction, and one with keyboard interaction. A study that investigated how audiences responded to the three versions showed that only half of the participants found the spatially immersive AR version of the game more engaging, while the other half found it overwhelming and preferred the desktop game. Even though Trip and Grace were fairly simply drawn animated characters, half of the participants in the study found that their psychological immersion in the AR game interfered with their ability to experience it as a play space. Instead, they preferred the distance created by mediation, with most choosing the keyboard interface over spoken dialogue as it allowed them to edit their responses. The added distance gave them the option to participate one step removed from the consequences of their actions in the game space, and with more control over their contributions to the dialogue than the real-time speech interface afforded (Dow et al. 2007: 1475–84). The evenly split preferences for an immersive experience versus one where you can remain aware of the artifice and maintain playful control map to the different approaches of Theatre of Cruelty and *Verfremdungseffekt*; one unsettling the subject position, the other emphasising critical distance and awareness of artifice.

Punchdrunk's emerging aesthetic

Robert Wilson, best known for his work in theatre, opera, dance and theatre design, created *H.G.* (1995), an immersive theatrical installation underneath the medieval prison ruins of the Clink in London, together with Hans Peter Kuhn. *H.G.* was realised as if recently deserted in 1895 in 20 of the underground rooms in Clink Street Vaults. The exquisite level of detail that was revealed when your eyes adapted to the low lighting made a profound impression on Punchdrunk's Felix Barrett, who saw the work at the time and noted how it gave space to imagination, together with the absence of actors or an explicit narrative (Machon 2013: 174). Wilson's meticulously crafted props and lighting came to influence Barrett practice at the University of Exeter and with Punchdrunk.[8] Wilson questions language and its control over what is knowable through a range of strategies, including silences, disjunction between visuals and text, discontinuity and decontextualisation that dramatises the gaps between visual and verbal representation. In *H.G.*, this central metaphor was articulated through lighting, absences and the space allowed for walking and creating your own interpretations (Hess-Lüttich, Müller and van Zoest 1998: 224–30).

Barrett was inspired during his A-levels by the work of Silviu Purcărete and Josef Svoboda, whose work with lighting, space, and time would prove to be a founding influence for Barrett (Machon 2019: 30). The architectural aspects of Svoboda's work, Purcărete's ritualistic approach to performance, and the working methods of 'laboratory theatre' inspired and anchored Barrett's artistic vision and aesthetic within the European avant-garde theatre tradition. He joined the Drama Department at the University of Exeter, where he met Peter Higgin, as an undergraduate student in 1997. Studying under

Stephen Hodge together with Higgin, Barrett experimented with theatre in unusual locations and intimate one-to-one experiences, including a piece at a swimming pool that referenced Debussy's *La Mer*, and which Barrett describes as the starting point for his exploration of the one-to-one format (Machon 2019: 109). For his final piece in 2000, Barrett created a production of *Woyzeck* (in which Higgin starred as the Captain) in the deserted barracks of the Territorial Army. For this first rendition of *Woyzeck*, Barrett worked with the building as text, and introduced an early version of the looping formula that is central to Punchdrunk's work.[9] The creative environment at the Drama Department at the University of Exeter, led until 2018 by Professor Hodges, has produced alumni that went on to work with Forced Entertainment and other experimental British theatre companies. The influence of European avant-garde performance on Hodge's work comes to expression in Wrights & Sites, which is a Situationist-influenced artist-researcher group with a particular interest in the relationship between people and spaces, articulated through walking art interventions (Wrights and Sites 2019).

Shortly after graduating, Barrett and Higgin formed Punchdrunk, and produced their first official show as a company, *The Moon Slave* (2000). This was a theatrical experience for one audience member at a time, based on Pain's horror story from *Stories in the Dark* (Pain 1901); an intimate mystery tour that played four times in one night, for a total number of four people. The audiences of one arrived at a village hall in Exeter, expecting a performance. Upon entry, they found themselves in a room with 200 empty chairs, all with printed programmes laid out on the seats and facing a traditional stage with a naturalistic drawing room set (Machon 2019: 191). A telephone started ringing inside a parcel on the stage, and upon answering, the audience member received the instruction that a car was waiting outside for them. A masked chauffeur subsequently whisked them away to a mansion where the rest of the experience took place as a gradually unfolding mystery; a format the company has continued to develop both in full-scale productions and their blended reality applications (Eyre 2011). The car radio delivered the first part of the sound score, a composition of Stravinsky's *Firebird Suite*, and a narrated story, the delivery of which continued upon arrival at the mansion through a headset, given to you by the driver. Guided on from that point by the narrator, you walked through theatrical installations, revealed to yourself as the central character in the play when your enactment merged with theirs in passing through a gate at the same time (Machon 2019: 191). The spectacle that followed lit up the sky with red flares, revealing 200 scarecrows and, subsequently, the return of your chauffeur. During the journey back via dark country lanes, you might have caught sight of another character in the play while the epilogue played, but only from one side of the car (Machon 2019: 192).

The Moon Slave received critical acclaim, and the company expanded to include the present senior members in 2002, when Barrett met Colin Nightingale and Maxine Doyle joined the company. With Nightingale and Doyle came stronger influences from music, choreography and live events beyond theatre, allowing the company to develop more physical forms of expression. In 2001, Punchdrunk produced *Johnny Formidable* and *The Tempest*, followed by *Chair*, *The House of Oedipus* and *A Midsummer Night's Dream* (2002), and in *The Yellow Wallpaper* and *The Firebird Ball* (2005) (Tomlin 2014: 279–80). These early productions explored what have remained signature elements of Punchdrunk's theatre: detailed performance installations, diffracted narratives where roaming audiences play a central part as directors-composers of their individual experiences, multiple narrative layers encoded into the performance space for exploration by audiences, and frame shifts within the artwork through nested narratives and confrontations between anonymous voyeurism and intimate one-to-one experiences (Worthen 2012: 79–97). During the run of *The Firebird Ball*, the company attracted the interest of Nicholas Hytner, then director of the London's National Theatre. Together, they produced *Faust* (2006), which was set in the period style of 1940s–1950s Americana. Having already established the haptic dimension of experience design as a key component of their work, with *Faust* the company developed innovative approaches to expressing complex ideas through the language of choreographed movement in space (Tomlin 2014: 273). *Faust* brought Punchdrunk to national recognition and played to nearly 30,000 audience members over a run of 119 performances. *The Masque of the Red Death* (2007), a site-specific production at the Battersea Arts Centre, combined several macabre stories by Poe, and culminated in a scene where the audience were evacuated to escape the plague, only to find themselves in a ballroom they had not previously known existed. The title theme extended into The Red Death Lates after parties, which ran at weekends during the seven-month-long, sell-out run. For Red Death Lates, Punchdrunk worked with Gideon Reeling to create a unique programme for each weekend (Baird 2008). *The Masque of the Red Death* incorporated an early, albeit not entirely successful experiment with an alternative reality game embedded within the set. In 2010, Punchdrunk collaborated with ENO on an adaptation of Webster's 1614 Jacobean tragedy *The Duchess of Malfi*, which they realised as a deconstructed opera with a score by Rasch. The performance was staged in a 1960s office complex, Gallow's Reach, in East London, and featured twenty-one singers and dancers, supported by a sixty-nine-piece symphony orchestra. The narrative was driven by the singers rather than the dancers and actors and received mixed reviews, mainly due to problems associated with integrating the orchestra within the larger vision created by Punchdrunk. The ENO performed the opera in two full cycles during the performance rather than the normal three of Punchdrunk productions, as the 12,600 metre-square set made it impossible to move the orchestra around fast enough; site management alone was an enormous undertaking. The ENO orchestra was also unwilling to be as closely involved with the development of the production as Punchdrunk would have wanted, leading Nightingale to conclude that 'bolt-ons' couldn't work, and that every new discipline integrated in the immersive mix needed to be 'embedded in the form and involved in the process' (Machon 2019: 93).

Ongoing Arts Council England support allowed the company to produce works on a larger scale from 2008, including an early version of *Sleep No More*, which opened in Boston in 2009. Also in 2009, Kevin Spacey, who was then the Artistic Director of Old Vic Theatre, approached the company with an interest to collaborate. This led to *Tunnel 228*, an immersive art exhibition with twenty-four contemporary artists in the tunnels underneath Waterloo Station. By now, Punchdrunk audiences had been inculcated, via past experience and the word-of-mouth reputation of the company, in the exploratory format for participation that the company asked for. They had come to expect deeply encoded sets with embedded clues to explore, and came prepared to act as agents within them, ready to create interpretations that may not have been planned. This relationship between the company and their audiences has developed to the extent that it often produces unscripted extensions of the performance space. One of the installation works created for *Tunnel 228* used the feathers of racing pigeons, which were marked with the breeders' telephone numbers. During the exhibition, the pigeon breeders found themselves inundated with phone calls from strangers who asked veiled questions in the pursuit of further clues. These types of independent extensions of Punchdrunk's storyworlds have become an important part of fandom activities,[10] and exemplify how instantiation of the particular, by repetition and individual points-of-view, creates difference and expands experience potential beyond what could realistically be created by a central authorial vision.

In the next chapter, I will discuss modelling and design for agency and its negotiation 'across the interface' in Punchdrunk productions, based on on-site research and interviews with designers and audience members that were directly engaged with the production of experience during the build and run of *The Drowned Man: A Hollywood Fable* at The Old Sorting Offices in Paddington, London, from 2013 to 2014, and a range of other productions by the company, historical and contemporary. Furthermore, Chapter 3 discusses the 'Punchdrunk formula' that allows the company to coordinate the movements of cast and audience over very large sets, and the way the company works with literary works to enrich their scenography.

Notes

1. Both Burke and Kant defined it as such in the eighteenth century, although they disagreed on its framing. Kant insisted on reason being the means to contain it, but Burke pointed towards the Romantic tradition.
2. In *Internal*, which was first performed in 2009 and in which the actors nominally seek partners, Ontroerend Goed invited audience members to interact one-to-one with actors in date-like situations. Subsequently, 'group therapy' sessions took place in which personal disclosures offered during one-to-one interactions were opened up for public discussion.
3. See Chapters 3, 4 and 7 for descriptions of processes and production of specific events.
4. See Chapter 3.
5. The Platonic revival in Florence was based on Plotinus' Neoplatonism, distinguishing the ideal from the phenomenal world, with the ideal world being the seat of the eternal transcendent.
6. COM2, COM3.
7. See Chapter 1, page 1.
8. Chapter 5 discusses this aspect of Punchdrunk's work and its importance to immersion.
9. See Chapter 3.
10. See Chapter 1.

3

Punchdrunk's Interactive Systems

While immersion in designed environments is commonly understood as a sense of vertigo or being sensorily overwhelmed, it was specifically associated by audiences in this study with investment and extension of agency, hinging on the willing suspension of disbelief. The vertigo one might expect as part of immersion flowed not simply from the sense of vastness or expanse but also from the uncertain bounds of this agency, and the destabilisation of what, or who, was in control.[1] The design rationale for 'self-abduction' (Chow 2012: 41) is clear when considering the duration of Punchdrunk performances, which is typically three hours (for one of the large masked shows) but can be longer (e.g. Kabeiroi): the impact of scale alone would not last. The sustained investment of agency, and the associated, sustained experience of vertigo as this agency seeks its bounds drives extended desire and awe, flowing from uncertainty. Mutual exposure brings performers and audiences into the immediate range of each other, which alters the role of both audiences and actors. Immersion, as a function of the scenography and the self-abduction of audiences, collapses critical distance and destabilises the audience position, which cannot be constructed as sovereign in the performance space, or immune to the consequences of actions within the drama.

The role of self-abduction in sustained immersion adds nuance to Chow's argument of capture in art (2012), in particular the importance of agency and the willing suspension of disbelief. The art-work of the skilled storyteller is not a trap in the 'dark play' sense, that is, not one that the audience enters unaware.[2] The suspension of disbelief found in this study is not one that flows from susceptibility to deceit but a compact into which the audience enters and sustains on terms intimated by the presentation of the performance. Punchdrunk's scenography communicates, through embedded attention to situated nuance, their ongoing commitment to this compact.

Disorientation, by way of its negative correlation with the experience of sovereignty (or control) is intrinsically controversial; a minor aesthetic that runs counter to representation of continuity. The frame that holds the artwork is vital to its experience, but not simply through containing or limiting it. The frame is a boundary, and play emerges *and is oriented in relation to* its bounds, whether in time and/or space (Huizinga 1955), by rules (Caillois 1961), the 'properness' of place (Certeau 1988: 188), in relation to the 'centre' or holding idea of a structure (Derrida 2001: 352) or the blunt edges of representation as it fails (Galloway 2012: 29). Moving or removing frames invites questions of the value of the art, and by expanding the frame to contain the audience of the artwork, it also questions their construct and relative 'value' in theatre and fine art alike.

Framing audiences in the capacity of their embodied affect and cognition, rather than the idea of their projected perception as a proxy for the disembodied mind, directly challenges the hierarchical implications of the mind–body dichotomy. Scenography, that is, the frame of the physical over, perhaps, the literary in theatre had already been dismissed as a lower form of art by Aristotle (McKinney and Palmer 2017: 5). Its suggestive effects on the embodied senses provokes and invites comparisons with the garishness of fairgrounds and amusement parks, which feature in the minor aesthetics of 'low' art as well as in early-twentieth-century Futurists, Dadaists, Modernists and Surrealists, all of whom explored variety theatre and circus themes. The association with popular or 'low' art and scenography's fundamental function as the frame or milieu for performing bodies resonate in comparisons of Punchdrunk's work with computer games (Hoggard 2013; Jakob-Hoff 2014). With the increasing availability of games and other applications for immersive platforms (e.g. virtual and augmented reality), theatre-makers and serious game designers share opportunities and challenges. Importantly, as greater artistic demands are placed on designed interactive and virtual experiences, their infrastructures will need to support more nuanced expression of the interactions by participating audiences as well.

While the idea of the *Gesamtkunstwerk* is a useful legacy within which to orient research and development of performance and computer games, expanded scenography does not necessarily produce immersion any more than a first-person shooter perspective does. Successful storytelling balances and integrates narrative and technology, with writing, acting, set design, sound and light design coming together in the repeating nexus of situated experience. Barrett acknowledges direct inspiration by Edward Gordon Craig, the British Symbolist innovator of scenography, lighting and mise en scène, and says, with reference to Craig's influence and the use of near-darkness in *The Drowned Man*, that 'every single theatrical element – the scenography, the music, the state of the mind of the audience, the auditorium itself – should be about creating the atmosphere' (Palmer 2017: 59). The immersive effect of active darkness (Palmer 2017: 50–4) on the focus of audiences in a traditional proscenium setting is exemplified in *Sun* (2013) by Hofesh Shechter Company, where the stage and auditorium is at times plunged in complete darkness while an amplified voice, projected from the perimeter of the auditorium, addresses the audience as complicit in the production of a culture that rests on war and exploitation. In the live performance, the darkness compounds the menacing voice and is almost suffocating. It appears to press inward and downward on the audience subject position, forcing one's focus to follow.

Punchdrunk also employ these features; pre-recorded voices were used in *It Felt Like a Kiss* (2009) and *The Drowned Man: A Hollywood Fable* (2013), and they employ active darkness to heighten the disorientating effects of labyrinthine scenography. Disorientation is further enhanced by separating audience members from their company before they are thrust, metaphorically and physically, into darkness: from that point on, they are complicit in their abduction for the duration of the performance, and responsible for piecing together a narrative from what they encounter. In Hofesh Shechter's *Sun*, both the provocations of audiences and their offering-up of complicity in response are projected, while in Punchdrunk's work encounters flow from the embodied exposure to one's own agency and that of others.

Punchdrunk developed their methodologies for working with free-roaming audiences over two decades. Felix Barrett founded the company with Peter Higgin in 2000, building on their experiments with theatre in unusual locations and free-roaming audiences as undergraduates at the University of Exeter, including a first production of *Woyzeck* (2000). Their first productions as a company were *The Moon Slave* (2000), followed by *The House of Oedipus* (2000). Between 2001 and 2005,[3] they continued to explore and develop what have remained signature elements of Punchdrunk's theatre: highly detailed performance installations that capture audiences within storyworlds in which simultaneous, and distributed storylines with textual elements that are embedded in the shared scenography of performers and audience (Worthen 2012). During the run of *The Firebird Ball* in 2005, the company attracted the interest of Nicholas Hytner, then director of the National Theatre. This was to lead to an innovative production of *Faust* set in 1940s–1950s America in collaboration with the National Theatre in 2006. Having already developed haptic scenography open to interaction by audiences, *Faust* established Punchdrunk's method for expressing complex ideas through the language of choreographed movement in space (Tomlin 2014: 273).

Punchdrunk's co-productions have not always been completely successful. Their collaboration with the English National Orchestra (ENO) and the National Theatre on the Jacobean tragedy *The Duchess of Malfi* (2010) took the form of a deconstructed opera with a score composed by Rasch and required adaptation of the methodologies of both companies. Even so, the different working methods of ENO and Punchdrunk made seamless integration difficult, and the show played to mixed reviews. The production took place in a 1960s office complex in Gallow's Reach, East London, and featured twenty-one singers and dancers and a sixty-nine-piece symphony orchestra who rehearsed off-site for longer than is typical for Punchdrunk performers. The narrative was driven by the singers rather than the usual dancers and actors, and ENO performed the opera in two full cycles during the performance rather than the three cycles that normally form the narrative structure of Punchdrunk performances. The 12,600-square-metre set made it impossible to move the orchestra around fast enough. The collaboration allowed ENO to gain contemporary relevance through immersive work and provided Punchdrunk with the opportunity to realise greater ambition and bring their work to the attention of new audiences at national and international scale. Their work was documented for TV for the first time, and the association with a national opera company attracted different and more middle-class audiences.

Sleep No More in New York (2011) and *The Drowned Man: A Hollywood Fable* in London (2013) followed; both were developments of previous work. *Sleep No More* is an adaptation of Shakespeare's *Macbeth*, and is based on earlier renditions; one in London (2003), which was also Maxine Doyle's first production with the company, and a later one in Boston (2009), which attracted interest from Randy Weiner, Jonathan Hochwald and Arthur Carpati (Machon 2019: 255). Following this, Weiner, Hochwald and Carpati went on to form Emursive, Punchdrunk International's New York production partners on the production of *Sleep No More* which opened in its present West Chelsea location in 2011. The New York production of *Sleep No More* is Punchdrunk's first commercially produced show and was followed in 2016 by a rendition in Shanghai. *The Drowned Man* is based on Büchner's fragmentary, unfinished play *Woyzeck* (Barrett produced his first version of this in his final year at the University of Exeter), and opened in partnership with the National Theatre in 2013. After several failed attempts to secure a suitable building for a large London production between 2010 and 2012, the company finally gained permission in December 2012 to use the Old Postal Sorting Offices by Paddington Station, which were empty in preparation for the Crossrail works. After an unusually short build period that created an unprecedented challenge, given the sheer size of the production, *The Drowned Man: A Hollywood Fable* opened in June 2013.

Both *Sleep No More* and *The Drowned Man* were ambitious in scale, accommodating 400 and 600 audience members per performance, respectively. *Sleep No More* has 158 people on the payroll, and around 100 performance and installation spaces over six floors (9,300 square metres) in the West Chelsea warehouse that the company transformed into the 1930s

McKittrick Hotel in a fictional Scottish town called Gallow Green, where the drama is set. *The Drowned Man* in London was Punchdrunk's largest production to date, with 170 individually created rooms over four floors (14,000 square metres), and a cast of thirty-five actors. A 300-strong crew of designers and stage technicians built the production over four months,[4] creating the imaginary world of Temple Pictures in 1960s Encino, a district in the outer parts of Los Angeles. Ninety people were needed to run each show, with an additional sixty to reset and maintain the set and props every day during the run, from the basement to the desert on the top floor. In total, about 500 designers, performers and stage managers worked on the build and the thirteen-month run of *The Drowned Man*.[5]

Concurrent with building their largest production to date in a challenging location under time pressure, Punchdrunk oversaw *Sleep No More* in New York and produced a new work, *The Borough*, which ran for sixteen days in June 2013 at the Aldeburgh Festival for audiences of one at a time. With *The Borough*, Punchdrunk revisited the one-to-one experience format that they worked with in 2000 for *The Moon Slave*. The audience members, again wearing headphones, were led on a solo journey guided partly by Crabbe's poem and partly by Britten's opera *Peter Grimes* (based on Crabbe's poem), woven into a sound piece focused on feelings of paranoia. *The Borough* audience journey started on a deck chair on the beach of Aldeburgh, and

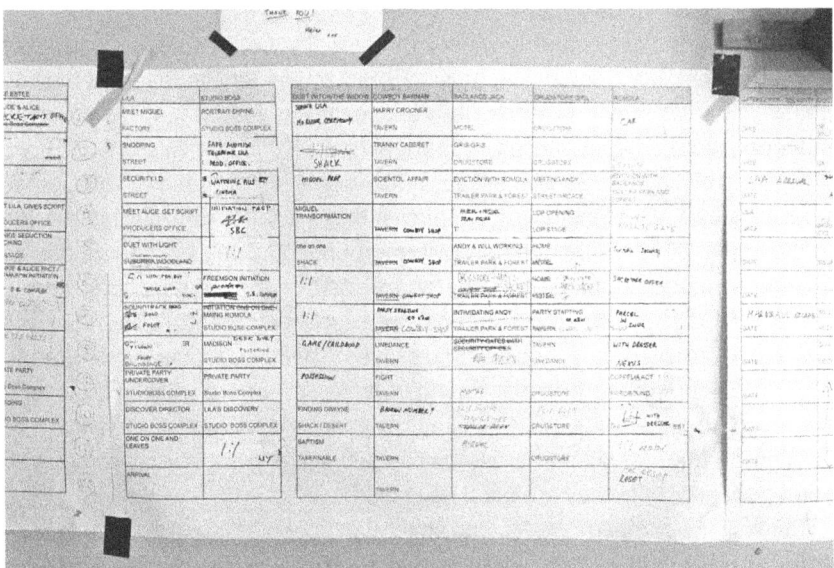

FIGURE 3.1 *Spreadsheet. A small section of the extensive spreadsheet that details scenes and changes of* The Drowned Man, *and which is used for planning and coordination according to the 'Punchdrunk system' (Credit: Carina E. I. Westling).*

ended in the dramatised experience of a community turning against the individual participant, with the contemporary world bleeding into the sound piece through interactions by actors and community performers (Drew 2013). Also produced in tandem with *The Drowned Man*, Punchdrunk created a one-off immersive commission to promote Jack White's album *Lazaretto* (2014) in collaboration with White's record company XL (XL employees are Punchdrunk fans). Again, at very short notice, Punchdrunk created an imaginary medical company called Vescovo for the event, with a history that was 'documented' by films set in 1948 and hosted by the Wellcome Institute, London. They recruited the audience for the performance under the guise of medical screenings via internet communities known to be frequented by fans of White's music. The entire campaign took three weeks to develop, from inception to the live event, with forty-five participants ultimately recruited to undergo medical testing in a London location just off the Strand. After they had spent thirty to forty minutes in the Vescovo centre, an emergency was announced and the audience was herded, wearing medical gowns, to a screened-off area, joined by forty-odd Punchdrunk performers who had just finished that day's performance of *The Drowned Man*. Suddenly, the plastic screens were ripped away to reveal Jack White and his six-piece band at arm's length from the audience, awash in blue stage lights as the band opened with the first line of the title track. The band proceeded to play a twenty-five-minute concert to a surprised and overwhelmed audience until Jack had a 'seizure' and was rushed away on a stretcher into an ambulance.[6]

The *Lazaretto* project emphasises the affinity between the company's work and the theatricality of live music. Creative director Stephen Dobbie and creative producer Colin Nightingale are invested in sound and event design and produced the critically acclaimed multimedia exhibition *Beyond the Road* (2019) at the Saatchi Gallery as an independent collaboration with James Lavelle of UNKLE, blending music and sound art with film and installation art (Gumble 2019). Although rarely foregrounded, Dobbie's sound design for Punchdrunk is a critical and operational part of their productions. It is a vital part of the ambience created by the scenography and keeps the time of the performance with near-inaudible cues. These cues are embedded in the sensibilities of performers during rehearsals, where initially clear and unambiguous auditory signals for key changes and movements within the clockwork structure of the larger performance are gradually replaced with quieter sounds, until they are barely audible.[7]

The way the company works with spaces and people is fundamental to their ability to adapt and evolve rapidly and at short notice, while maintaining an enquiring approach to audience experience, scale and milieus. Working with audiences of one to several hundred in different and challenging locations, over short as well as long periods of time and across physical and digital platforms, the company largely preserves an aura of secrecy and ephemerality. Their more intimate and evanescent performances, which are undocumented and may only occur once, draw much from the 'happenings' of Kaprow, while their large, masked shows evoke the *Gesamtkunstwerk* with epic scenography in which audiences perform as moving parts, acting, dance, sound design and innovative use of theatre technologies. An analysis of the immediate interfaces between Punchdrunk and their audiences in intimate encounters as well as participants in 'theatre machines' must take into account the infrastructures that make it possible. The practices and grounded knowledge that enables the company to negotiate emergence in one-to-one experiences and flows of crowd movements within the larger clockwork structure are of significant interest to designers and scenographers working in and across physical and digital materialities.

The shadow choreography and structure of Punchdrunk's worlds

The structure of *Sleep No More* and *The Drowned Man*, as well as most of Punchdrunk's large-scale productions, is based on hour-long cycles of distributed five-minute timed performance sections in twelve performance zones, organised like a repeating clockwork of moving parts.[8] The sixty-minute-long cycle repeats three times, allowing audiences to pursue different strands of the narrative, with the final cycle leading into the finale. Stephen Dobbie designs a unique soundtrack for each of the twelve performance zones, with nearly inaudible sound cues that time the performance transitions, and coordinates both the movements of 'travelling' performers (those that range throughout the performance space) and the actions of 'resident' performers (those that inhabit particular rooms and spaces).[9] The result is a clockwork scenography with a large number of scenes that guarantees that any one audience member cannot experience all performances even if they make many visits, and that unique experiences will be produced by different combinations and actors even if they return enough times to see all of the possible scenes. Their movements as individual audience members and crowds form a 'shadow choreography' – a flow that is neither fully predictable nor completely emergent, and which drives not the clockwork per se, but the production of new experience and adaptive responses.

In addition to the complexity of the 'theatre machine' and the inescapable production of difference by live audiences, the boundaries of possible experience are extended through an unknown number of story elements and are embedded into the scenography, which only become revealed through persistent exploration. Messages are hidden in books, bags and drawers; letters are scattered or hidden throughout the space that carry out correspondence between particular characters; contracts, address books, reports and other documents that exist within and expand the larger story can be found by inquisitive audience members; and countless other items that may seem trivial but which belong within the storyworld are imagined and created by the design team within its time and place. As well as layering multiple storylines into the set, the company weaves supplementary stories into the key texts of their productions. In *Sleep No More*, Macbeth is laced with references to Hitchcock's *Rebecca,* based on du Maurier's novel, and from the Paisley witch trials that took place in Scotland in 1697. The result is a darkly cinematic rendition of *Macbeth* that has become known for its intense physicality, from the raw power of Lady Macbeth in her private quarters to the tense, slow-motion precision of the all-cast banquet, rendered in chiaroscuro lighting and a 1930s aesthetic.

Also a composite of several stories, *The Drowned Man* combined *Woyzeck* with elements of West's *The Day of the Locust* and Bradbury's *Something Wicked This Way Comes*. Instead of the army milieu in *Woyzeck*, the story was set in the fictional Temple Pictures studio complex in Hollywood in 1962. Büchner, who died in 1837 before completing *Woyzeck*, features *in absentia* as the deceased George Buchanan, the author of a script called *The Drowned Man*, which, in the story, is to be filmed at Temple Pictures. The storylines of *The Drowned Man* are doubled up with reversed character pairs and staged on sets within the set; taking audiences through several levels of fictive reality as they navigate the performance area. As the build period was shorter than usual and the production was so large, the preview period of *The Drowned Man*, which is when company members participate as audience members or Black Masks (stage managers/ushers who populate the shadows of the scenography) to see how audiences respond within the space, was longer than usual, to facilitate adaptation:

> I think that's what's brilliant about the team; their willingness to change and the willingness to set up a system and have it in place, but understanding that it will change on a day-to-day basis. And an understanding that each element is as important as the others; it all combines as a whole. If the lighting is wrong it skews the sound, and it skews the design.[10]

The company aims to produce a stable system, but iterative change is accommodated and ongoing throughout a production run. Repetition produces difference in the most literal sense, as each instance of a performance, as experienced by their audiences, is unique. Its constituents (cast and audiences) change both in the absolute and in the relational sense, and in addition small adjustments are made to the execution, and sometimes even to the plan of the building to refine and optimise the production. All such changes necessitate further adjustments to rebalance the whole, resulting in a structure which, while designed to be stable, is only usefully so through understanding stability via balance, which is an active and adaptive approach, not a static state.

This complex network of interactions and situations, manifest at the interface level as a dynamic storyworld with substantive responsive capacity and hundreds of possible recombinations, is held within a clockwork structure, outlined on large spreadsheets that detail the movement of actors, scenes and performance areas.[11] The hierarchy of Punchdrunk productions is not vertical or centred on the frame separating the artwork and its audiences but instead on the different understanding and knowledge of the space afforded to actors and audiences. Actors understand the performance as one of narrative negotiation and opportunity, while audiences primarily describe their 'performance' of the shadow choreography as adaptive and emergent.[12] The resulting hierarchy is never fully set or immutable, as actors are exposed to the emergent responses of audiences. Consequently, they have to be open to improvisation to diffuse, diffract or reframe audience reactions to disorientation and the illusory absence of rules. Audiences are encouraged to explore and to follow characters they encounter, but the company tries to keep directives to a minimum, relying instead on the performance environment to shape and negotiate the flow and expression of agency.

Individual members of the audience sometimes disrupt or test the edges of the illusion in ways that could compromise the performance. More commonly, they get in the way of choreographed movement, remove or move one of the hundreds of interactive props used by the actors, and sometimes try to force one-to-one experiences. The Black Masks stand by ready to respond when actors want support with managing situations, while allowing close-range interactions to retain the essence of the encounter. Some actors prefer to negotiate their interactions with audiences more independently, others with closer support from the Black Masks; these discussions are had individually, as well as with regard to particular scenes, within the company.[13] The broad strokes of the 'shadow choreography' of the audience are developed and shaped through scenography and acting, and further adapted during the course of runs in response to how audiences move and interact with the space. Punchdrunk's significant body of experience and knowledge of working with live audiences has been gathered cumulatively during their many productions, but they continue to refine their methods under the different circumstances presented by each new work:

> We are learning what we need to do given that people are reliably, predictably kind of behaving in certain ways. We know that when people

follow us into this particular door into this particular room, they're likely to drift to the left for some reason, or something, this is like 'Okay that happens, we know that know, we can take advantage of that, or that's the thing we need to deal with. We need to stop that happening.' or whatever the situation. Human psychology is going to stay the same and that's something that we have to adapt to, we have to use that information to tell us how we have to do our job.[14]

As an object in its own right, the shadow choreography of the audience is at once shaped by the scenography and responsive to the movements of the performers; it both resists and depends on its form. It unfolds and orients within a structure that is sustained by an organising idea or centre, and which 'permits the freeplay of its elements inside the total form' (Derrida 2001: 351). The 'centre' is the company's vision, which materialises in their making culture and holds the total form of their productions. The total form is oriented and coordinated by the 'Punchdrunk formula' comprising the clockwork structure and the commitment to, and aesthetic of, making and interacting on either side of the interface. It is identifiable in the structure and texture of interaction behind the scenes as well as within the public-facing aspects of the work. This coherence allows participation to appear free to its audiences, revealing the exchange and essential tension between form and freeplay as at once emergent and repeating. It moves and shifts, like the story in de Certeau's writing, between place and space, unfolding in relation to form and time. Every live performance bears out this relationship: 'The audience can tell, even if they don't understand the rules of the game that's being played: they can tell when there are no rules.'[15]

Freeplay within the design schema becomes manifest at the edges of illusion, where audiences test how far they can go with the story. Here, the Black Masks play a unique role that articulates the shadows, both in the sense that they reveal the outline of the shadow choreography and in the sense of engaging with edge behaviours; actions that aren't central to the thought and designed affordances within the overall system of interactions. Dressed and masked entirely in black, they combine a traditional stage management role in performance that includes audiences with an intermediary role between the set and audiences. Black Masks occupy dark areas of the set where they remain invisible until their intervention is needed. When they emerge to guide or engage with behaviours that are unsustainable in the wider scheme, they interact wordlessly so to not break the ambience.[16] Rather than breaking the illusion, their interventions enhance immersion through diffusing the boundary between participant and system agency, creating a dreamlike sense of vertigo as these merge.[17] Embodying processes of negotiation and adaptation that flow into assemblages of human agency and technology (Hayles 2017), the

Black Masks operate within Punchdrunk's theatre machines to animate and articulate the shadows that might otherwise be thought to be empty, blurring the edges of the illusion. Making this boundary living and emergent, they engage with transgression at the edges of the shadow choreography to reorient it towards the centre:

> You know, I didn't feel out of control. [...] It was just so surreal, it was very dreamlike, and [...] I definitely felt like most of the decisions, like the control was kind of in somebody else's hands, and I had a diminished control. But it was cool, though. I didn't mind that. I really liked that.[18]

The urge to make obscure parts of narrative and scenography alive with potential is a driving aesthetic in Punchdrunk. The potency of absence informs all aspects of their productions, from physical design to acting: 'The notes that we aren't playing, or beats that we aren't playing, those are really important decisions.'[19] When Punchdrunk prepare a building for transformation into a performance space, their first step is to blacken out all windows.[20] Felix Barrett and lead designers Livi Vaughan and Beatrice Minns walk the darkened space,[21] visualising the narrative and marking it in a kind of founding, or *fas* ritual:

> He allows the building to speak to him. So he'll often discover that building in the dark, and he'll work out where the kind of energies and tensions are within the space, and he'll evolve the narrative from just ... listening to the walls.[22]

The company usually carry several projects in 'virtual' form, only realised and fully shaped as buildings become available: 'There are ideas for shows, but there isn't a show until ... I mean, we talk about all the time, until there's a building.'[23] Walking is an important part of preparing the 'theatre of actions' in which the dynamics of the space are formed; again, not from a fixed plan but as an evolving work of art to be experienced through its internal shapes and flows:

> There are different tones within the place, there's always a certain amount that is left completely blank, so when we come into the space ... it's like an axis from the door it's just ... left to itself, you know; it's left to breathe. A lot of the places are like that so. ... It can be kind intimidating, because in your head, you're thinking, 'yeah, we've got this amount of time, there's still so much unknown', but they do a daily walkaround [...] saying, like, 'OK so, the transition from this room to that room is going to be heightened' or it can lose its tension. But they have to kind of see it as it is, and as it's evolving.[24]

The scenography is shaped with a combination of broad and detailed strokes: first rapidly blocked out and subdivided, then gradually shaped and built in repeated, smaller gestures.[25] Designers work closely together on the sculptural or architectural aspects of the space and the depth of detail that creates grain and textural depth; cutting and shaping in one breath, seeding and layering in the next:

> I've always got the fear of approaching an empty room, and she's just great, she just bulldozes through it and makes really strong elegant strokes, and then, she's so quick as well, so I guess I'm kind of a slower pace, so I'll go back on it, and add another layer to the space.[26]

The senior design team has worked with this split responsibility for shape and detail since *Masque of the Red Death*, 'because you can't, kind of, operate the miniscule with the gigantic [...] they're always talking to each other so it doesn't feel like two separate roles'.[27]

The design role and its two closely interwoven parts already tell a story spanning space and place. The shape and contours of internal spaces create pressures and directions that enclose, release and fold the audience flows

FIGURE 3.2 *Red Moon desert. The desert on the top floor of* The Drowned Man, *with the lit Red Moon sign half submerged in a dune in the distance. The photo was taken at the beginning of the wrap party; no photos were taken during live performances (Credit: Carina E. I. Westling).*

within. Surfaces and spaces within this three-dimensional system of conduits and vessels are seeded and dressed with trees, caravans and indoors deserts, furniture, photographs and tiny personal items to draw senses and perception into play. Bounds and apertures create tension and build dynamics, while texture creates depth and almost infinite opportunities for exploration at close range.

Emergence and order

The tension between agency and control in Punchdrunk mirrors the dependency of play on its boundaries. Free-roaming audiences adapt and change their behaviours and actions in response to opportunities and limitations within the scenography created by acting and design to negotiate audience agency:[28] '[We are] moulding that material of the audience [...] it's like you're civil engineers, putting up structures, you know: installing systems of ... to direct that flow.'[29] The physical range of Punchdrunk actors stretches from high-energy and outwardly expressive (e.g. climbing or jumping off walls and other structures, or running at fast pace through the sets) to quiet and detailed, playing not only with physical space but also with audience perception. Gaze and intensity direct the attention and movements of audiences: 'You might decide to bring the pitch of your performance down to a very subtle, close up kind of level, so that you're giving them something that they know is just for them.'[30] When audiences misread or challenge the spatial language of acting and scenography, the Black Masks come forward from the shadows to reorient their focus through underscoring the embodied flow within a larger whole.[31]

The company's capacity for balancing adaptation and structure allows them to accommodate free-roaming audiences. Actors and Black Masks know their roles within the theatre machine,[32] while audiences typically find their part disorientating and unexpected.[33] This is central to heightened audience experience; most interpret this as exhilarating and intriguing, but a minority frame the same qualities in a negative light.[34] The difference in experience is dependent on frames, whether in the form of awareness of the whole (and your role in it) or in the interpretation of uncertainty as an opportunity or a challenge. When framed in trust conferred by knowledge and awareness of bounds, uncertainty can invite play and the suspension of disbelief, for example, between the boundaries of self and the performance environment. This is a form of spatial thought in itself, extensive and effortful: an aestheticised challenge. The effort of extension and negotiation that flows from the encounter is a central feature of the discourse of 'artificial hells' in participatory theatre and performance more broadly (Bishop 2012). Framing the encounter is a key concern of immersive experience design and requires adaptation for different materialities and different audiences. Physical and digital infrastructures support and create different conditions of possibility not only for making but also for participation and interaction. Thinking through framing is key to understanding these, particularly when the role and position of maker and audiences are taken into account in the larger schema. As we can see from audience responses to the live performances discussed in Chapter 5, as well as in *The Séance* (2012),[35] framing is key not only to the experience of immersion more generally but also for individual reception and interpretation of immersive experience as empowering, exciting and pleasurable.

The researchers who worked with *The Séance* proposed that the reason that the experience of immersion was diminished by technological mediation was insufficient 'ritual preparation'. Their analysis was based on Turner's anthropological thesis about ritual and its different stages (2017: 94–5) and they suggested that participants in the experience had insufficient induction into a 'liminal and playful' state. Liminality is fairly well understood as an ambiguous threshold state at the centre of rituals, while play has several theories. Within software culture, play is often discussed as *paidia* (childlike play), in contrast with *ludus* (rule-based games). This distinction was formulated by Caillois (1961) and is best considered alongside other play theorists, for example, Sutton-Smith (2001) and Huizinga (1955),[36] but it is relevant also in relation to Derrida (2001) who defined play (i.e. freeplay) as the degree of free movement within a structure. Play theorists and Derrida conceptualise play in relation to its boundaries, but instead of rules or limits in time and space, Derrida discusses freeplay as a potential that emerges in relation to the centre or unifying idea of a structure – or system of meaning. By comparing the way play theorists think boundaries and the way Derrida thinks freeplay in relation to the holding idea of a structure, the relationship between boundaries and frames becomes clearer. While these work in concert in ways that are eloquently articulated by de Certeau in his theory of space and place, they should not be conflated. The bounds of play in space and time create an essential condition for its emergence (Huizinga 1955: 9–10), and this idea holds in concert with Derrida's idea of freeplay or emergent movement in relation to the centre or 'holding concept' of a structure of meaning (Derrida 2001: 352). Whereas Huizinga and other play theorists primarily think of the containment of play as defined by 'outer' boundaries and rules, the limits that allow or produce play are more usefully thought through Derrida's idea of the centre as that which limits the degree of play within a structure of system.

The frame is also a limit, but it performs different functions than the bounds of play. It both focuses and occludes, and defines the art-space within which values of colour, shape, sound, movement and other forms of expression can be reimagined and repositioned in relation to each other. The frame implies subject position and gaze, and how gaze changes the nature of the object within the frame – and its value. The frame can be employed for critique, surprise and challenge, as well as for convention and stability. It can coexist symbiotically with the bounds of play and delineate play space as a privileged space, but the implied subject position in relation to frames is divisive. Looking in, the play inside the frame can look like a privileged space – but this position is transcendent, external to the artwork and its immediate circle of influence and consequence. In contrast, an immanent subject position inside the frame collapses safe distance into emergent exposure (O'Grady 2017). Artaud invoked an immanent subject position within the bounds of theatrical experience, containing the sublime threat to 'light, language' and 'life' (Lyotard 1991: 99) – without such bounds, emergence is an emergency. The frame is key to both Lyotard's and Kant's definition of the sublime, but the subject position is profoundly different. The Kantian sublime is produced when reason encompasses vastness, framing and controlling the possibility of chaos and dissolution. In contrast, Lyotard's sublime is a product of the bounded and thus bearable failure of representation and comprehension, including the self-representation of the subject as sovereign, that is, independent in relation to the object of its gaze. The latter is tentatively described by audience descriptions of their experience of *The Drowned Man*:

> I just felt at the same time so miniscule, my little eyes looking at this thing, but so infinite at the same time. And then kind of … quite thankful? But also, it was probably just kind of like, joyful immersion, as well – like forced immersion. […] If people can make you fall off the cliff face of consciousness, then you drop into this pool of like, eternal oneness.[37]

Positioning audiences within the frame and the bounds of play at the same time alters their perception of the event and their role within it in several dimensions, one of which is time. Ancient Greeks distinguished between *chronos* and *kairos*, or measured time and event time. Experientially, these correlate to the order of place and the extension of space (Certeau 1988: 118), with the former signifying limits and metrics of time and the latter concerning the emergence and extension of the perceived moment 'from within'. The difference can be seen in the analysis of *The Séance* (Dixon, Rogers and Eggleston 2012), in which researchers attempted to measure immersive experience with linear metrics based on how long it was remembered. However, the recollections of audiences in this study did not diminish much in intensity over many months, resonating with the idea of *kairos* or 'event time'. This cannot be explained by 'ritual preparation', as several mentioned attending in a sceptical frame of mind but willingly suspended disbelief in appreciation of the detail and complexity of the scenographic environment.[38] While ritual preparation might be one of many ways of framing an experience, there are no grounds in this study for regarding it as a necessary precursor to immersion, as speculated by *The Séance* research team (Dixon, Rogers and Eggleston 2012). Interviewees were quite explicit about the relationship between the scenography and their suspension of disbelief in terms suggesting that they were complicit in their own 'abduction' as proposed by Chow (2012).

Audiences are already disoriented when they enter the performance space fifteen minutes into the first loop of a Punchdrunk performance,[39] as they are separated from the company they arrived with and are left to navigate the labyrinthine spaces in near-complete darkness. Walking in on ongoing events underscores that the experience is not neatly organised for your convenience. You might find yourself alone in rooms for some time before you encounter actors, or fall in with other audience members to follow performers moving through the scenes at speed. Although you will find yourself one among other people in white masks at various times during a performance, the finale is the first time the entire audience is gathered in full. The effect is amplified by being directed to the finale by lights and sounds alone, often without knowing how it happened. Realising that you have been indirectly guided by and through the scenography across the designed landscapes within the building contributes to a sense of vertigo, as it confronts you with the shadow choreography and your role as a moving part within a theatre machine.

The dreamlike immersion of self-abduction and complicity with submitting your agency to blend into the larger art-work is described in encounters with the Black Masks, who call upon your agency to composition with their agency in situations where you approach the edge of the illusion.[40] According to Deleuze, composition produces joy when we encounter an external body that empowers us, whereas the opposite happens when we encounter an object or agent that opposes us. At the personal level, composition in Punchdrunk occurs in an event space framed in uncertainty. Encounters allow us to extend our boundaries into composition and threaten to disempower us through imposing 'subtraction or a fixation' on our agency (Deleuze 1970: 28), resonating with the idea of space as extension and place as bounded. The dreamlike sublime in encounters with the Black Masks flows from agency interacting with an-other, throwing its contours and the possibility of their failure into sharp relief.

Another example of vertigo in relation to framing and containment can be seen in the study of *Façade*,[41] which was released for desktop and AR (Dow et al. 2007). Half of the players found the desktop game preferable to the AR version, as they found it too immersive to be a 'play space' (Dow et al. 2007:

1476). Projecting into the on-screen interaction allowed them to play rather than embody the character:

> Here (in desktop) you feel like you are playing a role in an environment and (in AR) you feel like you are the role. You can say some stuff (in desktop) that you might not say (in AR) ... like you are somebody else. (Dow et al. 2007: 1482)

Seen from the perspective of the sublime, the differences in preferred subject position stem from how keenly the encounter is experienced, with a position within the frame being too close or unbounded for some players. While Lyotard's definition of the sublime as a threat twice removed ('deprived of the threat of being deprived') might be interpreted as a figure of speech, it bears out in the observation that Punchdrunk audiences enter the frame of the performance wearing a mask (which acts like an additional frame and offers the protection of anonymity), while the *Façade* players who found the AR experience too immersive to be a play space wore see-through headsets instead of masks.

The framing function of the mask and the protection it confers in Punchdrunk performances is emphasised by the effect of its removal by the actor in one-to-one scenes. It is immediate, as you have become accustomed to the feeling of the mask on your face and the disinhibition that anonymity engenders while moving around in the performance space.[42] The frame shift is punctuated with the sudden coolness of the air on your unmasked face or perhaps a quick sprinkling of water, which reminds the audience member of their 'real' physical boundary and marks the new arrangement of frames. The care taken in the negotiation of such shifts and the design of small movements by the actors serve to contain the encounter for both themselves and the audience members they invite into one-to-one experiences. As the disorientation and vertiginous possibility of the scenography at large are brought from external to internal space, it can be unsettling and, if not carefully executed, overwhelming. The spatial extension of possibility in the encounter with not only the agency of the other but also one's own, is key to the intensity of the experience:

> You know ... that's truly disorientating. If you put them in a position where 'I don't know why, what they're thinking ... I don't know why this person is doing this, because it doesn't seem like its calculated to be entertaining to me, and I don't know who I am, and I don't know who he is anymore', then it starts to feel real.[43]

The frame shift from external to internal space calls for a corresponding shift in scale of movements and actions by the performer. Every act needs to be minimised and slowed down, as the experience is amplified many times in the mind of the audience member:

> So I would never want to *ram* an orange, like suddenly *thrust* a piece of orange in your mouth, but people would always describe it in those kind of terms. [...] Your memory is writing its own version of events, based on what, sort of, how it feels and you only need to very slowly place an orange ... that was always quite a slow gentle movement every time. But as I say; you're invading their space, it is a bit weird, that's *why* you're doing it.[44]

As can be seen in the *Façade* study as well as in Punchdrunk's work across digital and physical materialities, the relation between the subject and the frame is critical for a comprehensive analysis of immersive experience. As in Hofesh Shechter's *Sun* (2013), an experience can be immersive without you being physically inside the frame. In *Sun,* sound and light were used together to shift the frame of the performance and bring the audience into complicity, with the experience of immersion flowing from the sense of exposure to hidden agencies. Immersive experience is less dependent on mechanical presentation than the destabilised subject position. Thinking it in terms of its structure allows for more agile story craft that 'cuts across' different platforms, materials and the topographies they present. Punchdrunk have developed this in their blended reality productions, for example, *Silverpoint* (2015), which they developed in collaboration with Somethin' Else and Absolut Vodka. With *Silverpoint,* Punchdrunk expanded on the model they introduced with *Goldwell* (2012). Audiences for the final three levels of live interactions across London were brought into the storyworld through a game for mobiles, where you unlocked different levels of the story by playing a points game that was based on Andy Warhol's early blotted-line 'Silverpoint' drawings. The experience was designed around the disappearance of a girl called Chloe and utilised the mobile phone application, email and phone notifications to blend the storyworld into the lives of the participants. Informally, a 'Spoiler' community expanded the storyworld onto Facebook with their own experiences. In *Silverpoint*, in contrast with *The Séance*, the story and the scenography stretched across time and different interfaces and environments that each presented specific affordances and limitations to both makers and audiences. The difference between the two projects can be seen in the structure of the story, as well as in the relationship between subject and event. Where *The Séance* created a plane of immanence outside of the event and kept the off-site participant external and not at any point subject to immanence within the event, *Silverpoint* invited the players to gradually project themselves into the storyworld: first, by way of time, which is a dimension of lived life, and subsequently their physical selves (provided that they could attend their rendezvous in London). The story enticed *Silverpoint* audiences to advance through and in between the features of the material topographies created by the software, devices and the physical locations designed for the experience in an 'art of operating and an art of thinking' (Certeau 1988: 77) that bridged from *chronos* to *kairos* time.

If immersion as an emergent phenomenon is the product of play, we need to think of play not as *paidia* in the simplistic sense, but as voluntary, exploratory adaptation in response to interpretative opportunities, gaps and frictions between different components of a story and ways of telling it. The nature of the in-between, and the elicitation of agency to enter and persevere within its uncertainty, thus becomes a key focus for designers of interactive systems in theatre and beyond.

Art-work and algorithmic audiences

The inclusion of 'moving parts' that one cannot fully control creates a problem space that is necessarily conceptualised in relatively rigid and rudimentary terms in digital design, compared with its centrality to Punchdrunk and others who create physical interactive systems. In live performance, the consequences of audience behaviours are immanent: they complete the artwork, integrating the image of cognitive 'moving parts' of theatre machines with the body as a site of production and experience. Thinking the whole as dependent on uncertain parts brings the question of how we configure audiences to the forefront; specifically, embodied audiences that are free to explore and fail within reach of consequence. Through its entanglement with time and gravity, the corporeal body will always resist the conceptual purity of the idea of mind and reason. Embodiment complicates self-representation with the untidy sensuality of bodily functions and its inevitable vulnerability to time and entropy. The grotesque in popular culture has often brought fertile impurity to what was later acknowledged as fine art, and continues to challenge representation in the present. It creeps into the postdigital aesthetic in art via games and screen applications that aestheticise glitches and the failure of representation (Apperley 2015: 236), echoing Bakhtin's analysis of the carnivalesque (1984). An early theorist of the minor, Bakhtin views the carnivalesque body – laughing, failing and fertile – with grotesque realism.[45] The rationalist occlusion of failure and the grotesque in visions of the digital modern is a function of remoteness, compounded by layers of representation that are at once technological and ideological. If the postdigital is to be life-affirming in the sense of the carnivalesque, it must accommodate, articulate and negotiate failure of rationality through modes of representation at the infrastructure level of interactive systems. In Punchdrunk's theatre machines, the contours of actions by human 'moving parts' that test the edges of illusion are met, traced and brought-within by the interpretative and reactive capacity of actors, Black Masks and designers, working in concert.

We can record and model all manners of actions as data objects in computational systems, but interpretative models fail when expressions are not part of their formal semiotics. Such systems are called technological, but much of interpretation in techne – that is, the skill in craft or art in relation to such systems – fall on their human 'moving parts', who carry over, synthesise and animate the whole. As computation and virtual assistants becomes embedded within our everyday habits, the personal and social habitat increasingly meshes with the machine habitat and its abstract topography, formed by the combined strategic and tactical forces of more and less visible virtual domains (Bassett 2007: 159). Within this composite habitat, human agents act like processors or algorithms that perform interpretative acts. Chun broadens software as a metaphor for programmatic code, and includes in the term the 'scripts' of mind, culture, ideology and the computational agency involved in the navigation of everyday life:

> Software's vapory materialization and its ghostly interfaces embody – conceptually, metaphorically, virtually – a way to navigate our increasingly complex world. (Chun 2011: 2)

If 'software' is an umbrella category for mediated cognitive expressions that connect and interpenetrate the social and technological, it also includes embodied interaction. Punchdrunk's 'theatre machines' depend on it: 'You set up an environment but they're nothing without the audience coming in, so suddenly you have to change so much, in terms of the space, and in terms of where they go.'[46] Casting the audiences as 'moving parts' in the theatre machine confronts them with a rupture of the familiar (Chow 2012: 47) as they are revealed, to themselves, as a part of the materialities of the artwork:

> I definitely felt like most of the decisions, like the control was kind of in somebody else's hands, and I had a diminished control. [...] Like being a spectator and an actor all at once [...] the stuff you do have to decide on is completely personal, but where your body is isn't [...] I wanted to be in the machine, in the software, I wanted to work with the algorithm, however you want to put it. I wanted to function, I didn't want to be the glitch that was in the bar, I wanted to function along with the rest of the machine that was going on, that was also a narrative.[47]

Through enclosure within the frame, the anxiety of performing (or failing to do so) is brought to the audience. Laying bare the possibility of failure invites, even without direct invocation of the carnivalesque, something of the un-beautiful and un-modern grotesque. Within the frame of performance, this can be sublime; the frame aestheticises what might otherwise be a form of terror.

Without the ready-made prioritisation of the proscenium stage, marked by the frame of the stage and the many decisions about what to amplify, the effort of selection and ordering is shared. Actors are not spared from adaptations to their part, and must expose a larger, nuanced surface to the audiences and the performance space: 'The wrong detail could shatter everything, and the right detail [...] can be so suggestive: just draw you into that world in such a powerful way.'[48] The hierarchy of taste (Bourdieu 1984: 264) is more difficult to maintain at close range and for the duration. Exposure invokes the sublime that 'threatens the very foundations of subjectivity' and 'destroys unity' (Zima 2010: 125–7); there is shared risk, as well as a lingering sacrificial element. Audiences offer up their social bodies and expectations to transgression and absorption into the 'machine',[49] while makers, actors and Black Masks speak with longing about belonging within the storyworlds of the company:[50] 'It gets completely ... it becomes your world, and you dream about it, and it's all you think about.'[51] Audience members describe a similar pull, even desiring to give up their everyday lives to immerse themselves beyond the performance:

> It's felt like a four-dimensional experience. It's all around you, it's in your head, it's also like, in your body. ... It's like, I don't know, it's so. ... You feel like you've been dropped into it like, and you're just, I don't know, it's kind of effortless. [...] I'm a total convert. As soon as I got back in, I actually signed up to be one of the people with the black masks on. As soon as I got in, I emailed them and said 'I would like to a volunteer' or whatever you call them. [...] I was just like ... I'll do that. I would stop DJ-ing for six months just to do that.[52]

The close-range affordances offered by immersive performance exert their pull by folding into itself and 'out of this world'. Storyworlds that fold inward, away from worldly affairs towards an idiosyncratic centre, suggest other types of places: churches and monasteries but also the home. Within such places, repeat patterns of touch lay down sediments of familiarity and wear, from prayer beads to familiar objects of the household. Bachelard's epistemology of touch within enclosed spaces describes how the internal space becomes a crucible for the 'synthesis of Memory and Will [...] *Iron Will*, not against the outside, or against other persons, but beyond all the psychology of "being against"' (Bachelard 1994: 85, original emphasis). 'Being beyond being against' is a kind of intimacy, antithetical to critical distance and a conduit for both affordance and containment. Intimacy situates agency inside of place, where touch, like de Certeau's story, can mediate between the two with the exquisite resolution that closeness affords. Similarly, touch, cultivated within a specific framework, is employed by the Black Masks to bring audience members back within the storyworld when they are at risk of compromising its integrity or their own safety:

> So, that was really interesting; how the psychology of getting an audience member to move ... it was quite clever. And as long as they feel safe, and they don't feel like you're, if you do that [demonstrates], then suddenly they're not in this magical created world, it almost like flicking channels on a television. 'Hang on, I was watching that, what are you doing.' There's always an initial like, 'I'm being moved, I'm being moved' and you can feel it. So you could move someone by the shoulders, and then if you wanted to ... if you ... instead of saying, 'stand here and you'll be safe,' all you had to do, was just push slightly down on their shoulders as if to say 'I'm rooting you to the spot'.[53]

Touch resonates in descriptions by designers and actors of crafting, moulding and shaping the shadow choreography of the audience as well as the space.[54] Layered repetitions of touch support the production of immersive space:[55] 'I can't overestimate the kind of .... Everything's planned [...] everything [...] has been distilled and processed.'[56] These repeated processes intensify metaphorical and metamorphic differential, and the potential for shifting 'the play of changing relationships between places and spaces' (Certeau 1988: 118). Using Chow's metaphor for the artwork as trap, the encoded layers in Punchdrunk's scenography disorient, snag and entrap the audience within a narrative structure, where play emerges to resolve the friction of entrapment. It is at the same time allowed within and limited by the structure (Derrida 2001: 352), as dependent on the extension of space as it is on the limitation of place. Conceiving audiences as an emergent and spatially expansive material complicates a totalising perspective and poses a challenge to digital infrastructures in particular. This is not due to an ungovernable extent of possibilities (Derrida 2001: 365) but rather through the supplementarity that flows from integrating the idea of audiences in the capacity of agency, unsettled by disorientation and unmoored from quotidian constraints. Each brings to the system their own inwardly folded space from which flows their capacity for completing the artwork and expanding its meaning.

The inward-folding intimacy that is brought to Punchdrunk shows by audiences is mirrored by Punchdrunk's designers and actors in the making of their productions. The next chapter looks at the making culture of the company in some detail, and how their practices embody what is asked from their audiences: repetition, touch, exploration and commitment to unfolding encounters.

Notes

1. See Chapter 5 for an in-depth analysis of audience experience.
2. Schechner calls forms of play where some of the players are unaware, or covertly co-opted into play as unwitting accessories 'dark play' (1993: 36).
3. In 2001, Johnny Formidable and *The Tempest*; in 2002, *Chair* and *A Midsummer Night's Dream*; in 2005, *The Yellow Wallpaper* and *The Firebird Ball*.
4. COM6.
5. COM6.
6. COM6.
7. COM5.
8. COM5.
9. COM3, COM5, COM1.
10. COM4.
11. See appendix.
12. See appendix.
13. COM3, COM5.
14. COM3.
15. COM3.
16. COM5.
17. AUD1.
18. AUD1.
19. COM3.
20. COM5.
21. COM2.
22. COM2.
23. COM6.
24. COM2.
25. COM2.
26. COM2.
27. COM2.
28. See appendix.
29. COM3.
30. COM3.
31. COM3, COM5.
32. COM3.
33. See Chapter 5.
34. See Chapter 5.

35 An R&D project between MIT and Punchdrunk between 2011 and 2012 on *Sleep No More,* New York. See Chapter 1 for an analysis of the project and the report by the research team.
36 See the discussion of play theory in Chapter 6.
37 AUD5.
38 AUD1, AUD4, AUD5, AUD3.
39 COM5.
40 AUD1, AUD2, AUD4, AUD5, AUD3, COM5.
41 See Chapter 2.
42 COM5.
43 COM3.
44 COM3.
45 Bakhtin bases his analysis of the carnivalesque on *The Life of Gargantua and Pantagruel,* written by the Renaissance scholar and writer François Rabelais as a collection of five novels between 1532 and 1564.
46 COM4.
47 AUD1.
48 COM3.
49 AUD1.
50 COM3, COM5.
51 COM2.
52 AUD5.
53 COM5.
54 COM3, COM5, COM4.
55 COM2, COM1.
56 COM2.

4

Behind the Interface – Making Punchdrunk's Storyworlds

The deeply layered detail of Punchdrunk's storyworlds supports the extension of the story by live audiences in and beyond the events, as evidenced by fandom practices. 'Superfans' (who visit dozens, even up to a hundred times) seek to experience and exhaust all possibilities that are offered. Rich detail invites those who visit the first time to suspend disbelief, even if they arrive as sceptics.[1] All audience interviewees described the detail of the scenography as important to their experience of immersion, as it reassured them that the performance and scenography would support them for the duration. The creation and maintenance of Punchdrunk's scenography, which, in the case of *The Drowned Man*, was distributed over 14,000 square metres and 170 rooms, is a staggering endeavour. Over 500 people contributed, the majority of which working with set design, build and stage management. *The Drowned Man* had an unusually short build period due to the short notice given to the company when the building became available (February–June 2013), and compressed the production schedule. *The Drowned Man* and other Punchdrunk productions are organised around the formula that is outlined in the previous chapter, beginning with directors and lead designers walking the space in darkness. Design plans are drawn by Bea Minns and Livi Vaughan together with the directors and distributed for development and implementation to design and build teams. From there, the storyworld thus born is extended to designers and performers who each devise and distribute their interpretations, all within the company's distinct making culture and aesthetic: 'I can't […] overestimate the, kind of instinctive element to it, that … every designer who works with Punchdrunk has to carry.'[2]

The reliance on distributed agency within the company reflects Rosi Braidotti's definition of contemporary cognitive machines as 'engines or devices that both capture and process forces and energies, facilitating interrelations, multiple connections and assemblages' (Braidotti 2013: 92). Within such machines, Braidotti's posthumanist subject is material and vital: 'embedded and embodied, relational and affective' (2016: 28), resonating with the description of the 'perfect Punchdrunk audience member' as 'someone who is aware of their own body, or their own sort of capability, and are willing to let that be taken over by the space, and taken over by the performance itself'.[3] In the frame of Laura Cull's performance philosophy which, like Braidotti, is informed by Deleuzean thought, the work of Punchdrunk is postidentitarian, as immanence is prioritised over transcendence (Cull 2012: 17):

> Transferring such philosophical and scientific concepts of the distinction between immanence and transcendence to the domain of performance might enable us to generate contrasts between top-down and bottom-up tendencies in authorship, as well as to distinguish between different kinds of artistic organizations. (Cull 2012: 29)

Within this organisational structure, the storyworld that flows from the initial walking and shaping of the performance space is promulgated and manifested through countless intimate interactions: conversations, movements, demonstrations, images, drawings; even mouthed non-verbal sounds:

> We both articulated what we were going to create by sounds, but it's a sound that imitated a characteristic of Bea, and it was just interesting because there is such a shorthand now [...] I think I've been taught these aesthetics, but I don't, it's not an imitation; it becomes your own.[4]

The shared storyworld begins as an image of thought and becomes manifest through acting, choreography and scenography, and the always-becoming shadow choreography of audiences. Acting and scenography are equally weighted and rely on distributed devising, and designers and performers are afforded considerable freedom. This allows the company to layer into the production a level of detail that would otherwise be unfeasible at scale. The information relay process that makes this possible is worthy of study in itself; during the design and build, the storyworld and its characters are discussed as existing in the present, and communicated by way of movement, sound-making and demonstration. Thus distributed, its realisation is shared by many hands.

FIGURE 4.1 *Design studio TDM where detail and smaller props for* The Drowned Man *were made. On the table you can see one of the models of the Red Moon desert that were used within the larger set (Credit: Carina E. I. Westling).*

The integrity of the storyworlds, maintained by distributed responsibility for its manifestation, allows the company to work with the very large numbers of designers who contribute to their productions. *The Drowned Man* was built in four months, shorter than usual due to limited access to the building. This compressed the build period and tested the production methods of the company. The team of 300 designers and makers who built *The Drowned Man* over four months comprised long-term members of the company who supported and managed scores of freelancers and students, many of which working a limited number of days.[5] The commitment to making by those who enter Punchdrunk's company culture for long or short periods, whether they do so as makers or audience members, is central to the processes of the company, as it upholds and manifests the storyworld:

> We did a workshop a few months ago, and one of the ladies there was describing the process of design as 'method designing', so you kind of embody everything that you do, so ... you know, Badland Jack, how would he write a letter? Scrawly ... like ... it would all be kind of frantically put together, a load more would be put on straight, you have to do that for every kind of item that you do, to make it exist properly.[6]

The introduction of new makers within the company is direct and pragmatic. They are inducted in health and safety, assigned to work with more experienced designers and tasks, and immediately start contributing within minimal explicit restraints:

> It's a thing that have to you kind of have to grapple with, because you've got exactly what it is, and how you need to create, but you have to kind of, allow the maker to possess it, because otherwise it's ... it becomes robotic, and there's no kind of freshness.[7]

The creative agency of each individual that comes to the making is accommodated within the overarching aesthetic, and enhances the supplementarity that is layered into the scenography. This creative and interpretative supplementarity expands the possibilities for interaction and thus the experiential space, and audience members emerge with unique narratives and experiences:

> We'd had completely different experiences, completely different stories. And so, considering there was two of us, how many times could you go and still have a completely different experience?[8]

> And all of us had different experiences, and we got to the end and I said 'Guys there's this amazing room in the attic, with this puppet in the bed', one of my three friends were like 'What, the attic?' 'Was that...?' 'Yeah, there's like, right at the top of the building, you went along this sort of wooden plank floor in this sort of attic space, and then you went down these steps into this old Victorian room, covered in suitcases and...' And they're like 'There's an attic?'[9]

> [...] like a deserted motel, and the bar, and everything, there was such fine detail in there, you know. So it ... it's very clever, and it would draw you into go back again, to try and, to try to recreate the memory that you had the first time, and perhaps, make, make it a different experience when you go back again [...][10]

The difference and repetition that Deleuze introduces in abstract terms is given physical form through performance and making in Punchdrunk's work: the many layers of interpretative touch by hundreds of designers and performers create storyworlds that are subsequently walked and experienced by the thousands who comprise their audiences. Even though the 'theatre machine' repeats, each repetition produces a different experience for the audience members who walk them, mirroring and overlaying the initial steps taken to block the space while the storyworld was still virtual, and a thought form waiting to become.

Building storyworlds

The building process in Punchdrunk generates interiority and inward-folding experiential spaces. It begins with blacking out the space in which the work is to be manifested prior to its mapping and continues with the labyrinthine scenography of rooms and detail. The shape of the space support 'abduction' through distortion: narrowings, openings, extensions, curvatures, elevations and descents exert dynamic forces on performance and audience flows. The dressing of the space, once the shape is forming, adds detail, depth and interpretative scope in textures and affordances for interaction and investigation. It also extends the promise of a compact to the audience:

> It made a massive difference for me, because it felt like I could trust them to give me the experience I had been promised. It did feel immersive, and it let me leave my cynicism at the door, by having so much detail. The sets were huge, you know, I was very impressed, and I felt very willing to participate in it, because it seemed like a worthy thing to participate in. It seemed like an experience worth having.[11]

Sustained investment in the performance by audiences for three hours while they pursue a fragmented narrative with little guidance requires perseverance in the face of uncertainty. Immersive states rely on self-abduction and yielding to the persuasive trap of the artwork (Chow 2012: 41). The detail of the scenography instilled trust in self-entrapment by audience members in this study, and sustained it for the duration of the performance.[12] The dressing includes large objects; trees, cars, caravans, large volumes of sand and foliage, through to small and medium-sized objects; for example, books, trinkets, clothes, letters, furniture, drapery, decorative lighting, pictures, plus about 400 props used by performers, in the case of *The Drowned Man*. These are created and customised from a wide range of materials including wood, resin, plastics, paint, plant materials, wax, textiles, paper and found materials. Hidden features and experiences that contribute to the story may never be discovered, like flipbooks in the corner of a book placed in a bookshelf, tucked-away letters or notes that reveal intimate communication between the characters in the play, or historical details that require further research to be fully understood: 'there's lot of stuff that we kind of design completely and it ends up being in the dark'.[13]

Vast amounts of materials are needed to create environments that participants can explore to the depth of physical reality outside the performance space.[14] An exception in *The Drowned Man* was the desert landscape on the top floor. It was a vast, symbolic gesture, with the Red Moon Motel sign half submerged in a sand dune as a metaphor for the nuclear testing that took

FIGURE 4.2 *The store. A corner of Punchdrunk's warehouse in the Silvertown store in advance of* The House Where Winter Lives. *The image shows some of the props in store for future productions. The amount of scenographic detail that is required to produce the requisite 'thickness' of sets needs layering over time. Organically patinated objects are mixed with hand-made, customised and manually aged detail over weeks or months, depending on the size of the production (Credit: Carina E. I. Westling).*

place in the Nevada desert in the mid-twentieth century,[15] and created an obviously fictive landscape. In the desert audiences were aware of the edges of illusion,[16] but chose to uphold the suspense of disbelief:

> It was the most beautiful installation, but it was not a space I wanted to be in, it was very much a space that I felt I just had to pass through, because if you look … too many of the details, you'd start seeing, you started seeing how that space works, like what are the. … How it was technically created.[17]

The tacit compact to uphold the integrity of the storyworld was generally upheld by participants in this study, even in the face of temptation to collect souvenirs. One interviewee said they removed a part of the set (a small paper card), and expressed this with a sense of guilt ('I think I maybe took one ... which I shouldn't have done').[18] The sense of importance given to small objects which are easily replaced reflects the sense that the storyworld was a manifestation of intense care and investment of effort:

> That was what I thought about taking, but I ... I was like 'Oh, I wish I could take this' but how could I, because someone else wouldn't have that experience. No, I'm glad I didn't. But I was like 'Oh, I'd really love to have this' and then I didn't ... take it. But there was a ... No, I didn't ... I mean ... Only with my eyes, that's the best way I can say it. Like, really like 'aaaargh' ... only with my eyes.[19]

The intensity of commitment from designers and actors, evident in the detail of scenography and performance, anchors the relationship between Punchdrunk and their audiences, and comes across in audience interviews as gratitude: 'I really want to say thank you, but I have no idea how to say it.'[20] Perhaps more surprisingly, the intimacy of touch that is layered into scenography seems to create the atmosphere of a strange home to which you long to return. This comes through strongly in accounts by audiences, but also by company members:

> It's the family, and I think that's how you ... it is like joining the circus, a bit [laugh]. It gets completely ... it becomes your world, and you dream about it, and it's all you think about.[21]

Repetitions of touch create and sustain the intimacy of the home but also immersion in Punchdrunk's work. In Bachelard's phenomenological and poetic imagination, the home is a 'vertical being' that challenges gravitational pull and defines a dualism between rising and falling and, through its external, singular form appeals to our 'consciousness of centrality' (Bachelard 1994: 17). In this image the outwardly singular form of the building, which stands in for the subjective body, is the vessel for inward-folding, idiosyncratic spaces, the experience of which extends beyond the physical outline.

Bachelard's description of the home that stands in for the subjective body echoes Hayles' definition of the posthuman (Hayles 2002: 319) that contains its own spatial entropy: the interior, as it folds in on itself, births new spaces that are defined less by their physical size than their experience potential. These shifts from place to space as you move from the exterior to the interior, take place as you enter *Sleep No More* (2011), which is housed within the six floors of a block of three adjoined warehouses in Chelsea, New York. The production has been managed since its opening by the US partner Emursive, overseen by Punchdrunk International.[22] The outside of the twentieth-century building is a flat, non-descript brick façade within the iconic, gridded urban landscape of New York. Within, twisting staircases and dark passages connect rooms and milieus; McKittrick's hotel and the village Gallow Green, where *Macbeth* is reimagined through a Hitchcock-clouded lens, both set in 1930s Scotland. The tension between the emotion of the drama and the space within which it is held is underscored by the choreography, which has the performers scaling, pushing and jumping off the walls. The McKittrick hotel takes up the first few floors, with the apartments of the key characters of *Macbeth*, the bar, the dining room and the hotel lobby. Moving upward, the fourth floor houses the village Gallow Green, laced through with themes from the Paisley witch trials and Hitchcock's *Rebecca*. The uppermost generally accessible (fifth) floor houses the sanatorium and the forest. The top (sixth) floor is inaccessible for general audiences; only one-to-ones are invited.

Presenting a similar contrast between exterior and interior, *The Drowned Man* ran in the Old Sorting Offices at Paddington Station, London: a man-made Victorian mountain of brick and sandstone that speaks of empire and solidity. Renamed Temple Pictures, the vast, open-plan floors were subdivided into nested series of studio sets-within-sets, representing multiple levels of reality and blurring the boundaries between layers of fiction, artifice and projected dreams. Like *Sleep No More*, each floor was dedicated to a specific location or theme. The basement housed the occult operations of Temple Pictures and their networked associations with powerful people, and the top floor desert was the setting for possible redemption. The expansive floor spaces had stairs in three corners and were subdivided to in disorientating series of rooms and spaces that were sometimes difficult to orient yourself in while working on the build. The sheer size, complexity and absence of daylight made the whole unfamiliar and disorientating. In *The Drowned Man*, spatial entropy was accelerated by nested stories within the overarching narrative and doubled up storylines with inverted characters, resulting in an inwardly diffracting space that multiplied the possible number of recombinations and interpretations by audiences.

Bachelard described the nest in Michelet's *L'Oiseau* as shaped from inside by the nesting bird, created 'by and for the body, taking form from the inside, like a shell, in an intimacy that works physically' (Bachelard 1994: 101). Similarly, Punchdrunk's scenography faces inward, a thickened interiority that is founded, created and sustained by repeated and layered walking, making and touching. The organic pressures of making and desire, embodied and articulated through perambulation and touch, lay down sediments over time. Like the birds in Michelet's *L'Oiseau*, Punchdrunk bring materials for nesting; furniture, textiles, books and other objects that they shape and form to expand the interior, protect and hold the illusion of its world against the exterior.

FIGURE 4.3 *Props composition. Examples of the countless props, large and small, on the build of* The Drowned Man *(from top left corner, clockwise): one of the caravans for the Woodchip Trailer Park; a miniature of the Red Moon sign, half submerged in sand; a selection of printed and hand-written prop detail including prescriptions by the Doctor; an eye test chart for the Doctor's surgery, letters and Temple Pictures scripts; props for the 'Frozen Lake' movie set at Temple Pictures (Credit: Carina E. I. Westling).*

The material thickness of the scenography must hold the outside world of the city at bay. As a boundary between the interior and the exterior, the scenography acts as a frame for the sublime and the boundary of play at once. The 'self-abduction' that sustains immersion over time rests on the particular qualities of the scenography. In interviews, audiences refer to the rich detail as critical to their willing submission to the experience.[23] Its duration, and the effort that Punchdrunk performances ask of their audiences, requires ongoing renewal of this compact, particularly as there is no promise of resolution or completion. This falls on the scenography as the experience unfolds, after the initial surprise and awe and between any encounter with actors. Its success can be measured in the enduring desire and/or longing to revisit the experience: 'It's just ... I would love to go back, I really want to go back and do it again, and not worry about the plot, and just see everything that I missed.'[24] Playful descriptions of this compulsion show self-abduction to be voluntary, just like the submission to immersion itself:

> If someone said 'oh, you have to go and see the Drowned Man every week' I'll be like, I'll probably, I'll be okay. I'll probably be okay: 'Allright then, fine. I'll live with this curse; this is one of the good curses, I think.'[25]

FIGURE 4.4 *Straw men in desert. The straw men in the desert on the top floor of* The Drowned Man. *After a show, the desert was full of footprints. Stage managers reset the scenography and props every day, combing through and smoothing 3.5 tons of sand in the process (Credit: Carina E. I. Westling).*

Devising and performing

Acting in Punchdrunk's 'theatre machines' is co-ordinated in choreographies that, together with the shadow choreography of the audience, connect and animate the scenography. Most Punchdrunk performers are both dancers and actors as the energy and shape of their movement in the space is central, and their movements form the clockwork of the 'machine':

> We imagine sort of energies of those journeys and how a character might guide an audience to all of these different atmospheres and ambiences. And we begin to plot this down almost mechanically, and we start with the central characters because we have much more information about them, because we can take very much from the text. And then we sort of build a grid, and we do the same process for each of the characters that we're going to be developing.[26]

Maxine Doyle leads the development of Punchdrunk's choreographic aesthetic and methods since joining the company in 2002. Her role combines directing and choreography, and she combines texts and other sources with devising in developing the movement vocabulary. Working off-site at first, Maxine establishes the foundations of the physical language together with the dancers in the studio, and move them into the space when it is sufficiently formed and safe to work in. Once they start rehearsing on-site, the building takes on a role in the further development of the choreography. The paths of central characters are developed with the different spaces and atmospheres in mind, and form interlocking systems with each other that become gradually more complex and detailed as the rehearsals progress.

Performers alternate in the characters they play as rotation of roles allows performers to switch between physically dynamic 'travelling' and less demanding 'residential' characters:

> Residents; they sort of inhabit, and they live. They were created initially partly in response to the dancers having … for the work to work … all those hours per week. So the dancers have two roles. They have one which is more choreographic and physical and dynamic, and then this other role which is kind of still demanding, but in a different way it – it protects the body in a different way, those … less sort of, physical investment; choreographic investment.[27]

The travelling and residential roles have different spatial dynamics; both active. Whereas the travelling characters express the narrative arc in broader strokes with higher levels of activity and influence more directly with the way audiences move through the space, the residential characters create slower, deeper rhythms:

> And there's a rhythmical thing, which is really important. There are always lots of rhythms happening in the building of the same time, and that's really important. To be able to go through the building and feel like things … the building is changing. And an empty space becomes a chaotic space, a calm space becomes a terrifying space, and all those things. So the residents have this … more consistent rhythm. They might have peaks and troughs in it. They're more lifelike, really, because that's more like we are – walking down the road; a little intervention might happen or it might not. They're kind of … more lifelike in that way, whereas the other characters, the travelling characters, because they travel they have more of an arc, more of a crescendo. So there's all of those … it's the melange of all of those rhythms that make it kind of interesting, I think.[28]

Once on-site, the choreography is developed with the characters and the space in mind. Small worlds are built for each character, and the company then 'invent other environments to support those worlds, that might stretch the life of the character'.[29] At the same time, they look at 'how that character might journey, and how you might journey with them as an audience, and follow them through these different worlds'.[30] Here, the legacy of dance is evident, not only in the conceptualisation of movement through space but also in thinking through the ensemble. Punchdrunk productions comprise several, nested 'wholes' within the larger totality, including that of the cast, who work with and even within a second circle, the audience. This can be traced in the system of interwoven trajectories that supports the shadow choreography of the audience:

> We basically build this grid; we spend a lot of time doing that, and we're thinking artistically and dramatically and about the impact, but also we are thinking very functionally in terms of flow. So we know that if we bring ten travelling characters together into one space, we know that will have a pull of audience, which is part of the formula that we developed a long time ago, and we kind of realised there's a strength in that. There is as strength in an isolated audience, potentially in an isolated individual, and then magically being put together with a mass of other people. [...] Someone once said that they thought we pulled a big magic trick. For that to be done well and smoothly, it's all about managing traffic. So, understanding where people coming from, what their timings are, what the rhythms are. It changes all the time in development, so we know that there's not going to be a dead-end or a block. Inevitably there are moments when there are ... but we try to minimise those. It's all about the flow of the audience.[31]

The acting is largely non-verbal, which means that the temporal linearity of language expression, as discussed by Deleuze and Guattari, does not overcode the process of experience (2004: 69). This allows the company to develop the text in several dimensions; it informs everything from choreography to scenography and is layered into the set as fragments. By contrast, the dialogue is limited to local and hardly audible utterances, supporting the simultaneous extension of story time in all directions within the building, and the distribution of composition and interpretation to audiences:

> If we were using dialogue and stuff, the dialogue is too on the surface, makes things too clear, too apparent. There's too much, you know ... laden with information. That kind of ... it doesn't work at all.[32]

While *Sleep No More* features little more than near-inaudible murmurs by the actors, *The Drowned Man* had some pre-recorded voice-overs by the character Leland Stanford, the director of Temple Pictures, around whom a web of other characters in the play was formed. Both *The Drowned Man* and *Sleep No More* explore themes of power and its abuse, but in place of the raw brutality in *Macbeth*, *The Drowned Man* explored dominance through the exploitation and commodification of desire and dreams in the Hollywood studio system. The indirect articulation of power was reflected in the portrayal of Leland Stanford by one of the long-term company actors:

> I didn't have a story myself, I was influencing numerous other people's stories; you follow me, you don't get the story of Leland, you know, you just get him … he's concerned with Wendy he's concerned with Frankie, Delores, Romula, Lila, you know … that's it. But he's going from one to the other of those stories; he's going between those stories, you know, having a sequence of impacts on them. But without a real … he's not really got a real story.[33]

Through 'not having a story', the character of Leland Stanford was at once nowhere and everywhere, and yet exerted a pervasive influence on the fates of other characters. Under his dominion, only white masks differentiated audience members from other performers. Defocusing language serves to reduce the distance between actors and audiences, and integrates the 'shadow choreography' with the choreography of performers. The partial 'un-coding' of the hierarchy of spoken dialogue in linear time supports situated emergence, and hones the focus on embodiment:

> I mean you can tell a lot about people; you can't see their face but so much is communicated with the body. You can tell if they're an interested, curious, and active audience member from the way they're standing, and where they're moving and where they're looking. […] People are very expressive with their bodies. If you wear a mask, you … as a performer, you learn how to express all sorts of emotions by putting the head tilted this way, sympathetic this way, all of, this is, there's so many … combined with gesture and stance, you know.[34]

While the aim is for performances to run like clockwork, routines continue to evolve during production runs, and improvised adaptations are incorporated as part of the routine.[35] Each instance of the form hybridises as it repeats, providing a concrete case study of Deleuzean difference as a function of repetition:

> Because of course, it's theatre, like any theatre, and you want to create this illusion of repeating universe, this closed universe that repeats itself. But the audience is excited by the fact that it's live. The audience is excited by

the fact that it's happening now, and it's that tension, one of many forms of tensions, that is interesting, and exciting for the audience. The fact that it is different each time, each scene is different each time, even if you are aiming for it not to be. Because it's theatre, and it's live, and it's messy and the audience is unpredictable, you can't help that it's different on the third loop from the first loop; it's a different kind of energy. [...] the show wouldn't happen, or it wouldn't be as good as it was, if it weren't for people creating in performance, and making these discoveries with each other.[36]

The accommodation of change and tolerance to improvisation within the clockwork structure that holds the scenes and transitions in Punchdrunk's large masked productions exemplifies the symbiotic relationship between play and its limits. This applies equally to the entirety of the productions as systems with moving parts and to human participants within them at the individual level. It affords a shift from thinking the personal through identity as a 'container' to one that is experienced as a possibility space through the immanent subject – or vantage position (Bignall, Bowden and Patton 2014: 31). In contrast with the transcendent idea of identity as a product of separation, it evokes being as 'not one *thing* at all, but process, change or difference' (Cull 2012: 7).

Bringing attention to the process of experience in Punchdrunk is aided by a range of devices, all of which flow from thinking and shaping the audience through potentiality. The idea of identity as an emergent or immanent process can be a device employed by performers in interactions with masked audience members:

> It's creating the illusion of drawing them into the world. You do that by kind of giving them a role to play within it. You've kind of cast them as a certain character; you create the illusion that they've been chosen for this scene for a reason.[37]

Audiences are invited into the process of change via unsettled identity and the potential for shape-shifting that this affords. This is a reversal of how interactions are personalised in digital systems based on stereotypes and makes possible experience that is not replicable even though the performance is scripted. The local 'overcoding' of identity in masked encounters is a device, like the disorienting scenography, to unsettle pre-existing orders and invite participation in the capacity of possibility or potentiality:

> It's an illusion obviously. But what you're trying to subvert is the reality of the situation, namely that they are an audience member who's bought a ticket, and you are a performer, whose job it is to entertain them, so

you're ... I'm always at pains to try to subvert that reality by not being overtly entertaining, particularly when in a one-to-one; trying to, you know, using things like, you know, not doing ... ignoring them for a bit, or just having a bit of a gap, silence and just sort of, or doing something that is not clear what ... they can't see it clearly enough, or it doesn't really concern them. [...] it's like as if you have to, kind of, scare them as an artist before you scare them as a character, so that they're, you know ... that's truly disorientating. If you put them in a position where 'I don't know why, what they're thinking ... I don't know why this person is doing this, because it doesn't seem like its calculated to be entertaining to me, and I don't know who I am, and I don't know who he is anymore.' then it starts to feel real. [...] You need to unsettle them as a performer, as an artist, to unsettle them as a character.[38]

Close-range encounters draw focus towards the interior of the interaction, and tiny details are devised, reviewed, adapted and incorporated within the larger body of knowledge in the company. In-show devising serves to refine and negotiate between the possibility of space and the definition of place, with a focus on the precise detail and articulation of interactions:

The wrong detail could shatter everything, and the right detail could. ... You know, the wrong word is like playing the wrong note in the key, it just doesn't ... but then the right way can be so suggestive: just draw you into that world in such a powerful way. It's all about details and accumulation of many, many, many, many, many, many, many details, and many, many small decisions, and the decisions that haven't been made, as well, the decisions to not do something: that would be the expected thing to do. The notes that we aren't playing, or beats that we aren't playing, those are really important decisions.[39]

Such encounters combine the close-up intimacy of film with the physicality of stage acting, without the mediating distance of conventional scenography. The fidelity of detail must therefore go beyond projected illusion:

It's why I think the dancers are ideal performers for this work, because a lot of actors, who've been used to work with traditional theatre or film or something; you know, have gone through a normal of acting training ... often would play too big. And they're emoting and narrating too much.[40]

With no visible boundaries between performers and audiences and no or little spoken dialogue, actors are required to simultaneously act and direct the audience as 'co-performers', using gaze and gesture to clear spaces, direct audiences and shift the boundaries of the performance to include or exclude participants:

> You can't take in that picture in any one gaze. The audience has to look this way and look that way, but without Wendy's presence there: seeing the orgy through her eyes, because her looking at it, and actually my character looking at her looking at it; that's where the meaning of the situation is. [...] you can tailor the pitch of your performance to their decisions so that if they come very close, even if you're still playing the game of invisibility with them, or you know, you're keeping up this pretence that you can't see them [...], so you might, if you have the leeway, you have the liberty, you might decide to bring the pitch of your performance down to a very subtle, close up kind of level, so that you're giving them something that they know is just for them.[41]

The cast works within the theatrical whole to negotiate the shape and flows of audiences, and characters may be added or adapted in production, just like the scenography, to enhance the working of the theatre machine:

> It's always an unpredictable thing, but the ... what we do, is our timings and our movements and the directions of our gazes to direct what the audience are aware of, how they behave, you know, makes all the difference. The audience is very directable and to manipulate them sometimes you just have to have a character like the Diva PA, who's, you know, got that job, OK you decide, you know, it's your job to clear this area. You need to you know, while this point in the ... music, you need to clear this you know, but getting this precision, by precisely arranging the performance, and you know, with help from lighting and stuff as well obviously, direct the audience to be where you want them to be.[42]

Thinking the audience flows within the affordances presented by the system beyond identity allows performers and designers to shape the shadow choreography as a material.[43] Mass audiences as a material has its own dynamic characteristics and requires that the designer or director steps back to view it as an elemental force:

> Someone once said that they thought we pulled a big magic trick. So, for that to be done well and smoothly, it's all about managing traffic. So, understanding where people coming from, what their timings are, what the rhythms are. It changes all the time in development, so we know that there's not going to be a dead-end or a block. Inevitably there are moments when there are ... but we try to minimise those. It's all about the flow of the audience.[44]

The idea of shape-shifting and the conceptualisation of audiences as capacity for change rather than identities effectively inform both the close-up perspective and the mass view of audiences. Punchdrunk as a company, incorporating all its constituents, continue to build significant artistic and pragmatic knowledge of how to negotiate and work with large and extremely small audiences as a dynamic material in mutually meaningful exchanges:

> I mean it is sophisticated, and we have developed it over the years, but however much … each project we do … we put more thinking into that area of it. Colin Nightingale is amazing at that … all of that management with us, but then we never know exactly how it will be until we put the show into play for the first time, with an audience, because some audiences are faster, and some audiences are slower. And then we really hand it over to the performers, and it's really … they really take responsibility for making that flow work. So they might … 'I need to actually…here there's a collision, I need to find a different route, I need to hold back, create a distraction for 35 seconds …' They become really, really adept, which is really why it's about dancers, or a very particular kind of actor with the right physical sensibility. And then the discussion becomes about your show in relation to the audience. Keeping them, losing them, or guiding them.[45]

One-to-one interactions are nested within the larger structure, and the performer needs to negotiate the shift in the audience members selected for these interactions from being part of an anonymous mass flow to barefaced encounters in small, enclosed spaces. To do so, the performer removes the mask, exposing the audience member not only to the intimacy of the situation but also the presence in the performance as 'oneself', underscored by the sudden rush of air on naked skin:

> I turned around, and the other guy had gone, and she was staring at me with her hands towards the door like she wouldn't let me out. And I was like 'ohhh god, oh I'm in an act … oh no, what do I do, do I go 'oh you're an actress, I'm a stage manager' do I strike up a conversation?' I was frozen! I couldn't say a word. And she took my mask off, and that's a really weird thing; when they take your mask off: you feel naked.[46]

The invitation to participate in one-to-ones is extended only to a small number of audience members each night. The exposure they engender heightens experience and is often described by participants in terms that suggest unexpected force, domination or transgression (e.g. 'dragged me into a room', 'forced an orange into my mouth').[47] By contrast, actors approach one-to-one experiences as tightly scripted events where their movements are minimised and carefully designed:

> I know with the Drowned Man one-to-one in particular, what I did every time from the beginning of the run to the end, was that I would unlock the door, push the door open and then sort of look at the floor. And I would wait for them to go in, and if they didn't go in, I would just maybe do a little tilt of the head, but I wouldn't even be doing eye contact at the point. Definitely not physical contact. [...] What you're trying to do is have the maximum possible impact with the minimum possible expenditure of any energy, of force.[48]

The one-to-one experiences demonstrate the complex effect of framing on experience, and its role in producing the vertigo of the sublime. The actor and the audience member share two frames in the one-to-one; the larger 'frame' or boundary in time and place of the show, and the smaller frame of the scene. They begin with one additional 'frame' each – performers have the scripted knowledge of the show, and audiences are masked. The removal of the latter in the one-to-one and the transgression of the immanent vantage point that this affords engenders awe and vertiginous distortion of scale in the audience member, while the actor experiences their movements as small, precise and aesthetic:

> If I do anything that is likely to make you move, or get lots of orange, like ... wrong, or like, I would drop the orange, perhaps, and then we'd have to look for it in the dark. ... Do you know what I mean? It's like you don't want to invite anything, you know, you're trying to minimise chaos. So, I would never want to *ram* an orange, like suddenly *thrust* a piece of orange in your mouth, but people would always describe it in those kinds of terms, the write-ups could be so inaccurate for that reason. Because they're talking about how they felt, and they're remembering it later. [...] Your memory is writing its own version of events, based on what, sort of, how it feels, and you only need to very slowly place an orange ... that was always quite a slow gentle movement every time.[49]

The Black Masks, stage managers and ushers who support the performers, interact with audiences as needed, and work during the day to reset the scenography are integral to Punchdrunk's masked shows since *Faust* (2006). They articulate and manage the edges of the illusion and intervene when audiences act in ways that threaten the integrity of the storyworld. They are dressed in black and use techniques that have been developed to keep their interventions within the overarching aesthetic and preserve the ambience of the storyworld. In the very low lighting conditions in most parts of the set, they can stay hidden even when you walk close by. The surprise element when they emergence out of darkness adds to the ambiguity of the edges of the storyworld, as you realise that you may have been watched throughout, when you thought that you were on your own. Rather than simply reinforcing limits, their interventions articulate the edges of the illusion in unexpected encounters: 'It was just so surreal, it was very dreamlike [...] like the control was kind of in somebody else's hands, and I had a diminished control. But it was cool, though. I didn't mind that. I really liked that.'[50]

Audience members sometimes try to remove parts of the set, and although is expected to occasionally happen when items are replaceable (e.g. notes or letters), such actions are monitored and, when possible, prevented:

> And how easy you can move an audience member or get them not to do something – just by shaking your head, making eye contact and shaking your head, and they'd put the prop back. And you couldn't talk to them either; it's all sign language. It's really clever. So instead of going up to someone going 'you can't keep that prop that you just put in your pocket, can I have it back, please', you sort of go up to them stand in front of them; make eye contact and just hold your hand out.[51]

In the interest of preserving the aesthetic of the experience, Punchdrunk have developed non-verbal techniques for the Black Masks that enable them to move and intervene in ways that are specific to the role they play and its situation between scenography and acting. They move in ways that establishes them as part of the shadows, bringing the negative of stage lighting to life:

> So you don't walk with the usual gait. Very slow and sort of within keeping with the show, you know, slightly mysterious, or slightly a bit of an enigma, in a way. And you want to blend in, so if you start, you can't run: if you run or walk quicker than normal, you stick out like a sore thumb.[52]

The guidance techniques developed for and used by the Black Masks in interactions rely on co-opting and reorienting audience members within the overarching narrative, and are communicated through changes in pace and tactile signals such as pressure applied to the lower arm or shoulder of the audience member:

> It's very calm; almost like someone's about to brush past you. And then you can ... what we normally do, is going up behind them, hands on their shoulders and grip, and just gently pull back, and you get them to move. [...] And there was another thing where if you wanted to walk with someone,

you could sort of run ... so, put your arm down, just put your arm down by your side. You would do that and just lead them, keep that elbow contact, so all your forearm is touching, rather than leading them like kids in primary school. You're keeping them quite close to you, and you would be able to steer them as well, with that forearm contact.[53]

The dreamlike vertigo described by audiences when encountering the Black Masks flows from destabilisation of their perceived locus of agency through composition with another agency and not being in control, yet moving around at will:

Yeah, I was just really ... I don't know, it was just amazing. It was so surreal; it was like ... the most surreal thing I've ever done. It was very dreamlike without being pretentious. Without kind of trying to be dreamlike. I genuinely felt, with the mask on, completely passive. That was a really new experience for me; feeling completely passive. Also, while walking around, and you know, like ... your body is really active but you're not expected to intervene unless asked, and ... and I remember at one point I tried to cross a room while the actors were dancing, and. ... You know, after being told 'explore!' like this, I thought 'I will just cross the room,' and I actually got stopped by one of the ... kind of 'bouncers' ... not bouncers, but the kind of people ... and physically stopped. They were like ... 'you can't pass the room right now'.[54]

Here, the shift in locus of agency within the whole is described as an altered state of awareness, like vertigo generated by the dissolution of the boundary between self and other (Lyotard 1991: 99); the experience of 'becoming-other' (Braidotti 2013: 3).

The sense of impending imposition by other agencies is elicited by the scenography and expressed in performance by both actors and Black Masks. It is not limited to audience members; Black Masks who worked regularly with *The Drowned Man* were also affected to the extent that they avoided certain rooms:

Well, you know, if you're standing in a really dark room, and the music is really scary, and your imagination starts to run away ... I'll say most of the stage management team didn't like being in the basement during scenes one or two, especially at the start of the show. There would be no audience down there, it's really fucking dark, and then the music is going '*dzummmmmmm* ...'.[55]

Commitment and extension of agency from company members and audiences are critical to the success of the work, making the storyworld a crucible of sorts where boundaries between self and other can blur within the larger frame of the performance. This manifests in encounters between self and other, where the emergent detail is heightened through careful framing. The scenography, the Black Masks, performers and the audience combine to form a material continuum of varying thickness or viscosity and response capacity, from dense and slowly changing to relatively volatile. The clockwork organisation and the bounds of the performance in time and space form the structure that simultaneously holds this continuum and allows it to be emergent. Play and its frame are interdependent; the movement of the former emerges in relation to the latter, and the material brought to live performance by its audiences is at once potentiated and shaped by the aesthetic conduits offered by scenography and 'shadow choreography'.[56]

Notes

1. AUD1.
2. COM2.
3. COM4.
4. COM2.
5. COM6.
6. COM2.
7. COM2.
8. AUD1.
9. COM5.
10. AUD6.
11. AUD1.
12. AUD1.
13. COM2.
14. COM4, COM2.
15. COM2.
16. AUD1, AUD2, AUD4, AUD5, AUD3.
17. AUD4.
18. AUD2.
19. AUD5.
20. AUD5.
21. COM2.
22. Punchdrunk's production company, set up in 2015 to produce and manage independent work by Punchdrunk, as well as collaborative partnerships, nationally and internationally.

23 AUD1, AUD5, AUD3.
24 AUD1.
25 AUD5.
26 COM1.
27 COM1.
28 COM1.
29 COM1.
30 COM1.
31 COM1.
32 COM3.
33 COM3.
34 COM3.
35 COM3.
36 COM3.
37 COM3.
38 COM3.
39 COM3.
40 COM3.
41 COM3.
42 COM3.
43 COM3.
44 COM1.
45 COM1.
46 COM5.
47 COM3.
48 COM3.
49 COM3.
50 AUD1.
51 COM5.
52 COM5.
53 COM5.
54 AUD1.
55 COM5.
56 COM3.

5

Audience Experience and Participation

Previous chapters discussed how Punchdrunk create their 'theatre machines' within which audiences are thought, addressed and incorporated as moving parts; an algorithmic material within a labyrinthine interior of deeply layered textures and texts embedded at multiple levels in scenography and dramaturgy. In this chapter, the structure of audience experience is in focus, particularly with regard to immersion as an expression of the sublime, produced by destabilised identity and extended agency.

Disorientation, and how we respond to it, is central to the experience of immersion in Punchdrunk's work and arguably beyond. It acts in tandem with the desire to figure out, persevere, and commit to the storyworld, and sustains emergence that is distinguished from emergency by way of framing. The centrality of frames is confirmed by descriptions by those who *do not* enjoy it, and who describe the same features in a negative light, as explored in the next section. The comparison, below, between descriptors of the experience and what audiences do in relation to it shows that interpretation and framing of challenge in theatre and experience design is critical in respect of producing 'value' – but in interactive systems that incorporate human agency within the designed vision, it is also functionally critical.[1] A more speculative exploration of how we might accommodate and leverage differential, divergent and even delinquent expressions of agency within the aesthetics of interactive systems concludes this chapter.

In her analysis of the participatory turn in performance, Bishop focuses on the self-exploitation inherent to the 'artificial hells' that were created by artists and performers in the twentieth century (2012), and outlines how performance in the participatory turn problematises late neoliberal or 'connexionist' capitalism (Boltanski and Chiapello 2005). The participatory turn in performance anticipated many of the questions brought by the acceleration of participatory and social technologies from the mid-2000s. Less than a decade later, social platforms had developed into contested new public spaces that commodify the performed self, resulting in tensions between instrumentalised participation and social structures in the physical world. Questions of representation in theatre and performance include how the self is conceptualised, modelled, performed and instrumentalised, offering a vital advantage when applied to interrogation of these new spaces.

The Drowned Man (2013) tells the story of self-exploitation and the commodification of desire in the Hollywood system in the early 1960s. It serves as a parable of self-exploitation and instrumentalisation of the performed self, mirrored in the tension between the transcendent and the immanent subject–event perspective that participants in Punchdrunk's 'theatre machines' are subjected to. Complicity with self-exploitation is articulated through an active and curatorial audience role in relation to the inescapable failure of 'completion'. The resulting exposure highlights the relevance of a Deleuzean system analysis of immanent and a transcendent subject position in tandem with, and enriched by, de Certeau's analysis of space and place which allows us to read emergent experience as a spatial operation. Deleuze's and de Certeau's perspectives on how experiences and our subject position in relation to them are framed come together in thinking the artwork as a trap, within which one self-abducts to experience the sublime (Chow 2012: 47).

The invitation to entrapment in Punchdrunk's work is expressed in every aspect of the design, from the labyrinthine spaces to the richness of textures, and invites its self-abducted audiences on a quest without given resolutions. Deleuze's idea of creative thought as intrinsically challenging and difficult, in contrast with problems that are formulated in relation to their solvability (Deleuze 2014: 209–10), finds physical form in participation that articulates embodied interpretation in the face of uncertainty and possible failure.

Analysing Punchdrunk audiences

Audience members I interviewed described their experience with enthusiasm and in great detail even months after visiting *The Drowned Man*. I kept the setting informal and allowed the conversation to flow around a mutual experience, to preserve the freshness of their accounts. As with my interviews with company members, I didn't take any photos; I wanted to conduct the research with direct exposure and sensory experience of the performance environment in focus, and leading conversations. These interviews yielded lengthy and detailed accounts of interacting with and making Punchdrunk's storyworlds. To gather negative as well as positive accounts from a larger cohort, I gathered and aggregated data from audiences who had attended *The Drowned Man* and *Sleep No More* and left reviews on TripAdvisor.

All the audience members that I interviewed described intensely sensory and aesthetic engagement with *The Drowned Man*; physically exhausting[2] but profoundly rewarding. They framed the experience as a challenge,[3] engendering a sense of mystery;[4] all foregrounding disorientation, uncertainty, confusion, deprivation and strangeness to a lesser or greater degree, as well as difficulty and discomfort. Of the thousand most common words used in interviews, those describing disorientation and strangeness were the largest subset, with subsequent groups describing enjoyment, difference and newness, and curiosity or interest. The remainder of commonly used words were distributed in smaller clusters describing awe, scale, sense of freedom, difficulty and intensity of emotion.[5]

While all the interviewed audience members framed their experience in a positive light, a subset of audiences who left reviews on TripAdvisor did not enjoy the experience. Of the total number of reviews of *The Drowned Man* and *Sleep No More*, approximately 15 per cent described negative experiences; they disliked the challenge to hunt and compose their own experience and were provoked and angered by the disorientation. A small number (~5 per cent) left neutral reviews, while the remaining 80 per cent left positive to extremely positive reviews (TripAdvisor 2015a, b). The split between those who enjoyed disorientation and uncertain outcomes suggests Bishop's description of critical audience participation as a field between 'opposition and amelioration' (Bishop 2012: 12). Those who disapproved used similar descriptions to interviewed audience members; they found the shows confusing, disorientating, alienating, disorganised, uncomfortable and tiring. The strongly polarised descriptions, as well as the specific descriptors used suggest the sublime aesthetic and the terror that 'nothing is happening, or is going to happen' (Bamford 2012: 123–4). The vertiginous thrill of the sublime flows from the vicarious enjoyment of fear, via relief that it is contained and thus did or does not happen. Disorientation compounded the fear of failure in audience members who sought to perform in the machine, and who wanted to be 'functioning parts':

> I wanted to be in the machine; in the software. I wanted to work with the algorithm, however you want to put it. I wanted to function, I didn't want to be the glitch that was in the bar; I wanted to function along with the rest of the machine that was going on, that was also a narrative, you know, so … I definitely had this really strong feeling that I wanted to keep up with everything – I didn't know what I was keeping up with, so that's where the … kind of anxiety, came in: 'what should I be doing now, what am I going to miss?'.[6]

In contrast with this audience member, TripAdvisor audiences that 'glitched' were intensely frustrated by what they felt was a demeaning and disempowering experience that 'made no sense' to them. The threat of failure in relation to the privation of recognisable coherence was experienced as an insult that compromised them personally, leading them to reject the event, reasserting dominion with anger. The framing of uncertainty is the fulcrum of the sublime in this study; the critical bifurcation where audiences shift their subject position into immanence with the event or react to their perceived loss of sovereignty and dominion with alarm.

The confluence of both positive and negative audience experiences in disorientation reveal this to be a feature, not a bug, and critical to the structure of the experience. The scenography of *The Drowned Man* was labyrinthine, extensive and distributed over four floors. Several similar-looking stairways made it more difficult to track your orientation, and audiences sometimes had to navigate more by feel than by sight.[7] In those who enjoyed it, the resulting disorientation generated a heightened sense of potential, with openness to hidden meaning and potential:

> Erm ... so yeah, there was a couple of really weird moments that I wasn't sure whether they were manufactured, or whether they had been intended or not. So, there was a bit where I was running around, kind of following a couple of the actors, and they were running past, and ... fell over something, and I tripped on a piece of wood or something, and I had to put my hand out, and I put my hand out against the wall, and when I took my hand off the wall, it was ... I had red paint all over my hands [laugh], and it was like I had bloody hands, basically, and I couldn't figure out whether it was intended, whether I was supposed to trip over this thing, or whether it was an accident. Because it was ... was such a ... I didn't know why the paint was still wet on the wall, you know, I just thought I'd just tripped over by accident, but when the paint was wet, it made me rethink 'maybe that was on purpose', that I was supposed to trip over it. Because it was obviously completely black, and there was just something in my way.[8]

The uncertainty about the origin and meaning of features can be attributed to the distributed and ambiguously bounded agency that flows both ways across the interface in Punchdrunk's performances. Posthuman embodied cognition, as discussed by Hayles (2002: 303), is grounded in the senses, receptive and subject to its environment rather than sovereign or inviolable. The receptivity in relation to the other and the richness of repetition in touch and movement by participants on either side of the interface presented by

FIGURE 5.1 *Room detail. One of the character rooms during the build of* The Drowned Man, *designed for contemplation or investigation by audiences, as well as ambience. All objects can be handled as normal; letters and cards contain messages pertaining to the character and the script and enrich the overarching plot with additional detail (Credit: Carina E. I. Westling).*

Punchdrunk's storyworlds produce interpretative space beyond the footprint of the building.

The suggestive power of this spatial potential affects not only audiences but also regular stagehands who work with the production, and for whom it cannot be based on surprise. Their imagination '[started] to run away' in particular spaces to the extent that they preferred to avoid them.[9] The tendency in audiences to read more into the productions that what was intentionally created is richly documented in the fandoms,[10] and lends the experience virtual properties. The scope for differential interpretation supports the formation of imagined possibilities, revealing the vertigo of ambiguously bounded possibility and agency as central to the experience, and the sublime as a leading aesthetic. The critical condition of possibility in Punchdrunk's work is thus dependent on framing and the subject–event relationship: 'within the frame', immanent and exposed to the encounter; or in a position of dominion and control, and at a safe enough distance from other agencies to preclude encounter and challenge of the sovereign self.

Active immersion

The difference between an artificial hell and an exhilarating storyworld is contingent on how it is framed by its audiences. Disorientation was a dominant feature in this study, and every interviewee discussed their actions within the storyworld in relation to it. Immersion as an aesthetic experience is an active state; it is not drowning. It requires complicity from the participant, and willing extension and commitment of agency to the performance. Without entering into an immanent relation to the event, the engineered disorientation that is facilitated by the scenography will produce, in place of exhilarating immersion, the 'artificial hell' of Breton's description of surrealist performance – alienating and threatening. Artaud's legacy can be traced most clearly in the fault line between Breton's artificial hell and sublime participatory experience; one is a strangely unwarranted form of terror, while the other orients us aesthetically within the vertiginous potential and limitations of our agency. The effect on the subject position by darkness and disorientation in the space and narrative together with the possibility of failure is perhaps more insidiously subversive than more easily dismissed taboos.

Action words used by the interviewees in relation to the space and its affordances emphasised exploratory approaches. The top categories included (in order of magnitude) words describing actions such as understanding, figuring or finding out; thinking, guessing; wandering and moving; followed by gazing and seeing.[11] Problem-solving actions associated with figuring out and understanding were symmetrical with the combined descriptors for confusion, disorientation, strangeness and newness, suggesting a proportional relationship. Although the interview sample was small in comparison with statistics gathered from TripAdvisor, the dominant descriptors used by interviewees conform with the stated reasons for both highly positive and strongly negative reviews by the much larger online sample, supporting the observation that these are key features of audience experience.

The largest subgroup of descriptors extracted from the interview sample concerned disorientation, unfamiliarity, difficulty and discomfort, showing these to be central to the experience.[12] In his discussion of Artaud's work, Deleuze argues that differential thought is challenging and difficult by nature, as it operates on and beyond the boundaries of recognition: '*difficulty* as such, along with its cortege of problems and questions, is not a *de facto* state of affairs, but a *de jure* structure of thought' (Deleuze 2014: 192–3, original emphasis). This analysis converges with de Certeau's definition of space in the set of descriptors and action words that were extracted from interviews. Differential thought, as opposed to thought based on recognition, is by nature challenging and uncomfortable, and not based on questioning that is formed in relation to the solvability of the enquiry; there must be the possibility of failure. De Certeau's definition of space as defined by extensive and exploratory properties resonates with the descriptions of immanent and close-range figuring out, crafting, wandering and adaptation, all of which occur immanently, or within the unfolding moment. Drawing on Deleuze, Cull argues that the encounter in immanent theatre replaces the dichotomy of authenticity and representation (Cull 2012: 5). Authenticity in theatre cannot be neutral or naïve and affirms, even in opposition, both the means and the purpose of representation. By contrast, the encounter is fraught with the 'powers of the leap, the interval, the intensive and the distant' (Deleuze 2014: 190). Inevitably effortful, it must involve 'self-abduction' and the extension of agency into the possibility of failure, which, in order to be meaningful, must be immanent and subject to gravity and time.

The embodied aporia produced by self-abduction to encounter such uncertainty may be experienced as an extension or a limitation. The difference lies in framing and its function in relation to play and perceived value, and where audience subjects – already 'framed' by their mask – understand themselves to be in relation to the art-work that is asked of them, and the overarching event in which they are 'moving parts'.

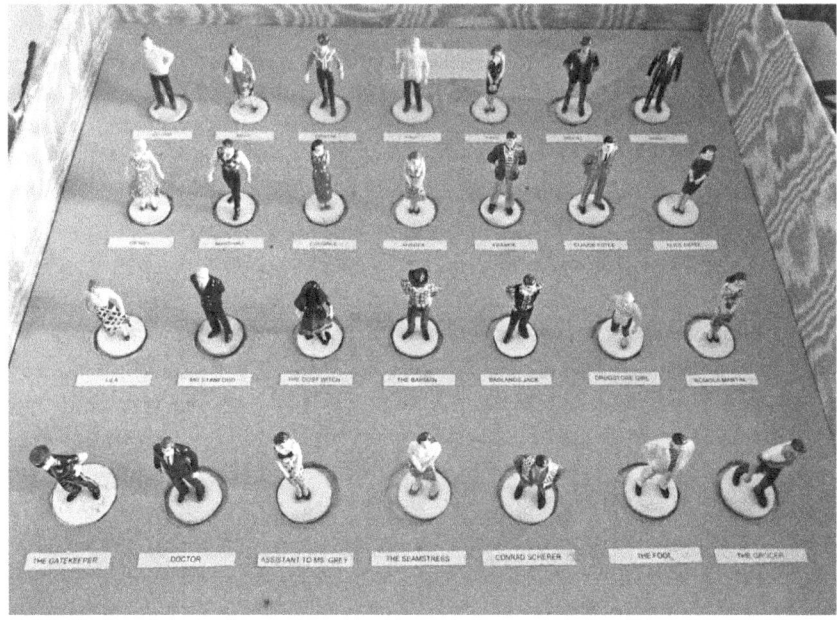

FIGURE 5.2 *Character models. Table-top size prop; tiny models of* The Drowned Man *characters from several nested plots, presented in a case like game figures or pawns. This is an example of one of the countless items that was designed and made with great care and with rich semiotic potential, yet simply placed on set in a discrete location for audiences to maybe happen upon (Credit: Carina E. I. Westling).*

The effects of anonymity

The masks that audience members are required to wear within the performance space (which is only removed during one-to-one episodes) are of a custom design; similar to the Venetian *Bauta* and not white, but a very light grey. They cover the entire face, although the lower part extends forward like a beak to leave the nose and mouth free, and you become used to wearing them over the three hours of a performance. Punchdrunk do not use masks in productions where audiences are given specific roles or missions within the work or in Enrichment projects but allow adult audiences to be part of the scenography without judgement (Machon 2019: 178). The Venetian *Bauta* is a masculine mask with a square contour, but the Punchdrunk mask has more ambiguous form with rounded extensions of both the lower part of the mask and the eye sockets, suggestive of a bird or the stereotypical 'grey alien' of popular culture, Barrett started experimenting with masks in his first rendition of *Woyzeck* (2000) while still at Exeter and evolved their design through eight iterations between 2000 and 2008. The design Punchdrunk settled on for *The Drowned Man* (2013) and *Sleep No More* (2011) was a refinement of the fifth iteration of the masks developed by Barrett and Simon Davies for the 2003 London rendition of *Sleep No More* (Machon 2019: 178–80).

Framed to themselves and each other in identical masks, the audience becomes part of the scenography, referenced and incorporated in the theatrical space as an Ancient Greek chorus of aliens via Venetian masques:

> And you take the masks, you know, they are – they're part of the form and that as an audience member you become ... there's a division between audiences foremost, but also there's a sea of white masks in a room, and they become part of the architecture, and they become a part of the performance in way. Also, they do – I think they do something to you, and they are like a filter and you can only see out in a certain way. And they make you more aware of what you want to do, and you can't see other people around you as much.[13]

Individual audience members are generally only made aware of their incorporation into an anonymised and de-individuated crowd when finding themselves among others in larger groups. When gathered, for example in the finale, audience groups of sometimes hundreds of identically masked participants form tableaux vivants.[14]

Used traditionally in theatre and ritual, masks allow their wearers to assume a different form (and sometimes spirit); they confer anonymity so that quotidian identity and the inhibitions that accompany and maintain it can be suspended. Punchdrunk masks are described as both protective and an aid to immersion:

> I like masks. I know some people freak out about masks. I don't know if anyone had that problem, but … Yeah, it's a nice barrier; it sort of makes things a lot less confrontational, and adds to the dreamlike quality of it, it sort of makes you feel distant enough to own the experience, rather than to have to interact. Yeah, maybe that's why it felt so, because we didn't … we weren't interacting with one another. It pulled us out of the experience, but we were definitely in it, and the actors weren't interacting with us in terms of responding to queues they were getting from us, they were just in their characters. So yeah, I think that is perhaps why it was so dreamlike in quality.[15]

All audience interviews but one talk about their experience as 'dreamlike',[16] as do several company members.[17] One audience interviewee traced their dreamlike state to being masked and finding their agency under question in interactions with the Black Masks.[18] The encounter between two masked individuals consists primarily of space and possibility of uncertain depth, eliciting a form of vertigo. Blurring of both personal and spatial limits, through masks in the first instance and convoluted darkness in the second, foregrounds the unsettling risk of 'becoming-other' (Braidotti 2013: 3). This risk is heightened in one-to-ones, and even by the possibility of being absorbed in the storyworld that an invitation promises.

During one-to-one experiences the performer invites the participant within an enclosed space that is usually small and proceed to unmask them. With the sudden unmasking during one-to-one experiences, your sense of invisibility is suspended, and you are brought to acute awareness of the proximity to the other person. While experienced as powerful and emotive, one-to-ones are discussed as desirable and sought-after:

> I didn't have any one-to-ones, which I was a bit sad about, because I knew that [name] had them, and I'd heard about, you know, whole scenes where they take your mask off, and they do all this stuff with you, but I didn't get anything like that, which I was quite … I was quite disappointed about.[19]

Those who do experience them describe how the performer collapses the distance through touch that is typically gentle and neutral, yet recounted with heightened intensity due to being enclosed and suddenly exposed:

> Yeah, and I was like 'no no no no no, I want it back, I want it back, I want it back; I feel safe with my mask on' and then she sort of got this sort of

holy water, and sort of sprinkled it in my face. I remember it like it was yesterday. She got my face in her hands and there's, when she was close enough to kiss me, she went 'you have to meet me at the castle, please meet me at the castle, we'll be safe there' I was going 'I don't know what the fuck you're talking about, what castle', but I just nodded slowly as if to go 'OK', but I wasn't like smiling or joking; I was deadly serious going 'OK' in my head going 'yeah, I'll meet you at the castle we'll be safe!' I had no idea. And then she sort of put my mask on, and sent me out the door, and off she went. It was incredible. I was like 'woooow, that was intense!'[20]

One-to-one experiences bring a startling sense of exposure: the mask constrains wide-angle vision and covers most of the face, and even though it protrudes away from the lower part of your face, the circulation of air around nose and mouth is reduced. Moisture builds up between the mask and your face, especially if you are physically active. When the mask is removed, the rush of air on the damp skin underscores the sudden nakedness of your face. Your vicarious belonging within the performance as an anonymous actor, free to roam and seemingly unseen, collapses as the dynamic is reversed: in the one-to-one, your entrapment within the story-space is revealed to yourself as the storyworld, in the form of the character played by the performer, transgresses the frame of the mask.

The baring of your face also alters your perception of what is permissible in the situation, ending the disinhibition of the masked state. The mask, which you are instructed to keep on unless instructed to remove it, induces a form of passivity that also absolves you:

> Like, how, I don't think if they didn't have masks on, I don't think they would have followed her that obviously. They had masks on, so they would just like 'oh, fuck it, and I am just going to follow this impulse'.[21]

Here, the interviewee was part of the crowd following the performer, but did not refer to his own participation in the pursuit of the performer as dependent on the mask that he was wearing: instead, he found her 'enchanting' to the extent that he did not immediately realise that he was part of a large crowd:

> I just thought 'I'm going to follow her' and then I realised that [laugh] everyone did exactly the same as me, like, she was getting followed by about 150 people: some were like running or falling over each other, which was really interesting to me.[22]

The implication here is that masking affects you without you necessarily thinking about it; you become rapidly habituated to wearing the mask, and only really are aware of it when you find yourself in a sea of white masks, or when you are unmasked in one-to-ones. The size of the performance space in *The Drowned Man* also played a part in forgetting about being masked, since you did not always see other participants.

Braidotti articulates the hierarchies of gaze within systems in her critical posthumanist analysis. Anonymity in Punchdrunk is superficially similar to that which can be assumed in digital interactive system, but the two states are distinguished by subject–event relationships. Digital systems have three key features of what Braidotti calls 'life-mining': visibility, predictability and exportability (Braidotti 2013: 62); the actions of participating subjects are typically continuously recorded, exported and aggregated with other data streams to form predictive data models. The 'life-mining' that Braidotti describes, and which defines the relationship between the watcher and the watched in digital systems, will always generate an unequal power relationship founded on the imbalance between the obscurity of the centre, or privileged vantage point, and the visibility of the participants in the system. By contrast, the participating subjects in Punchdrunk's large masked productions are anonymous, their 'theatre machines' accommodate emergence, and information about individual audience members is neither recorded nor exported. Observation of audience behaviour occurs continuously but is decoupled from identity.[23] The identity of participants is irrelevant to the interaction, but not their actions; observations of the quality and nature of these are noted and woven back into productions as iterative change. The scale and short lead time of *The Drowned Man* meant that the preview period was extended so that the company could incorporate more radical iterations and determine the amount of direction audiences would need. During and more slowly beyond this period, changes included added rooms and the layout of the space, character scripts and changes to lighting and sound.[24]

Punchdrunk tend to limit prescriptive directives and largely rely on in-show moderation of behaviour by the Black Masks,[25] who direct emergent audience behaviour as needed while preserving anonymity and the ambience of the performance as far as possible.[26] Audience behaviour is an important part of the design process, but it is viewed as a material force, unrelated to the identities of individual participants. The differences in perspective on anonymous audience behaviours in Punchdrunk and digital systems are clarified by an analysis of subject–event relationships, and the associated hierarchies of gaze. In digital systems, the 'identity' of the participant is a target; they may present anonymously at the interface level, but their actions are recorded and aggregated. In Punchdrunk performances such as *The Drowned Man*, the masks form a barrier between the performance and the identities of audience members; what concerns the performance is what they do, not who they are. Only the flows of agency are relevant to designed and emergent encounters, and the immanence of the masked gaze suggests kinship with

Cull's postidentitarian philosophy of difference (Cull 2012: 17) which clarifies Deleuzean ethics through performance that collapses hierarchies between stage and auditorium as well as mind and body.

Embodied meaning-making, supported by immanent subject–event relationships (i.e. acting from a perspective position 'within the frame'), shapes the system narrative of Punchdrunk's storyworlds,[27] with the distributed cognition of both company makers and their audiences meshing across the interface. This mutuality on a plane of immanence differentiates Punchdrunk's work from interaction design as typically configured in digital material culture, where there are few restrictions to the Cartesian image of the mind-body dichotomy and its contingent purity constructs:

> The emphasis on immanence allows us to respect the bond of mutual dependence between bodies and technological others, while avoiding the contempt of the flesh and the trans-humanist fantasy of escape from the finite materiality of the enfleshed self. (Braidotti 2013: 91)

Positioning the audience as ambiguously boundaried subjects within an uncertain milieu calls for participation on immanent terms: experiential and close range within flattened hierarchies that change imperatives for the expression and inhibition of agency. Exploration towards uncertain ends sums up the experiences of Punchdrunk audiences in this study as a voluntary crisis that is contingent on the absence of closure, aestheticised by the bounds of the performance and the mask.

Delinquent system aesthetics

Cull elucidates how Deleuzean ethics are clarified through minor theatres, and similarly Punchdrunk's theatrical worlds manifest how boundaries and edge conditions produce such play through interpretative movement and relational activities. The mask and the end points of the performance in time and space frame and produce conditions of possibility for sublime immersion in Punchdrunk performances. Within these frames, encounters with the agencies of the storyworld articulate the vertigo of possibility and failure, allowing the sublime to become a form of play with consequences for self-representation. Through differentiation and articulation, the boundaries of an interiority also speak of their exteriorities:

> We have only recently noticed that systems are inexorably coupled to the environments they distinguish themselves from to arise as systems. It

is as if the environments of systems had long occupied blind spots from which they have now been shifted into view. (Clarke 2008: 13)

Herein lies one aspect of the critical potential of the immersive aesthetic in theatre as a critique of representation not by way of *Verfremdungseffekt* but through engineered crises of the subject position. The encounter is complicit; the exposure requires willing participation and the extension of agency within its interiority. The mutual articulation of agency within the frame of the experience is a spatial operation that expands the unfolding present. The joy of composition that is described by Deleuze (1970: 28) flows from the experience of expanded agency in encounters. In Punchdrunk, encounters are afforded in interactions between the subject and vertiginous darkness and space, and in intimacy that draws focus to heightened detail. Both are forms of space, articulated through vertigo and possibility, and both counter the generalities of place and its orders.

The proximity of emergence and emergency in conditions of uncertainty magnifies and articulates the detail of experience. As discussed above, joy and the sublime in encounters with emergence/emergency are contingent on framing and containment. This holds in space and time: the hedonic upheaval of carnival, whether in Bakhtin's historical perspective or its contemporary expressions in music and performance festivals and durational events such as Punchdrunk performances, must be limited in time to serve the cohesion of *communitas*, but within its bounds it allows the delinquent old gods to temporarily upend quotidian order. The giddiness of fairground rides, an extreme but short-lived example of the carnivalesque at play, is vitalising, exuberant and enjoyable, but the upheaval of gravity would become a state of terror if it were permanent. Willing entry and complicity with the bounds of event- or storyworld is key to *kairos* and joyful composition with the other. It affords the projection of possibility space onto physical spaces, which places audiences in an immanent subject position in relation to the event, contingent on a leap of trust and the suspension of disbelief (O'Grady 2013):

Enjoyable but bizarre. It felt like quite a test, a challenge to your normative expectations of, not just what theatre is, but what, like I said, I've never been, I really, really felt like I hadn't been in a situation like that, ever, which doesn't happen very often. I've literally never experienced anything like that, apart from in a dream. Like, that sort of thing usually doesn't come out of my cynical mouth, so ...[28]

The nuance and precise detail of scenography and performances were discussed by audiences as critical for supporting suspension of disbelief: 'It felt like ... it was a high ... I suppose, yeah, because of the detail of the sets. It made me feel like I had more trust in them to give me a good experience.'[29]

Expanded upon, the perception of skilful effort and dedication was described as inspiring respect and gratitude:

> I had the utmost respect for the actors, as well. Because I've got an interest in acting; I'd love to do it. [...] I didn't for a second feel jealousy: just immense respect for the skill – and the kind of inverse of that was, or the other side of that, I also felt extremely happy for these actors that I didn't know [...] I was just like 'thank God this exists for them.' I was so like, so happy for them, I was like 'Oh, yeah guys!' I was like, part of me wanted to go up to them and say 'so great that this exists, because you get to just do it!'[30]

Even in disorientating circumstances and the typically dark scenography, audiences observed and interpreted the commitment of designers and performers to creating detail and precision as precarious generosity, which heightened their willingness to commit to the experience:

> And I remember the attention to detail in the set, so the set was just incredible. The production values of it was just amazing, and it was part of what made me leave my cynicism at the door, because I really did feel like 'ok, there's a lot of effort put into this, this isn't...' [...] I was very impressed, and I felt very willing to participate in it, because it seemed like a worthy thing to participate in.[31]

> I ... they were dancing up on the wall, and running, and doing really acrobatic almost, like very ... I mean insanely advanced stuff. Sitting at the bottom, I was like, all I could think was 'surely they are going to fall, surely they're going to fall over' [...] 'I'm going to have to catch these girls, because they're going to fall off' so it forced me into being present. [...] It was somehow like. ... You were forced into this feeling of, like, I was like in prison, in a glorious prison, for like, a few minutes because I was like 'I can't move, I have to catch them because they're definitely going to fall, because this is ludicrous behaviour.' But then of course they didn't fall, because they were amazing.[32]

Powerfully affective recognition and gratitude for extraordinary commitment was a recurring theme in all the audience interviews and also a leading theme in interviews with company members who were part of producing *The Drowned Man*. Some descriptions of audience experience were quite specific in their appreciation of imagined spaces, and how this triggered an expanded idea of space in their own understanding of how the performance worked, as a whole:

> I mean, and I could see the choreography when ... in the detail between the crossovers between actors, so that's when it really came out for me,

so. ... There would be different plots going on, there was you know, 5 or 6 different stories, and then you'd see all of a sudden two actors get together that were previously separate, and that made me just think 'how many ... how much detail has gone into the timing of making these actors, you know, collide at the right moments?' And considering there's probably more than one collision or interjection going on at once, there must have been an incredible amount of detail.[33]

The experience of manifest detail is particular and unfolds in the present. It is associated with the experience of space and potential through inviting and sustaining audiences' projection and extension of trust, gratitude and agency into the storyworld, bringing together Deleuze's idea of immanent repetition to produce difference with de Certeau's distinction of expansive space. The general, which Deleuze positions as opposite to the particular, is reductive and generic, whereas the particular is specific and infinite in resolution, resisting generalisation. Infinite resolution is a consequence of being manifest and actual (as opposed to virtual) and is available in any scenography and live performance. What makes a difference to Punchdrunk audiences is the depth of designed detail in both, which sustain the storyworld at close range. Even in low-lit spaces, audiences seem to 'read' the depth of possible exploration almost immediately:

> I've got quite a strong aversion to stuff that's trying to be something but fails to do it. [...] And without feeling like 'why am I here, and this feels like it's trying far too hard to kind of, live up to something that it doesn't.' But when I got there it really did, I just loved it; I just thought it was great ... I just left ... I was forced to leave all my cynicism at the door. I didn't have any, I didn't have any choice.[34]

Audience descriptions reveal a close association between the willingness to extend your agency into the performance and the degree to which you feel supported by the production, again underscoring the relationship between play and its boundaries. Understanding how the audience role is configured in Punchdrunk necessarily includes consideration of the company's making culture and how experience potential is brought into being in and through practice. Here we return to the idea of audience-as-agency, thought as an operative force rather than a collection of individuals. The image of the audience is present everywhere in interviews with company members as a zoetic flow that is given scope through design:

> And there's always in the back of your minds that ... you might be doing ten processes that no one is ever going to notice, but if it catches one

person's attention, then it's worth it, you know? [...] it's something that you're ... that without it you can kind of see, you know it's just like... there's something in the shadows, that you know is there.[35]

The concept of the audience as a zoetic flow feeds the ambition to create excess capacity for experience, even if it will never be discovered. The storyworld as a whole, with hidden niches that may or may not be found is discussed as a habitat that offers possibilities, not a spectacle or a front to create a sufficient illusion. The invitation to inhabit the storyworld is couched in terms emphasising embodied manifestation, a making-real to ensure that every object resonates with the storyworld, in order for audiences to do so, too:

You kind of embody everything that you do, so [...] you have to do that for every kind of item that you do, to make it exist properly. But as a model for doing things in a kind of efficient way, then it's terrible [laugh].[36]

'Existing properly' in Punchdrunk storyworld terms means that objects must be capable of anchoring the imagination of audiences holding, handling and investigating them, while also fitting in and adding to the narrative, however tangentially. This excess capacity is a form of delinquency in the transcendent 'gaze' of efficiency, and it is critical to sustaining investment in the storyworld:

It's a funny thing, because it's never an exact replica of the world, so there's nothing that's like, you know the walls ... the walls feel like brick and you know they should be, there should be a real tactile sense to the set, but it's interesting that the space is so abstract, but you're kind of still believing its total ... totality. And actually, if it was, kind of ... you know, an exact replica of reality, then it wouldn't take you in so much.[37]

Even with this level of commitment from designers to produce an interface of extraordinary materiality, the scenography evolves during a production. Members of the team participate regularly as masked audiences, and sometimes as Black Masks,[38] to experience from a first-hand perspective how the production works with the flow of audiences in relation to the experience:

You know, like it's constantly, you know, an unfolding thing, but you know ... it's never random. It's like, if this corridor is too large, and were not creating the kind of crescendos and contrasts in the space, then we'll ... 'build that now'.[39]

Understanding audiences as an operative force allows for particularity, as the production is, in a sense, instantiated anew with every live performance and for every audience member. As a result, experience potential expands through repetition. By contrast, digital platforms designed on the basis of predictive models of audiences within a paradigm that seeks to elicit generalisable data from their participation will create reductive feedback loops. Nominally, this data is gathered for personalisation in systems that are fundamentally inhospitable to idiosyncratic inputs from users, but data brokering is an industry in its own right (Kant 2020). The imperatives to personalise experience and gather tradable data combine with system fragility to drive audience modelling towards thin-sliced categories based on data from performative feedback loops. This reductive focus on the properties of the individual or agent draws predictive models ever tighter in response to demand for precisely targeted marketing and distribution.

Peggy Phelan's analysis of the 'marked' in relation to the 'unmarked', and the inflection of power by distance from the unmarked norm elucidates how reductive definitions of system users affects their potential agency within the system (1996). The normative unmarked is correlated with greater freedom of form and movement and translates into agency or potentiality to change and effect change (Sloane 2018). In contrast, those marked by their difference from the unmarked norm are rendered simultaneously more visible and less free to move and change. Within interactive systems, unmarked agency, invisible and free of form, becomes a proxy for the projected mind in relation to agents that are marked by their visibility or corporeality. The invisible networked data flows and protocols that pervade digital interactive systems (Galloway 2004) are, in effect, 'unmarked' agencies, and the data objects that represent human users within them are, in relation, 'marked' agents rendered visible by, and in the capacity of, their demographic characteristics. Conceptualising audiences not as agents, but in terms of their agency, as Punchdrunk designers and performers do in this study, gives their audiences a dynamic outline within the organisation or system of agencies that forms the whole. Were digital designers to think and represent their audiences in terms of agency or zoetic flows, participation might be called upon, invited and accommodated in the form of shape-shifting capacity or potentiality. Returning to the imperative of the designer in the quotation above to 'embody' every item for them to 'exist properly' in created worlds, digital systems, if they are to be folded into the wider socio-technological fabric of discourses, organisations and material production, must reasonably be expected to do so.

If assessed in the transcendent light of efficiency, designing environments for potentiality and emergence is a wasteful approach, but it is essential for the experience of expansive potential. Importantly, it shapes design practice. Rather than narrowing and funnelling agency into specific affordances, it forces the focus of the designer towards thinking around dynamic potential and instability of form. Garrett Wolf and Nathan Mahaffey think potentiality through architecture, an adjacent field to Punchdrunk's scenography, and propose an approach that may be applied also to designed digital spaces:

To reconceptualise the space between top-down and bottom-up as 'co-production', it is necessary to explore a non-hierarchical methodology, an indirect approach to problem-solving that embraces complexity, multiplicity of actors, processes, ideas and solutions. (Wolf and Mahaffey 2016)

They liken this to Deleuze and Guattari's rhizomatic model, the image of a distributed form of organisation with 'no beginning or end; it is always in the middle, between things, interbeing, *intermezzo*' (Wolf and Mahaffey 2016). While this brings to mind the image of distributed networks of unmarked zoetic flows, hierarchy is reasserted and even intensified in relation to co-opted human agents lest they are incorporated as potentiality or agency and not as data objects, marked by demographic characteristics.

The recording of actions within digital interactive systems to 'enrich' the data objects that are user profiles or identities falls within Braidotti's idea of life-mining. Personalisation, as currently applied in digital systems, instrumentalises and commodifies action and affect towards the creation of predictable models and data for brokering. The audience position within such systems is contingent on visibility, demarcation and transmutation of agency into saleable identities and actions and is, by definition, reductive. Braidotti articulates another vision for human interaction with technology that is based on play and 'unmarking' the human role in this relationship to elide efficiency:

> This machinic vitality is not so much about determinism, inbuilt purpose or finality, but rather about becoming and transformation. This introduces a process that Deleuze and Guattari call 'becoming-machine', inspired by the Surrealists' 'bachelor machines', meaning a playful and pleasure-prone relationship to technology that is not based on functionalism. For Deleuze this is linked to the project of releasing human embodiment from its indexation on socialised productivity to become 'bodies without organs', that is to say without organised efficiency. (Braidotti 2013: 91–2)

Masked participation in large Punchdrunk shows demonstrates the effects of a more profound 'unmarking' than anonymised participation on, for example, social media, where personal information is still recorded and fundamental to every interaction. Identity is genuinely deprioritised to foreground participation that is not organised according to transcendent efficiency and open to emergent interaction.

Without analysis of functional representation of audiences at the infrastructure level of Punchdrunk's interactive systems and digital platforms, they may be conflated in a critique of the attention economy that fails to address the inflection on conditions of possibility by how the audience is thought (Alston 2013: 129). The research presented in this study traces the fault line between identity mining and 'unmarking' and the consequences of this for the audience subject position. *Ou-topia*, or no-space focused on the question of identity itself provokes an ontological reconfiguration of participation. This is critical in an increasingly mediated world where participation, or rather its digital representation and monetisation within interactive systems, is co-opted. Consent to align platform providers with regulatory frameworks (e.g. GDPR, the General Data Protection Regulation) does not address the problem at root.

Bishop highlights the bifurcation in participatory performance since the first decades of the twentieth century between those who seek to disrupt and provoke, and those whose aim is to ameliorate and celebrate collective creativity (2006: 11–12). Critics of the immersive aesthetic in Punchdrunk and others have taken the latter position, arguing that the possibility of failure and the uneven distribution of hedonic 'rewards' for participation is symptomatic of neoliberalism (Alston 2013, 2016; Harvie 2013). Framing connectivity and communality over disorientation and the risk of failure as the social and political values of participation, they make a critical comparison between the two broad approaches in participatory art discussed by Bishop and locate, perhaps unintentionally, both the immersive aesthetic and neoliberalism within a dialectic with deeper roots. Adam Alston and Jen Harvie wrote their analyses of the immersive aesthetic prior to 2016, when real-world events demonstrated the importance of a critical interrogation of both participation and connectivity.[40] Since then, it has become increasingly clear that instrumentalised participation is core to advanced neoliberalism (Cadwalladr 2017; The Great Hack 2019), and that utopian connectivity inevitably comes with ou-topian exposure.

Critical interrogation of how participation and connectivity are represented in systematised encounters, including what does, does not and could occur, and between whom or what, is arguably essential to future-proofing experience design and the discourses it meshes with and inflects. Connectivity is essential to the demassified economic structures of advanced neoliberalism (Boltanski and Chiapello 2005), including the naturalised digitisation of production, management, distribution, consumption and performed social identity. This applies to interactions across digital and physical platforms for social and functional purposes, performance, VR/AR/XR experience design and games where the participatory component is of functional and critical importance to the completion of the artwork or application. Via networked infrastructures, we participate in storytelling systems as part of everyday life, where representation naturalises and shapes our projected 'being' within such systems as performed identities that are readily demassified for aggregation and commodification.

Sharply contrasted with this shape of being in the story; a projected 'identity' over a readily demassified 'body' of data points, Punchdrunk audiences are embodied but anonymous. Their shape of being in the story is shared with performers and Black Masks on a physical and consequential plane of immanence, where connectivity and exposure are integrated and concurrently articulated. Failure is possible, and immanence is critical; the process of developing theatrical spaces in which audiences are instrumental, critical and living parts creates an intimate imperative to negotiate and harness emergence. This principle is embedded in design thinking for audiences that are depersonalised but fully present in their capacity of embodied agency: the not-knowing of audience members is balanced by the not-knowing of designers and performers, levelling the shared field of potentiality.

In large masked productions from *Faust* (2006) onward, the fulcrum of this balance is embodied by the Black Masks. Their role as stage managers and stewards has gained increasingly dramatic expression (Machon 2019: 268), and is designed for the shadows and edges of both the scenography and audience behaviours. Their interventions are described as enhancing the experience of immersion, by putting agency into question in surprising encounters:

> And the bit where I got told to not do something was really funny, [...] it just totally fucked with my already fucked-up expectations about what was going on. So, like I wasn't allowed to cross the room – I thought I was, but I wasn't. It was just stuff like that; it was like the whole three hours were spent renegotiating your surroundings. [...] Every so often you got these moments when spectatorship was punctured with moments of realisations that you were there, and you were a body, and that you were actually in the space. So, that experience was really weird. I have not had anything like that before. Like being a spectator and an actor all at once, so your mind is working, but not with, you've got that ... the stuff you do have to decide on is completely personal, but where your body is isn't. ... You didn't feel like you were 'safe' at any point.[41]

Lyotard's definition of beauty that is destroyed or threatened by the sublime include rationality and efficiency, which he describes as the performative principle of legitimation in late, or neoliberal capitalism (1984: 45–6). According to de Certeau, the delinquency of the old gods lies in their resistance to rationality and thus implicitly the efficiency dictate. A delinquent system aesthetic may be one that perversely rejects the efficient in service of the effective, manifest in the observed and described actions and responses of participants on both sides of the exchange in this study:

> I don't think you'd get this in many other set design jobs; you're forming the story as it is being created, and one reason for that is the scale of it: it all has to be put into departments of who's kind of in control of it, and also the process necessitates for it to be constantly evolving and changing, which

can be hugely frustrating. You could be going down one thread and then it would change, but that allowance keeps it fresh. I think that's why it has the result it does on people; it's never kind of, nothing remains stagnant, because if your performer's developed some new story, then the whole thing's got room for manoeuvre, so it's that kind of working process; you're going back and forth and you know, it can take ten times as long.[42]

Always-becoming art-work drives Punchdrunk's theatre machines; immersion in their work is contingent on the compulsion to make. Legible to audiences even in darkness, their commitment to making and devising is read as life-affirming in the sense described by Bakhtin; a delinquent commitment to corporeal becoming that hides in the inversion of the contemporary order:

> I know it's for entertainment, but it needed to exist. And it felt like this culmination of so many different talents. They must have been influenced by so many other different talents over the course of their careers. It felt like my tiny little pinpoint experience of it. ... I just felt at the same time so miniscule, my little eyes looking at this thing, but so infinite at the same time. And then kind of ... quite thankful? [...] like when the world stops, like generally when you fall in love or when you experience real art, it feels just like time stops – there's no outside. There's no yesterday, there's no tomorrow, and you're just kind of floating through space. And 'aaah, it's ok' [laugh].[43]

The hedonic qualities of their work flow not from consumption, but from making and becoming; a perverse, against-all-odds, delinquent delight and commitment to making that hides in the dark, beyond the reach of an efficiency rationale that measures, divides, contains and prices every effort. Like all systems, theirs tells a story of the broader situation in which it exists; one of inversion, but also possibility. The next chapter discusses critical perspectives and potential for interactive experience design in this light.

Notes

1 See comparative data in Appendix.
2 AUD1.
3 AUD1, AUD5, AUD3.
4 AUD2, AUD5, AUD3.
5 See Appendix.
6 AUD1.
7 See Appendix.

8   AUD1.
9   COM5.
10 COM2.
11 See Appendix.
12 See Appendix.
13 COM4.
14 AUD2.
15 AUD2.
16 AUD6, AUD1, AUD2, AUD4, AUD3.
17 COM3, COM2, COM5.
18 AUD1.
19 AUD1.
20 COM5.
21 AUD5.
22 AUD5.
23 COM3.
24 COM4.
25 COM4.
26 COM5.
27 COM4.
28 AUD1.
29 AUD1.
30 AUD5.
31 AUD1.
32 AUD5.
33 AUD1.
34 AUD1.
35 COM2.
36 COM2.
37 COM2.
38 COM4.
39 COM2.
40 The impact of data aggregation and targeted political messaging on social media and their complex interactions with instrumentalised behaviours and monetisation of user data came to broader public awareness during and after the British 'Brexit' referendum in June 2016 and the US presidential elections in November 2016.
41 AUD1.
42 COM2.
43 AUD5.

6

The Shape of Agency in Interactive Storyworlds

Performance is a privileged space in which we can experiment with a non-utilitarian use of the senses, an education of feeling that enlarges the senses as well as consciousness. This is not about escaping the world, but about constructing a space within the social that turns away from utilitarianism towards intuition; an island where the experience of duration can and does happen.
GOULISH AND CULL 2009: 142

The development of Punchdrunk from a theatre company to designers of participatory experience across physical and digital media is grounded in working with and interrogating embodied imagination, subject positions, gaze and relations of power across the stage and the auditorium. The location and nature of 'the stage' and 'the auditorium' shift as we look towards virtual and augmented platforms, but the functional framing that these concepts perform, applied to the design process, remain critical. An understanding of modes of seeing and modelling experience on digital platforms through critical performance theory can be applied to the integration of digital and virtual technologies to extend visualisation and interaction in performance, whether for artistic reasons, documentation or broadcasting. In participatory theatre and digital design alike, the 'part' played by audiences is shaped by how they and their actions are conceptualised. In interaction and game design, this in turn shapes their representative form and how it is instrumentalised within code infrastructures (Bogost 2007). Whereas digital design for human interaction is thought through game physics, demographic modelling and what Ian Bogost calls simulation gaps (2007: 43),[1] live performance audiences present themselves in their embodied capacity: weighted bodies that bring nested frames of interpretation to the art-work (Lehmann 2006: 17). Understanding audiences *as* agency is more intuitive to those working with live audiences than to those working with the idea of remote system users, and fundamentally shapes how experience is thought by the designer.

Perspectives on agency in interactive systems

The many events and possibilities for interaction that comprise Punchdrunk productions remain discrete and distributed until connected and articulated by audience members, acting as moving parts or narrative agents. The embodied curiosity of audiences flows into the gaps and tensions between acts, scenes and objects to interpret and connect them into a new whole, unique to each recombination. Punchdrunk audiences are thus functional and expressive 'moving parts' within the production, and active participants in the art-work. This is the role of human participants in both physical and digital interactive systems, but the way they are thought and modelled is profoundly different. The reasons why this is so are many, some of which have already been discussed in this book, but the different relationship between designers and their audiences in digital, remote performance and that between designers and audiences in live, physical performance is a critical source of the thinking in either discipline. To the designer of live performance, audience agency is not only material to the function and completion of the interactive system: it is a key material, present in the work in evident and consequential form. By contrast, digital audiences are remote, and typically conceptualised around the idea of identity and discourses of the self for functional and aesthetic purposes (Kant 2020). Observations and ethnographies of Punchdrunk's work in this study show that identity is primarily relevant to immersive experience design through its destabilisation, and not from a functional point of view.[2] The temporary destabilisation of identity and the disorientation that flows from a challenged subject position undermines the illusion of sovereignty, described in terms that suggest the sublime.[3] Thinking the subject in terms of emergence and the negotiated extension of agency are central themes in descriptions of immersion in this study.

The body is a site of contested agency and control, and 'deeply mediatic' in its capacity for perception and sensation (Parikka 2012a: 22). It mediates our interaction with what Christian Ulrik Andersen and Søren Bro Pold call metainterfaces; logistic structures and designed habitats that are also cultural expressions built on templates and generalised ideas (2018: 35–7). These are already always-on interactive systems that require our naturalised, embodied participation. Existing metainterfaces are acquiring virtual layers, embedding new expressions of efficiency as a transcendent, organising principle in the everyday. Through interaction with interfaces and metainterfaces, we participate in what Nick Couldry calls 'reality work' that is performed through 'the embedding in practice of specific organising categories' (Couldry 2012: 135). Their pervasion on the personal is increasing by way of interactive systems that allow the 'reality work' of system agencies to close in on the already narrow parameters of system users (Galloway 2012: 137). In an attempt to elide the organising principles closing in on the subject within such systems, Alexander Galloway proposes 'the whatever' as an alternative way of thinking about system users to escape totalising holding patterns (Galloway 2012: 139). Drawing on Deleuze and Agamben, he describes the 'whatever' as 'a figure of pure singularity' that is determined only in relation to the totality of its possibilities (Galloway 2012: 140). Galloway stresses that this position should not be confused with anti-essentialism: it rejects not difference but systemic generalisation, and is intended as a position of aesthetic and political incoherence that resists easy incorporation into normative central myths (Galloway 2012: 141–2). Similar to Rancière's dissensus in negation, Galloway's proposition however stops short of a positive alternative. Addressing the question from another vantage point, Jill Dolan proposes utopian or, rather, ou-topian ('no-place') performance, linked to a 'reconstructed humanism [that] is multiple, respecting the complexities and ambiguities of identity while it works out ways for people to share and feel things in common' (Dolan 2005: 22). Dolan places immanent and emergent experience as central to utopian performance: idiosyncratic prior to recognition and articulation as social and shared, uncertain, and generative of difference and emergence (Dolan 2005: 65). Like Galloway, Dolan's vision of emergence focuses on formlessness and undoing place to allow for the production of space; it is clear in its formulation of resistance, but vague with regard to what might follow. As discussed below, the modelling of systems in which human participants are essential 'moving parts' requires a functionally coherent articulation of their role; it cannot be positively accommodated as a negation.

Rancière, in frustration with the 'misadventures of critical thought', proposes a way forward that invites participation not in no-place, but in 'scenes of dissensus' where the sensible is organised without 'a single regime of presentation and interpretation of the given':

> It is the collectivization of capacities invested in scenes of dissensus. It is the employment of the capacity of anyone whatsoever, of the quality of human beings without qualities. As I have said, these are unreasonable hypotheses. Yet I believe that today there is more to be sought and found in the investigation of this power than in the endless task of unmasking fetishes or the endless demonstration of the omnipotence of the beast. (2009: 49)

Peggy Phelan's *Unmarked* (1996) addresses the central challenge in Rancière's proposition; she names the normative subject position that minor others are marked in relation to and investigates its everyday power in and through language and visibility. The 'unmarked' mirrors the transcendent organising principle that needs no mark, as it is the norm rendered invisible and ungraspable by its distribution and abstraction (Galloway 2004: 31–3). Whether applied to the ideal or normative human subject or the normative, organising principle in interactive systems, its ubiquitous and thus ungraspable presence makes it transcendent in relation to those who are marked or defined by their difference in relation to it. Similar to the unmarked hegemonic norm, the transcendent agency of unmarked networked system protocols, being both present and remote, remains at once undefined and unrestrained in form in relation to human participants. A simple example of how unmarked agents, who require no descriptors other than their specific role in a given context (e.g. 'the author', 'the artist'), are afforded a greater dynamic range than those who are defined by their deviation from the naturalised norm can be seen in the narrowing of readily accepted expressions when the agent is marked (e.g. 'black author', 'female artist'). Looking to de Certeau's analysis of place and space, we see that power relationships are associated with degrees of fixity, and that 'unmarking' in order to shape-shift confers differential capacity.

Unmarking through masking recruits 'the quality of human beings without qualities' (Rancière 2009: 49) and is a trope in performance, theatre and the carnival; all potential scenes of dissensus. In participatory forms of performance, anonymity serves to not just destabilise subject positions across the stage and auditorium, but also to flatten hierarchies of agency. As identity is meshed with the social compact, masking is instrumental to the temporary suspension of dominant orders during carnivals and fêtes and is also employed in Punchdrunk's large shows. Thinking the mask as a frame for *ou-topia* of the subject position allows for the translation of this function to other dramatic devices that unsettle identity, thought as a sovereign transcendent, to afford metamorphosis. Laura Cull proposes a 'postidentitarian philosophy of difference' for performance (2012: 17) that draws the transcendent subject position into an immanent and relational one. In Cull's words, Deleuzean immanence is the 'participation, multiplication and extension of the human body' that is 'produced by relations of force and encounters with the affects of other bodies' (2012: 10). This reveals a shared provenance of ideas with Hayles, who defines posthuman embodiment as dispersed 'through the body and its environment' (2002: 319). In immanence, the posthuman subject embodies difference as an 'emergent phenomenon created in dynamic interaction with the ungraspable flux' of distributed cognition (Hayles 2002: 304).

In Cull's interpretation of Deleuzean ontology, the immanent subject position and aesthetic in theatre is a minor one; not in numbers, but in nature. It is an emergent vantage position from which the language and tools of theatre are subjected to a greater degree of variations that diverge from conventional narrative structure and representational techniques (2012: 20):

> [Deleuze] suggests that the revolutionary nature of a minor usage of theatre lies in its affirmation of the primacy of cross-categorical mutations, its emphasis on the tendency of life perpetually to differ from itself, alongside its tendency to congeal into recognizable or categorizable identities. (Cull 2012: 21)

The emphasis on emergence begs a comparison with Galloway's description of play as behaviours to overcome systemic contradictions (2012: 29), and also Bruce Clarke's discussion of the minor as 'a species of meaning systems in their own right' that co-emerges with and mediates between psychic and societal systems (2008: 19). Focusing on metamorphosis within narrative systems through shape-shifting (2008: 11–12), Clarke's narrative theory of un-modern posthuman archetypes nods to the delinquent old gods of de Certeau (1988: 129). Within the brittle formal rationalism of the digital modern, the un-modern old gods are relegated to the shadows of technological narrative systems, where they roam with relative freedom. Acknowledgement and articulation of the irrational and un-modern is typically resisted, as neither infrastructures nor business models are built with sufficient resilience or response capacity to do so. Were this a carnival or a performance, the result might be regarded as dark play.[4] However, as always-on, distributed networked systems that rely on pervasion of bounds in time and place make the possibility of opting out remote, the resulting imbalance of power is more accurately described as misrule. One way to flatten the hierarchy of agencies in dark play and misrule is to reconfigure the way participation by human 'moving parts' is modelled in systems that create such conditions of possibility. This brings us back to the confluence of Galloway's 'whatever' and Phelan's unmarked with Rancière's unreasonable challenge to create scenes of dissensus in which the capacities of 'human beings without qualities' can be invested (2009: 49).

De Certeau's image of *metaphorai* (from the Greek μεταφοραί; to carry, transfer) frames live, embodied audiences as story-vehicles that mediate between place and space (1988: 115). In this image, the human subject navigates and negotiates narrative systems with emergent interpretative and cognitive acts. Thought like this, participation flows from the capacity for dynamic change, countering stultification (Rancière 2009: 9–14). Configuring participatory audiences as *metaphorai*; vehicles for transportation and meaning within theatre machines, prioritises their agency and capacity for interpretative acts over their form. In an adjacent strand of thought about and through systems, Clarke stresses the fundamentally metamorphic nature of human agency in narrative assemblages and compositions with non-human agencies, located somewhere between the natural and the social. Articulating the compositions that occur in interaction between the ideal subject and imagined non-human counterparts, Clarke suggests the 'daemonic situation of medial contingency' as an allegory of the human in narrative systems (2008: 54). Clarke's analysis nods to Phelan's unmarked and its shape-shifting capacity, but the question of who is and, more critically, who isn't afforded this dynamic range in interactive systems looms large.

The dynamic range of the unmarked is afforded by lack of determination, which is given, or rather un-given, the normative or unmarked subject. The audience position in Punchdrunk allows for fictive and temporary physical invisibility and suspension of quotidian identity, afforded by the bounds of the performance and the mask. It brings about a state of play and of the carnivalesque, which are framed and made possible by such bounds. Cull's Deleuzean minor and Galloway's interpretation of play in relation to systemic tensions are emergent states; intensive rather than actual, and as far as that is possible, the 'form of difference' (Bonta and Protevi 2004: 14). Shape-shifting or mimicry is a key form of play (Caillois 1961: 19; Sutton-Smith 2001: 127), and meets the delinquent in the carnivalesque (Bakhtin 1984), where masking represents metamorphosis (Clarke 2008: 46). The mask, whether a physical barrier to recognition or a role played in character, confers anonymity and serves as a frame – it empowers the masked in relation to the object of the gaze from behind the mask, and is at once a provocation and a power play. As indicated by Rancière in his unreasonable proposition, it might be afforded all participants in scenes of dissensus or bounded play spaces. But when play – and the players – are invisible to some of its participants, the result is what Schechner calls dark play (1993: 36); a hierarchical imbalance that becomes a ubiquitous state of misrule in always-on, systemic interaction that penetrates our private spaces. The relationship between frames (boundaries, containment), visibility and representation, and how these are encoded into the infrastructures and affordances of interactive spaces, are thus central to an analysis that includes the audience as a critical material element. In the case study offered by large masked Punchdrunk performances, the hierarchical relationship of agencies is redressed by affording audiences anonymity. Analysed through frames and boundaries, actors perform 'behind' their character, just like audiences participate 'behind' their masks, positioning them on a shared plane; the intense, not the actual, and taking, perhaps unreasonably but nevertheless functionally, the 'form of difference' within the bounds of the play.

In his analysis of representation and the logic of recognition that underpins it, Deleuze argues that the thought that is forced to think its central collapse must be engendered if it is to think into being that which does not yet exist: difficulty is not 'a de facto state of affairs, but *de jure* structure of thought'

(Deleuze 2014: 192–3). This sits within a broader critique of problems that are formulated according to their solvability, with self-representation as the ultimate target for interrogation. This critique of the dogmatic image of thought, which Deleuze defines as a self-reinforcing representation of a problem or question that 'betrays thought' (2014: 209–10), echoes in Rancière's critique of critique, which calls instead for practice in dissensus, in which it is possible to 'reconfigure the landscape of what can be seen and what can be thought' (Rancière 2009: 49).

Critical to Rancière's analysis is the idea of human capacity over social identity, applied here to physical and digital systems. Knowledge generation of human subjects in the type of designed interactive systems that produce big data is based on the figurative representation of audiences from data points as profiles, identities or stereotypes. Such knowledge generation must look back, rather than to the unfolding present. To optimise system resources, it must also analyse data with the objective of generalisation, rather than articulation of the particular. Bringing Deleuze's differentiation of the general and the particular (Deleuze 2014: 2–3) to this query sheds light on the conflict between generalising or totalising representation and emergence. In his thought, generality is a totalising perspective that is afforded the subject that assumes a removed, or transcendent, point of view in relation to the observed event, or unfolding situation. The event thus becomes the target of the subject's reductive gaze; it is reduced by generalisation and becomes an-other. By contrast, the particular is perceived from an immanent subject position in relation to the event, that is, within the event and its immediate circle of influences and consequences. The immanent subject–event relationship is associated with repetition, which occurs in the moving present, never in the generalised idea of 'continuation, perpetuation or prolongation' (Deleuze 2014: 202); that is, emergence. The immanence of repetition produces the particular and thus difference which, to Deleuze, affords theatre the potential for anti-representational movement and continuous variation (Chiesa 2009: 72). Applying this perspective to interactive systems and to the question of how we conceptualise and configure the critical role of users or participants prompts us to think of agency in differential rather than identitarian terms. If we, as Deleuze suggests, are to free the differential, identity cannot be thought as 'that' or 'not-that', but as a dynamic property. It cannot accurately be conceptualised on the basis of a prior horizon of identity – that is, recognisable, or working within the dogmatic image of thought, if it is to escape or elide representation. Here, Deleuze's immanent encounter converges with Rancière's scene of dissensus, and the confluence therein of collectivised capacity.

Storytelling, even when it describes the past, necessarily reflects the present moment in which it unfolds, reimagined (Aherne 1995: 25). Computer games and digital platforms inspire Felix Barrett and Punchdrunk (Hoggard 2013), similarly to how experimental performance art has historically incorporated novel elements of popular or 'low' culture. For a dissensual critique of self-exploitation (Bishop 2012: 277) that looks beyond the physics, mechanics and motifs of computer games and interactive platforms, the form of participation and the frames and boundaries of experience must be included, as they shape conditions of possibility for participation. The extension of networked systems, and the blurring of boundaries between game and not-game in both contents and procedural rhetoric put to test the legacy of critical methods that focus on the complicity of audiences in the construction of narrative and meaning. Avant-garde theatre has a long-standing relationship with 'low' culture, represented in the present moment by cross-fertilisation between performance and computer games or social platforms.[5] We see this in the work of Punchdrunk, Blast Theory, Agency of Coney, Ontroerend Goed and others, and also in LARPing and cosplay, and in public events such as the now-defunct Igfest in Bristol. Some remind audiences of the artifice, while others seek to go beyond conventional representation; both or either can be applied to designed interaction with technology (Galloway 2004: 99). Brechtian methods have informed postdigital critiques focusing on artifice and glitching, but Punchdrunk's work with audiences directs us towards a critique of always-on pervasive connectedness, frustrated emancipation and occluded exposure through uncomfortable negotiation of contested place and compromised space.

Discomfort, uncertainty and the possible failure of the subject position is at the heart of dissensus in Punchdrunk's work. It might not be an actual emergency, but emergence is not, and perhaps cannot be comfortable, since its possibility is born in dissensus between transcendent dominion and immanent encounters. As the idea of the sovereign subject is a central myth in Western post-Enlightenment culture, its destabilisation is unpalatable outside extraordinary situations. Within a wider discussion of artistic modernity and aesthetics,[6] Rancière concludes that emancipation through art-work must be achieved through collectivised capacity, invested in 'scenes of dissensus' (2009: 49). Applying Rancière's critique of the stalemate in critical thought (2009: 25–49) to the digital modern is exquisitely relevant. Its promise of emancipation, in spite of surface appearances, cannot escape replicating the mechanics of commodification, and must instead produce a standoff between 'left-wing melancholy' and 'right-wing frenzy' at either end of the battlefield of critical analysis (Rancière 2009: 40). His analysis offers a road map, supported by preceding theories of representation in theatre. These interrogate not just the locus, but the nature and mode of subject positions in performance, including those of audiences, directors and actors.

In his analysis of the sublime as a key aesthetic in avant-garde art, Rancière emphasises unavailability and the immaterial essence of our relationship with the material. He locates the sublime in the 'break of the mind's capacity to take hold of its object' (2004) and, via Sloterdijk, as an anti-gravitational desire that fails into the human condition (2009: 31). Jean-François Lyotard describes the sublime as being 'deprived of the threat of being deprived of light, language, life' (1991: 99); an aesthetic that compromises the subject through failure of reason. Narrowing this focus further, Peter Zima describes the sublime as a threat to 'the very foundations of subjectivity' (2010: 125). The sublime subject position, like the one described by Gilles Deleuze in *Difference and Repetition* (2014) and Jacques Derrida in *Writing and Difference* (2001) in their analyses of Artaud's Theatre of Cruelty, is precarious and immanent. Interviews with Punchdrunk audience members describe a sense of vertigo and awe through the embodied sensation of possibility and challenge as boundaries between the self and the performance environment blur.[7] We might infer from this that immersion is a sublime aesthetic that flows from the destabilised subject position and the transient sense of being subsumed or captured within the performance environment. Otherwise undesirable experiences like disorientation and a dreamlike disassociation are made tolerable by their containment within the storyworld, making destabilisation of the subject position a form of play. Sublime play requires bounds as well as edges, precipices and the possibility of falling, features and themes that recur in this study of Punchdrunk and their audiences. Following Lyotard's analysis, exposure to the possibility of failure and falling is essential to sublime immersion, and the voluntary 'abduction' of audiences not only completes the artwork; it also contains and aestheticises challenge (Chow 2012).

Edges and containment are critical to an analysis of the sublime, focused on the subject position. In *Unthought* (2017), Katherine Hayles discusses the assemblages we form with tools and technologies as mutually meshed agencies, in contrast with visions of technology as an extension of the transcendent, sovereign subject. In her view, the subject is ambiguously bounded and exposed to situational influences and agencies; human and non-human. When naturalised, assemblage with technology is occluded, for example, books, which we take for granted as part of our world. Reading and writing are deeply meshed with thinking and communication as actions and extensions of cognition and allow us to form narrative systems with books that incorporate our senses, cognition and imagination. Books shape our way of thinking and our way of thinking about ourselves, but before the printing press and movable type, they were rare items of high value, and scribing was an occult skill that afforded specific privileges, similar to how many view coding today. Both books and digital systems are information technologies and vehicles for storytelling, but the book can be closed and put away, as theorised by Derrida in the idea of *clôture* (Lehmann 2006: 61). By contrast, embedded technologies and their infrastructures are always-on and integrated within distributed networks; 'texts' that at a glance share the open processuality of post-dramatic theatre (Lehmann 2006: 61), but with key differences in the relationship between text and audience. Whereas the open processuality between text and audience in live performance is immanent, that of distributed network interaction is fundamental to the generation of data as a commodity, extracted from the flow of interaction that is generated by our participation and use of games, social media, search engines and other digital platforms, and which is subsequently processed and brokered.

In *La Monnaie Vivante*,[8] Klossowski discusses voluptuous emotions and cognitive processes as generative of economic production. The attention economy that is built on this commodity reifies Klossowski's argument, and the normalised elicitation and extraction of attention and emotion that Rosi Braidotti calls life-mining (2013: 62) naturalise exposure from always-on connectivity. The commodification of 'voluptious emotions and cognitive processes' in technological systems based on formal logic and the idea of pure reason embeds a reductive perspective on human participants that allows for occlusion of that which does not serve the transcendent. In the name of efficiency, behaviours that fit the business model will be 'seen', while those that fall outside of it can remain 'unseen'. Here, a parallel can be drawn with Phelan's 'marked' and 'unmarked' to elucidate the power differential between the two conditions and the consequences for our projected selves as data objects or identities. By contrast, embodied participation by masked Punchdrunk audiences is articulated as a material, and identity is occluded. Thus, participation can occur as an 'organisation of the sensible' that does not rely on representation of identity and its relation to a transcendent or totalising perspective (Rancière 2009: 48–9).

Such interrogations are critical to the digital un-modern, or postdigital mode of design thinking. A critical theory of representation and gaze that is specific to interactive systems in physical and digital media must move in and out of the 'blind spots' caused by the particulars of each medium (Clarke 2008: 24). As discussed above, such an interrogation must look at how participation is modelled, both with regard to the subject position and the event presented to the subject within the design schema. Even prior to making, the way audiences are thought informs their representation at the infrastructure level of interactive systems, whether these are live events or digital artefacts, and how this inflects conditions of possibility at the interface level.

Scenography as experience infrastructure in physical and virtual worlds

Play within designed environments is at once interpretative and compensatory; 'the thing that overcomes systemic contradiction but always via recourse to that special, ineffable thing that makes us most human' (Galloway 2012: 29). It might be an emergent response to the breakdown of representation – a tactic to meet crises of meaning in post-dramatic theatre as theorised by Hans-Thies Lehmann (2006). Efficiency was defined by Lyotard as the performative principle of legitimation in late capitalism (Lyotard 1984: 45–6): a transcendent that structures a moral argument and frames certain types of 'beauty' in political and economic discourses. A contemporary transcendent, efficiency decrees representation that minimises the friction of interaction and obscures the possibility of failure. In this light, the excess capacity and deliberate frustration in Punchdrunk's work is a delinquent, even obscene aesthetic. These qualities are, however, essential to the sustained experience of vertiginous possibility in their productions in emergent encounters and the temporary meshing of one's agency with that of others, or 'joyful composition' (Deleuze 1970: 28). The rich possibility space that flows from deeply layered and differentially articulated expressions of agency, converging in and flowing across the interface between makers in the company and their audiences, is central to the experience of immersion in Punchdrunk's work.

In lieu of efficiency there is effectiveness, which also distinguishes between ritual and performance. Ritual has a clear purpose and outcome; it is scripted and relies on non-critical enactment by its participants. It is formulated to produce *communitas* under a transcendent organising principle, and typically reinforces or naturalises 'good' or 'common sense'. By contrast, performance affords the possibility of disbelief and what Rancière calls dissensus (Schechner 2013: 80; Couldry 2012: 72). Following Schechner's argument, digital interactive systems are ritualistic in that they are configured for anticipated and predefined, that is, scripted inputs from human users. Bogost calls this procedural rhetoric (2007), which requires the audience to enter into the 'breaks' in the scripted experience – the simulation gaps – to complete it. The simulation gaps are shaped by the scripted narrative and the capabilities of the infrastructure of the interactive system, and shape participation.

Bogost's analysis of the procedurality of interactive narrative systems focuses on the limitations and possibilities offered by the computal, but the structure of his argument and its emphasis on analysis of the infrastructures of interactive systems applies equally to physical materialities. The shape of participation that is afforded by design in Punchdrunk is influenced by multiple modalities, from the architectural aspects of the scenography to the fine grain of detail, by Stephen Dobbie's soundscapes, and by the acting and interaction of performers. Like interactive theatre and performance, digital experience design is founded and 'crafted from a multitude of protracted, intersecting cultural processes' (Bogost 2007: 7). Scenography, which in its fullness spans the stage and the auditorium, allows analysis of how audiences are conceptualised and configured, and we can read physical or digital infrastructures of interactive experience as texts in their own right.

De Certeau understands storytelling as the performance of spatial transformations in relation to structure and emergence. In Punchdrunk, the story is performed not only by the company but also by their audiences as *metaphorai* or story-vehicles. The story moves and mediates between place and space, or structure and emergence, in de Certeau's analysis: 'What the map cuts up, the story cuts across' (1988: 129). The concepts of place and space follow the French *lieu* (place), and *espace* (space). *Lieu* is derived from the Latin *locus*: location in relation to a definition or ordained purpose, and a subdivision of social space. It can refer to an occasion or a specific instance within a context, that is, an appropriate moment for a particular action or statement, bound or contained by order. Place/*lieu* thus describes locations within hierarchies, situations and other constructs that stabilise and establish positions and create social orders. The French noun *espace* (space) is derived from the Latin *spatium* and is close to the meaning of the English 'extent', as in 'extension of (time or space)'; a field of directions and dynamic properties such as movement and time. Space/*espace* is a product of dynamic time and location, and only exists as it is performed, or practised:

> Space occurs as the effect produced by the operations that orient it, situate it, temporalize it, and make it function in a polyvalent unity of conflictual programs or contractual proximities. [...] caught in the ambiguity of actualization, transformed into a term dependent on many different conventions, situated as the act of a present (or of a time), and modified by the transformations caused by successive contexts. (Certeau 1988: 117)

Participation in Punchdrunk productions is a 'play of changing relationships between places and spaces' (Certeau 1988: 118). Its shape is configured around immanence and emergence, supported and contained by scenography and performance. In Ancient Greek myth, *metis* signifies a form of tactics; a combination of skill and cunning that is emergent and, as a story practice, allows the story to transform the order and stability of place into emergent space (Certeau 1988: 83–8). *Metis* uses metaphor, metonymy and synecdoche to re-order and shift interpretative frames and registers (Certeau 1988: 81–3), and draws on memory and intertextual references to create polyvalence. It comes to expression with every repetition of a Punchdrunk play in the variations afforded both company and audience members within the scripted whole, including the possible inflections of meaning that comes from different combinations of the many story elements. The scenography and its richly layered detail hide countless more opportunities for interaction and touch, and performers and the Black Masks create, through enactment and adaptation, further variations each time and in response to the spatial interpretations of audiences.[9]

In digital media, the potential of *metis* or 'emergent story tactics' is inhibited by the comparative rigidity of digital systems in response to emergent, ambiguous or polyvalent inputs from human participants. Everything is precisely scripted in procedural rhetoric, including non-player characters (NPCs) in games and other game-like applications. More complex modelling, scripting and incorporation of AI in NPCs can create an enhanced simulation of autonomy (Posada Trobo et al. 2019), but human agents typically realise their limitations quickly. The idea of personalisation in digital communication developed to compensate for the rigid formalism of digital systems but quickly became the rationale for intrusive gathering of audience data (Kant 2020). Even when seeking to learn from human users, digital systems depend on limiting inputs to what the system can read. User modelling, even when cumulative, is based on identities; a composite of stereotypes plus data of past actions (Kobsa 2001; Galloway 2004: 114; Kant 2020). Predictions are based on inferences from the data object of what was, projected by way of aggregated generalisation of past behaviours by other identities with sufficiently similar characteristics. Together with the limited capacity for differential user inputs, this creates and reinforces behavioural conventions that shape the participation of the data object or identity by which each system user's actions and interactions are mediated.

Mediation of actions and interactions is inevitable in any system, physical or digital, and infrastructural factors inflect the degree and nature of agency that is afforded human participants. Limits also frame, and boundaries support or even produce play; the expression of space occurs in relation to place. Likewise, procedural rhetoric is expressed in relation to the underlying processes and constructs that form its infrastructure (Bogost 2007: 24–8). Infrastructural processes thus found spatial transformation in what de Certeau calls 'theatres of action' (1988: 125). Here, de Certeau draws on the Roman *fas* ritual for auspicious military or diplomatic campaigns (1988: 124). It made actions lawful to the gods by enlisting divine support, established space for the intended action to take place and founded the campaign or *coup*. Performance that unsettles and undoes representation and identity alters an existing social order (Certeau 1988: 122–6), and the *fas* that prepares for the *coup* (Certeau 1988: 85, original emphasis) occurs in design, rehearsal and resetting the scenography for each performance. Punchdrunk's storyworlds, like digital ones, are founded by subroutines and processes that 'found expression of a higher order' (Bogost 2007: 5). In Punchdrunk, these subroutines are performed and processed by human agents who bring their capacity for interpretation, memorisation and adaptation to the play. Their collective *metis* or tactical skill generate the place and space through which the unfolding stories enacted by each audience participant move with 'the subtlety of a cybernetic world' (Certeau 1988: 88).

Here, de Certeau alludes to the abstract or virtual nature of digital territories, not capacity for nuance or necessarily fluidity. While data is extremely fluid in form and reach, the shape afforded human agency in 'cybernetic worlds' is relatively rigid as their infrastructures, even when the interface layer suggests otherwise, are based on formal logic that requires predefined inputs. Further comparison between Punchdrunk's storyworlds with digital worlds highlights the lack of transparency in code and the potentially global reach of local expressions as they are scaled by distributed networks. The global is collapsed into the local, extending local platform logic and the effects of user representation and modelling at the infrastructure level of interactive systems to remote human participants and their communities. The critical nature of this query becomes clear in light of the effects of scaling on immanence beyond small interactive systems, for example, performances that are local in time and space, to the effects of how audiences are thought at scale and over time. An analysis of how Punchdrunk frame immersion across performance for one audience at a time to audiences of several hundred is a rare opportunity to explore functional mechanisms of representation and capture, and how these inflect conditions for play and the sublime across media.

The postdigital sublime: beyond the digital mythos

Rancière's 'unreasonable' hypothesis of dissensus nods to the sublime which, as Lyotard and Zima argue, is a function of the possible failure of reason and subjectivity itself. The sublime and its undertow of aestheticised submission is a product of framing or containment of this threat. It hinges on the vertigo of failing comprehension and contextualises our smallness, rather than our greatness. Nature, in both the spatial and cultural sense, typically invokes the sublime, but it also finds expression in many areas of design, including the arts, architecture, mathematics and technological systems. It can be felt looking up into the inverse vertigo of a Gothic cathedral, across the horizon of oceans or by projecting imagination through time. It invokes awe and existential vertigo; it is unsettling, but tolerable and even thrilling when framed and aestheticised. The sublime discussed by Lyotard and Zima is not beauty in the conventional sense and falls outside of totalising systems of representation that foreshortens rather than poses questions (Zima 2010: 127). Central to the sublime is the possibility of falling or losing oneself, or rather, one's self. In the Kantian analysis, the frame that produces the sublime by way of containment is reason and its capacity for extension and comprehension, whereas Lyotard instead traces it along the fault line of reason, where the soul is 'deprived of the threat of being deprived of light, language, life' (Lyotard 1991: 99). The sublime is thus a bounded encounter with the possible failure of representation and the rational self that 'threatens the very foundations of subjectivity' (Zima 2010: 125).

A functional understanding of both play and the sublime needs to be thought through and in relation to frames and boundaries (Galloway 2012: 29). To Derrida, play disrupts presence, or the centre (Derrida 2001: 369). In any historical moment, the mythical centre is recursively shaped by that which defines a culture and its boundaries: it simultaneously allows and limits play. Play occurs in relation to boundaries, with ambiguity and the tension between dissolution and rules informing its mechanics and conferring much of its appeal. Drawing on Derrida, Sutton-Smith draws attention to this tension:

> There is an endless play of signifiers of which children and all other players are capable [...]. All players unravel in some way the accepted orthodoxies of the world in which they live, whether those orthodoxies have their source in adult or child peer groups. (Sutton-Smith 2001: 166)

Roger Caillois locates play between the polarities of rule-based games (*ludus*) and the informal spontaneity of child-like anarchy (*paidia*) (1961: 14–16, 27), reflecting de Certeau's story that negotiates between the tension between the order of place and the extension of space to produce ambiguity, transgression and multi-variancy (1988: 85, 129–30). To Johan Huizinga, whose *Homo Ludens* established play theory as an object of study in its own right, it is a fundamentally human activity that simultaneously depends on and produces boundaries in time and space, whether social or physical (1955). Huizinga's analysis emphasises the adjacency of play and the carnivalesque, where upended orders within the bounds of time and space allow, even invite irreverence and dissolution (Bakhtin 1984).

Positioning the experience of art as capture; a temporary suspension or upending of sovereignty within bounds, Rey Chow describes the encounter with art as an 'abduction' (Chow 2012: 41), with the implication that the artwork is a trap that captivates and entangles its audience, whose entrapment completes or fulfils its design (Chow 2012: 43). Resonating with Lyotard's definition of the sublime experience in art, capture enforces a rupture within the entrapped and self-ensnared, caught between the impact of ensnarement and the fear of annihilation (Chow 2012: 47). This is particularly relevant to transmedial dramatic staging that contains and erases distance, reintroduces illusionism and appears to run counter to critical reflexivity. Instead, Chow focuses on the 'crudeness and primitiveness' employed by both Brecht and

Artaud to alienate and reach beyond conventional representation. While the former enforces critical distance through failure of representation, the latter immerses the audiences within a multi-sensory dramatic environment to strip audiences of their socially oriented and embodied constructs of good sense and taste (Chow 2012: 27–8). The ensuing rupture confronts audiences with their normally withheld crudeness of instinct and emotion, exposing them to the vertigo of possibility that issues from within. The 'cruelty' of such voluntary capture aligns with Claire Bishop's idea of self-exploitation (2012: 277).

Capture in Punchdrunk comprises several 'minorising' components, including disorienting scenography, prevailing darkness, perspective shifts (in scenography and audiences) between vastness and intimacy, distributed narrative and occlusion of identity (through masking). These are reinforced by ongoing exposure to agency; one's own and that of others. Agency is centred in lieu of the identity of the subject, by conditions that challenge, recruit, engage and, in interaction with the Black Masks, sometimes overwrite it.[10] Phelan's hierarchy of visibility (1996) orients the marked subjects in relation to the unmarked; the 'supposedly universal model of Man' (Cull 2013: 20), or 'so-called Man' (Kittler 1999: 16), placing agency, or the executive power of the subject, in a contested or even inverse relation to visibility: '[if] representational visibility equals power, then almost-naked young white women should be running Western culture' (Phelan 1996: 10). The negative relation between visibility and power finds further expression in de Certeau's argument about space and place, where definitions that issue from a totalising ordering principle create place, whereas immanent, or emergent extension of space is 'unmarked' and open to the unfolding story. Marking flows from the transcendent gaze of the unmarked, and in relation to it:

> Identity emerges in the failure of the body to express being fully and failure of the signifier to convey meaning exactly. Identity is perceptible only through a relation to an-other. [...] In that declaration of identity and identification, there is always loss, the loss of not-being the other and yet remaining dependent on that other for self-seeing, self-being. (Phelan 1993: 13)

Identity-as-marked thus affirms its own failure and the unmarked norm, returning us to Herbert Blau's challenge: escaping the commodity form of the body, marked as it is by visibility (1992: 4). The mechanisms of capture in Punchdrunk's work converge on the form of the subject to produce the possibility of failure and escape at once. Temporarily suspended, embodied dissensus is staged in scenes where audiences swarm in crowds, and where agency is confronted with itself in encounter with an-other; the dark mirror image provided by the Black Masks, or the sudden baring of the naked face in one-to-ones. It is revealed to itself through self-exploitation and capture as employed by Bishop and Chow, respectively.

Social rupture between identity and embodied experience can be dramatic or mundane; frames determine whether it is breakdown, performance or play. Jorge Luis Borges' classes of animals; those we watch television with, those we eat, and those we are scared of, underscore that our understanding of ourselves as human is a matter of framing (Braidotti 2013: 68). Within Braidotti's broader post-Cartesian critique of the liberal humanist idea of Man, this reference underscores its dichotomy with the body and those defined by their difference from the unmarked, or 'supposedly universal model of Man' (Cull 2013: 20). Taking aim at the frame that upholds the illusion of sovereignty of mind over body, Artaud sought to remind audiences of our shared minor state, occluded and assuaged by representation:

> A theatre difficult and cruel for myself, first of all. And, on the level of performance, it is not the cruelty we can exercise upon each other by hacking at each other's bodies, carving up our personal anatomies, or, like Assyrian emperors, sending parcels of human ears, noses, or neatly detached nostrils through the mail, but the much more terrible and necessary cruelty which things can exercise against us. We are not free. And the sky can still fall on our heads. And the theatre has been created to teach us that first of all. (Artaud 1958: 79)

The reality work of representation serves to soothe precariousness, typically through reinforcing prevailing orders under a transcendent or totalising organising principle. By contrast, sublime destabilisation through capture within the artwork aims to disturb. In late Western capitalism and the largely parallel digital modern, efficiency is both an organising principle and a proxy for ideological purity in relation to which its opposites, complex continuities and resistance to demassification, are 'impure' and near-heretical. The impassioned superabundance of layered detail in Punchdrunk's work is a perverse expression within this order, as is its function to abduct and seduce the subject, robbed of identity, into embodied states of emergence.

While the sublime of Lyotard and Zima flows from embodied disorientation and the possible failure of identity and comprehension, the digital modern fetishises the idea of transcending the human condition through hyper-rationality and technological transmutation: establishing sovereignty over the delinquent abundance of life and its twin, entropy. The sublime that may be produced within this vision flows from Kant's definition, where the subject assumes a vantage point of reason from which the vertigo of awe can be framed and contained. Building instead on Lyotard's and Zima's sublime, where the subject faces failure of coherence from a position of immanence, a postdigital sublime might draw on the threat of demassification of the self and its systemic representation. In this vein, Punchdrunk's aesthetic embraces disorientation in convoluted and detailed scenography that elicits the sublime in spatial articulation and hidden encounters that require perseverance in the face of dissolution.

If we regard the abducted subjects as 'spect-actors' from Augusto Boal's *Theatre of the Oppressed*, design for participation in interactive systems provides opportunities for rehearsing emergence under exposed conditions (Bishop 2012: 122–5). Arguing that we have already entered the postdigital moment, David Berry bases his position on the observation that the digital no longer 'stays put' in its encoded, modular form, or remains contained within vessels that we can understand as physical phenomena. This suggests that such exercises are timely, even overdue. Embedded, always-on computational process flows already invisibly extend and pervade social and physical space (Berry 2014a). In contrast with the artwork, which is bound in time and space, distributed networks capture the digital representation of its human actors within an unbound 'trap' (Chow 2012) that replicates endlessly, without ever living:

> The lines of a distributed network continue off the diagram. Any subsegment of a distributed network is as large and as small as its parent network. Distribution propagates through rhythm, not rebirth. (Galloway 2004: 94)

The open-endedness, speed and reach of electronic media collapse time and space, disassociating the physical properties of place from the social 'place' that confers its meaning (Meyrowitz 1985: 115). Meyrovitz argues that the narrative space of electronic communication disrupts social frames that were previously maintained by physical distance and locale (1985: 125). Social behaviours that were previously characterised by degrees of isolation (e.g. the domestic sphere, prisons, and convents) have been particularly influenced by the dilution of importance given to physical places, as the 'opening of closed situations' formed during several hundred years is facilitated by electronic media in the last century (1985: 308). More recently, mobile and embedded computation exposes unrehearsed intimacy, a state of immanence held within the habitual, to this change. Rather than simple communication devices, these are presentation technologies connected to distributed computational networks that expose people and systems to each other in ways that we have only begun to understand. Exposure is necessarily as mutual as connectivity, and Artaud's demand for its articulation to remind us of precarity remains timely, particularly as these technologies are designed to be ubiquitous and as seamlessly integrated with everyday life as possible. As discussed in the next chapter, Punchdrunk have incorporated mobile phones and tablets in participatory performance outside conventional or adapted performance spaces. They work carefully with cross-platform transitions, that is, between electronic media and physical reality, to create narratives that bridge the two without exceeding credible illusion.

The most radical intervention that can be derived from Punchdrunk's work to enhance design for digital platforms is a critical re-imagination of audiences not as individuals or demographic categories, but as a material force in design: un-modern, delinquent and sometimes volatile, but also vital, dynamic and with unparalleled capacity to process and respond. This may not fit design schema that serve the transcendent, whether this is efficiency, rationality or Kittler's 'so-called Man' (1999: 16), but failure to articulate the possibilities that remain outside of the frame of 'good sense' leaves de Certeau's delinquent old gods unaddressed and free-roaming, and depletes aesthetic potential for the sublime. Towards this critical re-imagination, postdigital systems must either problematise totalising efficiency or articulate the emergent properties of human participation. Rigid representation of audiences betrays their nature; human participation is the 'softest' and most readily expressive material of interaction design, embodying a flux of 'signs, meanings, attractions, desires' (Parikka 2012b: 97–9). Instead of thinking audiences as stereotyped users or identities, we might think of human agents in interactive system as *metaphorai*: vehicles for transportation and transformation across the physical and cognitive dimensions of storytelling. If we think not in terms of identities, but what types and modes of participation are accommodated, we invite a shift in interaction design towards modelling agency and its expression.

Moving away from the agent model in software systems and instead representing human agents *as* agency would entail a paradigm shift with profound consequences and new possibilities. If participation can be modelled as a dynamic force in relation to possibility spaces within interactive systems, it might support a postdigital sublime that is informed by immersive performance such as Punchdrunk's and the longer historical arc of participatory theatre and performance. These play spaces serve as laboratories for understanding who we are, and what we might be, when we interrogate totalising orders, and ourselves within them. What makes us most human is perhaps our facility for negotiating systemic contradictions (Galloway 2012: 29) or, as Latour asks regarding the definition and form of the human: 'A weaver of morphisms – isn't that enough of a definition?' (Latour 1993: 137).

Tempered by Artaud's vision of pure theatre; 'an intense equilibrium, a wholly materialised gravity' (Artaud 1958: 65), perhaps it is; at least for the purpose of design. As audiences are incorporated as actors and become critical parts in the totality of producing performance and interactive experience, the intensity and cruelty of Artaud's vision instils a sense of awe before the material that accommodates both the tragedy and comedy of Man, Artaud's model subject and target. He writes, in 1938, of the Warrior, 'bristling from the formidable cosmic tempest' and his Double, who 'struts about, given up to his schoolboy gibes, and who, roused by the repercussion of the turmoil, moves unaware in the midst of spells of which he has understood nothing' (1958: 67). As it expands from physical to digital platforms, scenographic design that acknowledges, addresses and engages the collectivised capacity of 'human beings without qualities' in dissensus (Rancière 2009: 49), that is, human agency in all its dynamic expressions from hubris to foolishness, is perhaps not only not unreasonable but essential. In this vein, the next chapter looks to design for physical and virtual spaces with intense equilibrium and materialised gravity in mind.

Notes

1 What Bogost calls 'simulation gaps' are the designed affordances of procedural rhetoric that leave out certain narrative actions that are 'outsourced' to the audience to enact in order to complete the designed narrative.
2 See Chapter 4 for analyses of how audiences are thought and modelled in the design process of Punchdrunk performances.
3 See Chapter 5 for analyses of audience experience.
4 'Dark play' is Richard Schechner's term for play where some participants are unaware that they are co-opted into a game or performance. Dark play typically exploits unaware participants to a greater or lesser degree (Schechner 1993: 36).
5 See Chapter 2.
6 Rancière, in his discussion of artwork as the anticipated reality of a new, political people that do not yet exist but may be found in its audiences, discusses modernism, postmodernism and the sublime as the three major interpretations of 'being together apart' in expressions of artistic modernity and aesthetics (Rancière 2009: 59–60).
7 AUD1, AUD5, AUD6.
8 *La Monnaie Vivante* was originally published in 1970 and translated to English as *Living Currency* in 2017.
9 See Chapter 4 for a close description and analysis of the role and function of the Black Masks in Punchdrunk.
10 The role of the Black Masks in Punchdrunk is discussed in detail in Chapter 4, and audiences' responses in Chapter 5.

7

Impure Futures

Data from our performance as agents within computational systems is no longer contained, any more than those systems are or realistically can be. Scrutiny of how we are represented as data is essential; not just what information is gathered and aggregated, but its form and structure. As their perspective is sharpened by the immediacy of consequences, theatre designers and actors have an empirical advantage over those who try to model audiences remotely. There is no functional or aesthetic imperative, as this study of Punchdrunk audiences shows, to relentlessly think audiences through their demographic characteristics and gather personalised data of their every action, outside of certain contexts (e.g. transactions that require direct access to personal records for financial, health or security reasons, or where safeguarding is concerned). Moreover, the study shows that it is possible to design interaction for agency beyond identity if the precise detail and nuance of how agency is expressed in interaction is articulated immanently in systems that are is designed for response capacity.

We do not have sufficient understanding of the effects at scale of representation as reductive stereotypes at the infrastructure level of interactive systems. It stands to reason that failure to represent us beyond such data objects is scaled to the reach of the networked systems that rely on human 'moving parts' to fulfil their design and function. Scaling effects in complex systems are difficult to model and comprehend, and involve many decisions that cannot be neutral, especially so when the critical material, the individual and social human, is fundamentally dynamic and unstable. Punchdrunk's large masked shows combine features that suggest an alternative way of thinking and designing for participation as agency in interactive systems: they are small enough to model, big enough for crowd effects to occur, and robust enough over time. Rather than a critique that stops at pointing out where and how digital systems fail to represent human participants in interaction, this presents an opportunity to formulate a positive, if challenging alternative for interactive systems across physical and digital media. Punchdrunk, who with Barrett have developed from a theatre company with roots in live art events and spatial practice to experience designers across physical and virtual media, are now redeveloping their R&D village in London as partners in the UKRI Audience of the Future programme.[1]

Human participants that are incorporated in active roles within the design schema must be modelled in the capacity of both success and failure to fulfil the design schema as envisioned, or perhaps even to perform as 'human' at all. To live events designers working directly with live mass audiences, the abstract-sounding potential for the 'distinction between the human and the daemonic to lapse' (Clarke 2008: 54) is a pragmatic perspective. Rather than a vision of the technologically extended posthuman seen through the lens of the digital modern (Klich and Sheer 2012), a 'postdigital posthuman' is one that problematises the un-modern human in relation to technology and un-human expressions that fall outside of idealised projections. With increased connectivity and reach comes proportionate exposure, and often disproportionate consequences to the naïve users that participate in the capacity of themselves. Interrogating the composite metainterfaces that are formed as virtual and physical realities are blended in design through the lens of scenography allows for analysis of subject positions across figurative 'stages' and their 'auditoriums'. Scenography has moved from the illustrative representation of the renaissance stage to be recognised as a critical material contribution to the event that goes beyond simple representation. 'Theatre machines' such as the ones designed by Punchdrunk offer us a rich source of grounded knowledge for design of experiences that draw us into close relations with screens, mobile and wearable technologies, via the infrastructures that support interaction. Using the machine as a metaphor for a system in which human participants perform as moving parts provokes necessary questions around conditions of possibility and, in Derrida's terms, the amount of freeplay that is possible within them.

The extent of surveillance and data harvesting was not public knowledge until Edward Snowden's NSA leaks entered mainstream horizons in 2013 (The NSA Files 2018) and marked the public end of the digital modern. Since then, initial questions around the impact of always-on surveillance have been rendered almost trivial by revelations of the entanglements between social media and international politics (Cadwalladr 2017; Bradshaw 2019). Events in public and private spheres seem to confirm the critical perspectives of Braidotti and Hayles who, rather than propagating the illusion of the sovereign subject, emphasise its permeability and exposure to other agencies. The imperative for hyper-connective efficiency in late or demassified capitalism occludes both the capacity and vulnerability of embodiment. By contrast, Punchdrunk foreground embodied agency and defocus identity, which profoundly alters conditions of possibility. The combination of anonymity and intense articulation of detail in their designed interactions allow them to negotiate and harness the un-modern, and its vital capacity. Through centring embodied agency (as a grounded capacity for change and process), rather than the agent (as a persistent identity and sovereign source of will), the performance space becomes a crucible of sorts; a vessel for change that maps to the sensate body.

Bridging from physical to virtual scenographies presents profound creative and ethical challenges. The effects and consequences of making data a commodity through the technologies that deliver both personalisation and surveillance are in part products of scale. Scalability can be understood in different ways that broadly fall on either side of the distinction between repetition and generality, as described by Deleuze. The type of system or theatre machine that Punchdrunk create is scalable according to the principle of repetition, but not according to generality. A replicable formula does not preclude difference in the sense implied by Deleuze; repetition produces difference (2014: 375): 'In every respect, repetition is a transgression. It puts law into question, it denounces its nominal or general character in favour of a more profound and more artistic reality' (Deleuze 2014: 3). The association between repetition and transgression suggests de Certeau's delinquent story-space (Certeau 1988: 129–30), which resists and disrupts the order of place. Side-by-side analyses of Punchdrunk's R&D project *The Séance* (2011), *Goldwell* (2012) and *Silverpoint* (2015) show the different effects of scaling by extension and scaling by repetition. Whereas the latter two projects (blended reality experiences that incorporated mobile phones for games in the initial stages and messaging throughout) were relative successes, *The Séance* (which sought to extend the experience of *Sleep No More* in New York through technological portals and interlocutors) failed to communicate immersion to the external participants.[2] The experience of replicable formulae remains particular to each instance or repetition, and supported immersive experience in *Goldwell* (described below) and *Silverpoint*.[3] Replication does not in itself cause loss of quality in participant experience; this comes from insufficient particularity. Provided that the interface offers sufficient detail and affordances to support encounters, each participant brings their own particularity to the interaction. In *The Séance*, the project partners at MIT attempted to extend and transmit the experience of the on-site audience member, and ultimately reframed an immanent experience within a transcendent subject-even relationship.

Garrett Wolf and Nathan Mahaffey call for theorisation of architecture to enhance design for potentiality and difference, which is equally, or even more relevant to digital spaces:

> Co-producing spaces of potentiality and difference is an effort to further the closure of the gap between the design and planning professions and

their understanding of the production of space as a larger scale process. It is necessary to further develop the theorization and methodologies of co-productive practice. Not only do we contend that this would allow the 'current' intended use of the space to flourish, but we also contend that as the space transforms into the many versions of itself in the future it will be malleable enough to serve the shifting purposes. (2016)

The agency of human participants, who are vital components not only in the connection between but also in the production of space in virtual and story domains, must reasonably be considered in design as a dynamic material. The following sections discuss these and other implications for scenography and performance in physical, digital and blended media (including AR, VR and XR), explored and taken forward in R&D and full productions by Punchdrunk and other artists and designers.

Condemned to change

Punchdrunk's masked shows present an opportunity to observe and understand not just how mass audiences operate, but also how individuals respond out of their comfort zone. For the purpose of interaction design, a mass of people cannot be functionally understood as multiples of individuals, and an individual cannot be understood as the fraction of a mass. Following Deleuze's argument of generality versus the particular, subjects of actualised generality can only determine their resemblance, and particular subjects can only illustrate the generality imposed upon them at the cost of their capacity for difference. Particular subjects (as opposed to the 'pure' or conceptual subject) are condemned to change as a function of being particulars rather than concepts. This change is difference, and inherent to repetition as defined by Deleuze. The 'pure subject' that is excused from change (i.e. participants modelled as generalities) is an abstract concept, and affordances designed for pure subjects cannot empower the actual or particular subject. In performing a role designed for a stereotype, no matter if it is enhanced with aggregated data from past performance, the performance of the actual subject must enact their own powerlessness to repeat (Deleuze 2014: 2–3).

The audience members in this study shared the observation that the detail of the designed experience supported their voluntary commitment and investment of agency, which came to expression in exploration and encounters. Beyond the shared appreciation of detail, interviewed audience members were united more by their capacity for process and responsive change than any other type of description. As demonstrated by the 'Spoiler' and Superfans social media discourses,[4] behaviours within a particular interactive system (or interface) primarily reflect that on system and are not necessarily transferrable to other systems. A theory of agency in interactive systems should include analyses of the systems in which it is expressed, as platform effects limit how much one can reasonably generalise. Moving away from personalisation and projections predicated on past behaviours to modelling agency as a dynamic and potentially even volatile material would require that we rethink how participation is conceptualised at the infrastructure level of software platforms.

In response to this problem, theorists of the in-, or un-human suggest that a language that issues from the animal may go towards practice beyond representation:

> Isn't such an ethology precisely what Derrida has searched for as a language beyond logocentrism, a language that is trace in all its complexity? And isn't language that erupts from the animal already a language beyond the signifier, such as Deleuze seeks, a language linked, not only to the signification of what is absent, but a language that acts and transforms, more amenable to a pragmatism than linguistics? (Grosz 2011: 14)

Grosz is not suggesting that we imitate animals but proposes that we rethink representation with reference to a framework beyond the Cartesian understanding of what it means to be human. Observation of live audiences, particularly where they share the performance space, support the idea of emergent representation of what they 'are' in the unfolding present, and pushes against notions of what they 'should be'. Interviews with Punchdrunk company members suggest that thinking of audiences, or rather, their capacity for actions as a material is not only critical to the designed experience but also functional, particularly when audiences are large. Thinking audiences in this fashion is particularly relevant to designing for movement, which, as Grosz suggested, can be seen as a language that issues from 'the animal'.

A query that orients concepts of thinking agency around movement in physical spaces is relevant also to thinking about navigation in digital systems and online environments. The swells and flows of voices and discourses on social media and other distributed networked systems may be better understood if considered in the light of not just human agency, but other physical forces. Klossowski's analysis in *Living Currency* (2017) speaks of desire as a driving force of production in capitalism, and the demassified participation of prosumers in the attention economy gives form to his theory. Jussi Parikka argues in his critique of media archaeologist Wolfgang Ernst (Parikka 2011) that crisp disciplinary delineations can offer depth in particular areas of interest, including the study of digital media, but that the psychotechnics of cognitive capitalism require an inter- or cross-disciplinary approach (Parikka 2012a: 73–4). In an un-human frame, computational methods in physics and mathematics might be extended to theorising and modelling human agency as a dynamic fluid with properties such as pressure, velocity and density, modelled as functions of time and space. Moving beyond stultifying stereotype modelling at the infrastructure level may support design for interpretative participation (Rancière 2009: 9–14), where audiences can be 'story-vehicles' in de Certeau's mould that travel through the unfolding of narrative, mediating between experiential place and space. Understanding and representing audiences as an embodied force may also ground the hubris of the digital modern and enhance the resilience of interactive systems through shifting narratives, aesthetics and methods away from over-centralising ideals of reason, symmetry and efficiency (Mackay and Avanessian 2014: 42–3).

The sublime versus efficiency

What makes man human is the power of reason, of speech, of response, of shame, and so on that animals lack. Man must be understood as fundamentally different from and thus as other to the animal; an animal perhaps, but one with at least one added category – a rational animal, an upright animal, an embarrassed animal.

(GROSZ 2011: 12)

Lyotard's sublime is the possible failure of reason to the minor other. It is a hierarchical fall, not a gravitational one, and the illusion of sovereignty is the primary loss. When Grosz asks how a theory of language beyond the 'European, masculine, upright, and erect' might look (2011: 14), art that has strived to not just go beyond representation, but beyond the representative format for its appreciation by audiences comes to mind. Artaud's desire to rescue theatre from its servitude to human interest (Artaud 1958: 90) was a call for theatre that does not uphold the upright and sovereign, the transcendent image of Man. While performance art has challenged this image on- and often offstage for a century and more, digital design remains committed to representation in the Cartesian mould: the sovereignty of mind over matter is indulged, and the consequences for misconception outsourced. The cost of this is aesthetic and functional, as well as ethical. Even visual representation of human agents remains a problem, with immanence to date most satisfactorily addressed by a first-person point of view. Companies such as Chinese Room (of *Dear Esther* and *Everybody's Gone to the Rapture* fame) produce acclaimed work where the subject position is defined by absence, and Punchdrunk's augmented reality productions (e.g. *Silverpoint* or *The Oracles*) invite audiences to take the place of the subject in the game, in a world where people are quite specifically missing.

While VR invites participation from a first-person point of view and does not by default rely on representation of the subject, it struggles to articulate human participation in a way that makes sense on its own aesthetic and functional terms. Limitations to physical movement restrain movement and embodied feedback, and presence still depends on projection, which often results in nausea or migraine when the experience is not room-based, that is, movement and vantage positions in the storyworld are not mirrored by the physical situation of the viewer. The interaction mechanisms are frequently buggy or incongruent with immersion in the storyworld. For example, navigation devices must be visually represented but may not blend well with the aesthetic, or the VR representation of physical objects from which the viewer receives haptic feedback drifts or is misaligned from start. The best VR work acknowledges the limitations of the medium and chooses subject matters and narratives carefully. In *Chalkroom*, Laurie Anderson and her collaborator Hsin-Chien Huang moved towards an aesthetic that doesn't over-rely on the spectacle of three-dimensional illusion, only to struggle against the limitations of the display technology. In *Chalkroom* (which is delivered via HTC Vive headsets), Anderson and Huang work with a surface aesthetic based on chalk letters and drawings on slate that accommodates the grainy texture of the image resolution. The resulting virtual spaces are sufficiently abstract to slip the closer criticism invited by hyper-realism, but the meshing of embodied and virtual experience suffers from navigation glitches and misalignment of feedback from the physical environment (e.g. the stool you sit on) and the virtual objects that should map to the physical environment (e.g. the virtual representation of the stool) (Anderson 2018).

By contrast, Blast Theory's award-winning *Desert Rain*, which was created in collaboration with Nottingham's Mixed Reality Lab, successfully negotiated many of these challenges (Tomlin 2014: 244–6). Like *Chalkroom,* but arguably more successfully, the aesthetic of *Desert Rain* employs material limitations and affordances to communicate its subject matter: the mediation of the Gulf War and the blurred boundaries between reality and screenic representation. Each performance played for an audience of six, who were given headsets with ear- and mouthpiece and hooded parka jackets to 'overwrite' their identities, much like the masks do in Punchdrunk shows, swipe cards with the name of their target on the back, and instructions on a TV monitor. They were then led, one by one, to zipped-up netting booths in front of a large rain screen on which the VR world was projected. To navigate the VR world, participants had to use their weight to lean on balance plates (Shaw et al. 2000), which integrated the embodied experience with the audio-visual world in a similar way to Char Davies' *Osmose* (1995). After the game, in which they had to navigate a virtual desert, they crossed through the rain screen, to find their path over a raised sand dune, perfectly smooth as if no one had ever walked there (Shaw et al.

2000). The desert motif frames the subject within a vista marked by time and gravity, and was also used in *The Drowned Man,* where it marked the natural habitat beyond the artificial worlds of Temple Pictures. In a different form, the latter device is elegantly and poignantly used in Daniel Libeskind's architecture for the Jewish Museum in Berlin (1998), where floors and corridors have a twelve-degree-tilt, giving the visitor a sense of disorientation and increased weight as they travel through the building, particularly along the passages named *Axis of Exile,* the *Axis of the Holocaust,* and the *Axis of Continuity* (Libeskind 2011). After climbing the sand hill, *Desert Rain* audiences reached the last installation room: a palimpsest walled with full-size photographs of the walls of a hotel room, empty apart from a monitor cut into the wall, precisely aligned with the TV monitor in the photograph. The swipe card triggered stories of the Gulf War, told by their 'targets'; or rather the real person behind the name – a soldier, a tourist, a peace worker, a television viewer and an actor in a drama about the war (Shaw et al. 2000). The successful blend of display technology and traditional installation materials in *Desert Rain* underscored that immersion is a function of the complex integration of subject matter and materials, including the embodied experience of audiences, in the design schema.

The work of Blast Theory and Punchdrunk, while aesthetically, thematically and methodologically different, demands commitment and perseverance from their audiences within a design schema that underscores complicity. The possibility of failure to perform, to complete your mission, or simply to keep your balance is part of the experience. The aesthetics of failure are critically explored by Elevator Repair Company, Forced Entertainment and other postdramatic companies, and in immersive theatre the possibility of failure is brought to the audience. Punchdrunk audience members in this study discussed challenge and extended effort as important parts of their experience, often framed as sublime; awe, disorientation, vastness, depth (of detail), and the unknowable in interaction with Black Masks and performers.[5] *Desert Rain* and Punchdrunk's large masked shows are read by their audiences as generous; a condition for immersive experience that is frequently overlooked. The perceived generosity reassures audiences that the experience will support their suspension of disbelief, sustained by the scenography over time. The importance of superabundance (within a coherent artistic vision) to immersive experience implicates efficiency as false economy and puts several challenges to software designers who seek to create immersion.

We can trace the critique of representation in aesthetics of light and dark, and how they resonate with the Kantian and the postmodern image of the sublime. The idea of the 'light source' and the 'dark source' is reflected in the interaction between scenography and the audience in conventional proscenium staging and. immersive spaces: the former projects towards us, while the latter draw us into receding shadows. The use of light and dark in theatre has historically reflected social and technological factors, and from the late nineteenth century, the convention developed to light the auditorium and the stage separately, clearly setting the two apart (Palmer 2017). Punchdrunk return to unified lighting of stage and auditorium[6] but reverse the earlier convention of them being more or less equally bright and plunge both in darkness and sublime disorientation.

The Kantian sublime frames the vastness of possibility in reason, while the sublime of Lyotard and Zima traces the limits of comprehension. The former seeks to transcend, through reason, the vastness of the possibility space of knowledge, while the latter is produced by the threat of incomprehension. A transcendent vantage point allows the subject to frame the event in rationality, reducing complexity. Punchdrunk audiences describe precariousness or the possibility of failure of self or others as central to the production of meaning.[7] By contrast, digital worlds are notable for the absence of gravity and embodied consequence. Similarly, virtualisation of war – the subject of *Desert Rain* – renders it a form of entertainment through occluding the real consequences of events and actions (Favret 2009: 24).

The possibility of consequence and failure are key to the aesthetic of audience experience in Punchdrunk's work. They may 'fail' through inappropriate actions, but primarily through insufficient commitment to the experience.[8] Behaviours on the edge of what the performance environment can accommodate are addressed by the Black Masks, who articulate this boundary in both the physical and narrative sense of the word. They might, for example, connect their arm to the side of an audience member's arm with a light pressure to guide their movements by creating a temporary composite of jointed parts. In doing so, they articulate the possibility of consequence by simultaneously marking the boundaries of agency and diffusing the edges of illusion. The resulting ambiguity appears to support a dreamlike experience in which participants are lucid and physically active, while feeling as if they are being controlled by agencies of the performance space. Such encounters both connect and expose, creating a sense of vertigo as the moment contains both a question and an invitation carrying the possibility of risk and potential.[9]

The postdigital perspective expands the frame around makers and users of interactive systems beyond the image of rationality that is associated with the modern, mirroring the shift that occurs between the Kantian and the Lyotardian sublime; the latter framed in the failure, rather than the perseverance, of reason (Rancière 2004). Zima defines the sublime as an aesthetic outside ordered beauty, where beauty is understood as a unifying concept that contributes to the 'constitution of the subject' via good taste and good sense (Zima 2010: 125). The sublime, as an experience that 'destroys unity' (Zima 2010: 127), relies on the threat to self and reason by dissolution and is often represented and described in spatial terms. The unifying 'good sense' of the modern flows from a transcendent subject position that is sufficiently removed to contain, in idea and ambition, the grain and complexity of immanent experience within a totalising, purifying vision. This perspective produces both extremes of the digital modern: the reductive 'good' and the grotesque 'old gods'. Clarke describes this as the splitting of the 'real, discursive and social' narrative middle ground into the two dichotomous, but equally mystified, realms of the angelic and the daemonic (Clarke 2008: 51), neither of which are hospitable to immanent encounters.

A postdigital encounter, if conceived as a meeting between immanent agencies, must occur on the same plane or 'level ground'. Deleuze's description of joy rests on the extension of agency and requires that it is empowered, in the moment of composition with an-other, by the absence of prescription. Phelan notes the trap of visibility: 'There is real power in remaining unmarked; and there are serious limitations to visual representation as a political goal' (Phelan 1996: 6). Through this, Phelan clarifies the power of interrogative totalitarianism that Derrida discusses in relation to the visible and the invisible. Within interactive systems where control is disseminated and exerted via protocols (Galloway 2004), 'unmarked' agency is the distributed locus of executive power. While diffuse and imprecisely located, this agency occupies a transcendent perspective that both produces and is defined by the unmarked norm.

The Chinese Room, with *Dear Esther* and *Everybody's Gone to the Rapture,* and the game component of Punchdrunk's *The Oracles,* address, through the absence of human characters, the problem of human representation and its conflict with emergence. Bogost identifies this dichotomy in mainstream games, and speculates that the rise of the latter has influenced a broader shift towards identitarianism:

> The very idea of the gamer assumes that identity is predominant, even before that identity seeks either protection or expansion. And then, for everyone, games primarily become an apparatus for exercising self-identity. [...] Maybe the obsession with personal identification and representation in games is why identity politics has risen so forcefully and naively in their service online, while essentially failing to build upon prior theories and practices of social justice. And perhaps it is why some gamers have become so attached to their identity that they've been willing to burn down anything to defend it. (Bogost 2015)

Bogost argues that stereotypical representation via fine-sliced demographic profiling splits the 'middle ground', which introduces and reinforces distancing in several dimensions while creating a distorted and demassified fairground mirror image of the self in online social discourses. For a postdigital middle ground, we might ask that infrastructures for blended, extended and virtual scenographies support ambiguity and emergent agency as it unfolds in the moving present. Towards this, we may draw on theatre and performance and the performative function of hyperstition (Lütticken 2017), the facility of digital media for imagined futures, collapsed chronologically into the present:

> The best games model the systems in our world – or the ones of imagination – by means of systems running in software. Just as photography offers a way of seeing aspects of the world we often look past, game design becomes an exercise in operating that world, of manipulating the weird mechanisms that turn its gears when we're not looking. (Bogost 2015)

In place of techno-utopian accelerationism, which has rolled back its previous calls for revolution in the face of resurgent populism, new accelerationisms have emerged which embrace eccentrication over speed, moving away from even the notion of a central, totalising vision (Mackay and Avanessian 2014: 42–3). This change in focus is reminiscent of the early twentieth century, when the revolutionary ardour of Futurism was cooled by war and Dada emerged, followed in due course by Surrealism. Here the idea of the story that moves between place and space is invited (Fuller and Goffey 2009: 150). Aesthetic stratagems such as enhanced capacity for metaphorical shifts, polysemy and articulation to accommodate nuance may allow us to fold the digital into the impure, fecund complexity of the social and historical. A postdigital perspective on software and its cultures thus brings them into the human, social condition. In place of the call for everyone to 'become digital', the postdigital task is to place the computational within the continuity of history, immanent to the social. A critique of representation, or cybertyping, is critical to the success of this task (Galloway 2012: 137).

In Punchdrunk's systems, actors and stagehands engage immanently with their audiences and we might ask that digital agencies do the same, but not from behind Wizard of Oz curtains, but immanently. In the academic report from Punchdrunk's collaboration with MIT in 2012, the authors suggest that 'digital performance needs digital performers' (Dixon, Rogers and Eggleston 2012: 7). Such digital agents could, based on this study of Punchdrunk, 'perform' in narrowly designed, highly specialised functional and narrative roles. In *Resisting Reduction: A Manifesto* (2018), Joichi Ito, former Director of MIT Media Lab, debunks the idea of Singularity as a transcendent religion. 'Singularitarians' seek to invoke a godhead in the same mould as that of existing monotheistic religions: a disembodied über-controller, destined to dominion over its subjects, and promising if not immortality, at least 'amortality':

at some level, all Singularitarians believe that with enough power and control, the world is 'tamable.' Not all who believe in Singularity worship it as a positive transcendence bringing immortality and abundance, but they do believe that a judgment day is coming when all curves go vertical. (Ito 2018)

We are, at this junction in time, at a point where the field of software engineering appears to not be able to design alternative solutions, as they would require unthinking its own founding myths. In *Unthought: The Power of the Cognitive Nonconscious*, Hayles reflects on the idea of cognitive assemblages and the infrastructural, technological 'subconscious' as analogues of the human nonconscious; heuristic schema that operate within, or rather behind human consciousness (Hayles 2017: 11). In cognitive assemblages with technology, human nonconsciousness meshes with the structuring influence of the 'nonconscious' of technology:

> Cognitive assemblages are inherently political. Comprised of human-technical interfaces, multiple levels of interpretation with associated choices, and diverse kinds of information flows, they are infused with social-technological-cultural-economic practices that instantiate and negotiate between different kinds of powers, stakeholders, and modes of cognition. (Hayles 2017: 178)

The act of unthinking is frustrating and without an end point but nevertheless an essential and radical interrogation of the problem at its root: representation. Applying existing critiques of representation in art, theatre and literature to digital technologies requires translation or transposition for application to the 'grammatical' level of interactive systems.

We might query the modelling of human participation as agents, and propose that they are represented as agency, the 'raw material' of participation within interactive systems. Thinking beyond the 'so-called-Man' that is contingent on the rationality principle, we might consider if our models need to be 'human', or if our representation within digital systems would be more true to form if we were modelled as the dynamic fluids discussed by Punchdrunk performers:

> They're like water or something, and we have to design this aqueduct [...] it's like you're civil engineers, putting up structures [...] to direct that flow, or to block it, or to do whatever. But the property of the water is a constant: water behaves in a certain way, you know, for whatever reason. You start to realise that people, individuals, and a body of people an audience, do have certain predictable characteristics in terms of the way they flow around the place, or the way they respond.[10]

Modelling of mass audiences must, if we are to heed Cull's call for a postidentitarian philosophy of difference for performance and participation (2012: 17), resist fixity and afford dynamic form in order to be functional and empowering. We might instead think and describe audiences in terms like volatility, viscosity, force and pressure, expansion and flow. The social identities of masked Punchdrunk audiences are unimportant to the designed interactions: what *does* matter for the purpose of design is what they do and how they do it.

This observation is even more critical for mass audiences. A functional understanding of large groups of people for live experience design cannot be formed by multiplying representations of individuals – the properties of a mass of audiences is not a larger amount of the properties of an individual but a different 'material'. It follows that projections based on aggregated reductive representations of individuals can only yield a base representation of crowd behaviours. Reflecting Deleuze's argument of the particular and the general, individuals cannot be faithfully represented based on crowd data – so-called big data will always present a reductive and ultimately stultifying image of individuals. The current paradigm of representation thus fails in both dimensions. Another paradigm could be formed on the basis not of individuals or crowds, but of the dynamism and changeability of human agency in relation to designed environments. A postdigital sublime aesthetic could leverage the failure of Grosz's man-ness of Man through articulating the possibility of falling, or failing, into the other – stepping out of the human frame to look at other ways of modelling what and not who, but *how* we are in motion and interaction.

Harnessing the un-modern

For a functional empirical relationship with audiences, we need to unthink identity in the transcendent mould. The surveillance afforded by pervasion of networked technologies is widely researched and a genuine concern, but even the corporations that own the platforms that generate and own the information gathered don't appear to have an entirely functional vision of what to do with the data, beyond selling it to advertisers of ideas and goods. They are struggling, and largely failing, to monitor and control the sheer volume of activity on their own platforms, and the promise of a 'god-mind' AI that will intervene with a higher rationality is at once unlikely and luridly evangelist, redolent of the twin ideas of apocalypse and the second coming.

Arguably, the digital modern and the transcendent image of thought that shaped much of its narrative from the latter half of the twentieth century reached its autumn years in the second decade of the twenty-first, in no small way due to the fallacies of its foundation myth. As digital systems are scaled up, their rigidity becomes apparent in relation to the complexity of the physical world. Connectivity and exposure work both ways, and as networked technologies mesh with the social and physical realities of the unbound world, the nature of play must change. To the technological evangelist and the digital refugee this is a challenge and perhaps anathema, but entropy and difference will persist. All articles of faith must eventually yield to the fertile impurity of life. Underscoring the dependency of innovation on stability, Grosz says: 'It is this relative stability and orderliness, predictability, that is the very foundation or condition for a life of invention and novelty, a life in which pure repetition is never possible' (2011: 30). Thinking technology through clean lines and Platonic logic, we may mistake it for a promise of control, stability and order. In a reverse, or even perverse *détournement*, the comparative rigidity of representation and the lack of nuance at the infrastructure level of interactive systems seem to engender a desire for transgression and disruption. In real-life, physical interactive systems like those created by Punchdrunk, where the consequences of dysfunctional interaction cannot be outsourced, we find more accommodating terms of engagement. Punchdrunk's large masked performances are crucibles of sorts, not just for personally transformational experience, but ways of thinking and working with human agency in interactive systems where physical consequences are immanent.

The creep of the transcendent requires vigilance in live events, just as they do when working with remote audiences – otherwise both ethics and aesthetics suffer. Good design builds on good quality information and acute sensitivity to your materials. Punchdrunk members take part in performances as actors or Black Masks, or as masked audience members, to see how and where the experience can be improved, but they do so within the immediate reach of consequences, and on shared terms with their audiences. The company cultivates this sensitivity to the vulnerability and trust that is inherent to immersion as an active state, and the grounding precariousness of immanence. It guides rehearsals and devising and infuses the 'micro-culture' of the company. In place of a stag party before the wedding of one of the senior members of the company, they designed a unique experience for him that played out over three months:[11]

> It would be midnight, or it would be at five o'clock in the morning or it would be at his lunch break; someone would pop up, or something would happen to him, and so by the end he was a bit of a broken man, because. … His whole world was that show. He didn't know what was happening. And … yeah, he had no handle on what the rules were, because there were no rules, and it was all happening on the same. …
>
> I think he got quite emotional when it was all over.[12]

While performed in good faith and a spirit of generosity, this custom production was not delineated in time and place and was thus a more extreme version of what Punchdrunk offer their wider audiences; durational, unpredictable, and unlimited by the physical bounds of the scenography. In a hierarchy where the transcendent hierarchy is unchallenged, seniority might have ensured a privileged position; distant to the event, and less exposed to consequence. In a culture that celebrates immanence, the privileged position, as in this example, might instead be one of extreme proximity to and within the event, and with more, not less, exposure. Apart from celebrating a momentous life event for a colleague with a generous display of ingenuity, creativity and determination, such custom performances are grounding reminders of the encounter and the vertigo of exposure: a reconfigured memento mori.

Punchdrunk's work invites the un-modern imagination with dramatic themes that tend towards the dark and typically revolve around passion, madness, jealousy, abuse of power and superstitions. Their aesthetic and reputation invite the imagination that any transgression is possible. While the company's interactions with their audiences are carefully designed and considered, the reverse is not always the case; audiences occasionally transgress.[13] Their scenography, supported by performers and Black Masks, is designed to accommodate and negotiate the un-modern, with much *metis* to offer designers of digital experiences and systems. Conditions of possibility that don't depend on personalisation and the ever-tighter definitions that supports it can, as shown in Punchdrunk's work, be created through putting the quality of experience over efficiency, and layering detail and response capacity to invite and negotiate immanent encounters. In a bounded and mutual encounter, the invitation does not necessarily require that we know who the audience is; with sufficient immanent response capacity, it is of greater interest who or what they might become.

The experience potential that comes from a destabilised subject position is demonstrated by the pioneering VR work produced by The Mill; notably *6 x 9* (2016), which was created in collaboration with Guardian VR and presented at Tribeca film festival to critical acclaim. *6 x 9* integrates the individual aspect of the designed experience and motivates the audience to project themselves not only visually but also psychologically, into the virtual space, and elides the 'novelty trap'. It was designed for mobile-based VR for seated audiences and built in Unity. The sound was modelled to map to the visual space, and included a soundscape composed from first-hand accounts from former prisoners who had spent time in isolation. Much effort was dedicated to getting textures right in the modelled space, from the concrete walls of the VR 'isolation cell' to the projection of quotations from the interviews with prisoners who had been isolated and other visual motifs onto these virtual walls. Rather than opting for free-floating text, the decision to render it as projections allowed for the written narrative to mesh with the virtual space. The demands for authenticity meant that all narratives were developed from first-hand accounts, and all visual references were carefully researched, including the titles and covers of books and magazines piled up in the cell. Critically, *6 x 9* avoids sensational effects, with visual features such as blood on the floor (which was described in the voice recordings) being deliberately understated. It uses time carefully and leaves the participant to wait in the cell at times, limited to contemplating their surroundings. This underscores the suspension of social interaction and the self you believe yourself to be in isolation. Psychotic episodes, taken from real-life accounts by prisoners, were given form through shifting points of view. On one occasion, the spoken narrative retells an out-of-body experience and the camera view follows, creating disassociation between the embodied feedback from the actual berth created for the display and modelled in the virtual simulation, and the minds' eye hovering underneath the ceiling of the cell.[14]

The VR team at The Mill developed these methodologies further with *Paraiso Secreto,* which was created for a corporate client (Corona) in Mexico City in 2017. Ideas generation began in March, and the experience was delivered in August of the same year. The VR team at The Mill in London worked in tandem with Cocolab who created the physical scenography in Mexico City, and together on-site for a month of quality assurance before launch. *Paraiso Secreto* blended location-based, room-scale VR, built in Unreal, for a mobile audience of approximately 400 people per night. The full theatrical experience was realised in an old colonial mansion that was turned into an elaborate party venue. The physical scenography for the VR experience gave embodied feedback, and as audiences created their own movement there were no problems with nausea. As in *6 x 9*, the designers at The Mill were keen to avoid awkward in-world controls and instead devised a small motion-sensitive, AI-driven hummingbird to guide attention as needed through the VR experience. The hummingbird motif was repeated in the décor and scenography of the mansion and marked small gold coins that were used for entry into the VR part of the experience via a doorway hidden in a large standing fridge. Once inside, audiences were 'on-boarded', or equipped with backpacks connected to HTC Vive VR HMDs so they could move around inside the physical set. The physical scenography was divided into two physical areas through which the VR experience looped twice, resulting in four zones, each with a different habitat: jungle, vista, cave and beach. The four VR vistas were superimposed on the same structures in the two physical areas, with the route carefully guided by the hummingbird to ensure audiences received matching physical feedback. The audience flow was a key part of the design and required guidance by stewards who, like

Punchdrunk's Black Masks, remain unnoticed as far as possible by walking closely behind, but not touching the participant wearing the HMD, unless it became necessary. The VR experience was reinforced by sensory feedback from rocks, plants, underfoot materials such as sand and water, and motion triggered infrared lights and fans that mimicked the sensation of sunlight and winds. To ameliorate drift, the physical scenography was designed to accommodate a two- to three-centimetre discrepancy with the VR world. In the penultimate vista, the cave, the Vive controller was visualised as a hand-held torch, and voice-activated crystals glowed as audiences spoke or sang. Existing the final vista, the beach, audiences had their equipment removed by the stewards walking behind them as they stepped into a 'decompression zone' with intense red light, mirroring the sunset scene in the VR world.[15]

Minimalistic, 'lo-fi immersive' digital artefacts at the other end of experience design can also close the 'space between spectator and performance' (Aronson 2018: 216) by drawing the audience in through framing and intent (Aronson 2018: 203), thought through the sublime. The un-modern can be harnessed by drawing on the superstitions and metamorphic dreamings that haunt the distributed imagination of network infrastructure. An example of how such hauntings can inform both the narrative and the distribution of an artwork is the born-digital *9MOTHER9HORSE9EYES9*, which emerged unannounced in 2016 as an unfolding dystopian story across the comments sections of a number of seemingly disparate Reddit communities. The literary style resembles H. P. Lovecraft and draws on science fiction, 'creepypastas' and online conspiracy horror stories. The full story is captured in *The Interface Series* (Reddit 2016), a wiki that was quickly developed to enable followers to gain an overall understanding, and which documents all the entries to piece together the narrative of *9M9H9E9*. While not physically immersive, the intense interest and perseverance with which new followers took the documentation and interpretation of the phenomenon on board marks *9M9H9E9* as a particularly economic blended reality application, relevant to the immersive aesthetic. The author, _9MOTHER9HORSE9EYES9, uses the term 'Flesh Interface' to describe embodied gnosis, or the 'opening of someone's mind after an experience that allowed their consciousness to transcend their physical body' (Motherboard 2016), suggestive of the monstrous-posthumanist literary genre (Clarke 2008). In a self-post in their subreddit, the author performs a *fas* ritual of sort when they defined the 'theatre of actions' (Certeau 1988: 125) for the storyworld of *9MOTHER9HORSE9EYES9*, putting the existing social order under question:

> I should clarify that this information is not fiction. Nor is it true. It is a mix of things which happened and things which almost happened. Things which

were and things which could have been. You must understand that the present moment in which we exist is simply a nexus from which trillions of possible pasts and possible futures branch out. The important thing to realise is that these unreal pasts and unrealised futures are related to each other. By examining what might have been, we can come to understand what might come to be. (Reddit 2016)

Here, the purposeful diffusion of fact and fiction invokes the sublime by way of the vertiginous, even monstrous, potential for extension brought to the interaction by the imagination of its participants, who are co-opted in the creation of experiential space. They took up the challenge quickly; the first post was made on 18 April 2016, and the wiki was set up within a week. *9M9H9E9* is an example of how a narrow focus on the detail of interaction and working effectively with and within the conditions of possibility engendered by digital infrastructures can leverage metaphor to destabilise place in favour of space and co-opt participants to take up the art-work of extending the storyworld.

Punchdrunk are inspired by perspectives for experience from computer games (McMullan 2014; Judge 2019) and their shows already share the affordance for composing your own version of their performances with open-world computer games. Barrett is open to exploring a 'meritocratic approach' through 'playable shows' in order to articulate questions that were, arguably, already suggested in *The Drowned Man* (Judge 2019). The company's work retains important differences with the typical structure and design processes of computer games and other digital platforms, particularly the emphasis on careful design research grounded in embodied experience. In recent years, they have developed work in a territory occupied by companies like Blast Theory, Rimini Protokoll and Invisible Flock, exploring game theory in and across city spaces, and situated R&D in Fallow Cross, a full-size indoors village housed in an industrial estate in Tottenham Hale, north London, where the company is based. Fallow Cross was run 2017–19 as a site for research and collaborations with creative practitioners, industry partners and the local community to produce innovative R&D projects and a workshop programme for artists and educators. There, they produced work for smaller audiences to expand their trademark approach to theatre with blended and digital technology, for example, *Kabeiroi* (2017), a live performance based on R&D work developed at Fallow Cross that played out in central London over four to six hours for audiences of two at a time. Combining many of the dramatic devices used in large Punchdrunk shows, distributed across central London, the British Museum and Fallow Cross, *Kabeiroi* was a scenographic experiment with sound design, one-to-one interactions in public spaces, site-specific installations and endurance performance that culminated in a set-piece finale at Fallow Cross.

Punchdrunk Enrichment develops work for diverse audiences, including children and the elderly. Under the direction of Pete Higgin, they create productions that typically appear and disappear suddenly in schools and other institutions. Examples of Punchdrunk Enrichment's work include the productions *Under the Eiderdown* (from 2009) and *The Lost Lending Library* (from 2013) for schools, *The House that Winter Built* (2012) that was first created for Discover Children's Story Centre in Stratford and *Against Captain's Orders* (2015) that was produced in association with the National Maritime Museum. The village of Fallow Cross was the physical story world in the blended reality production *The Oracles* (2017), another Punchdrunk Enrichment project that was created in collaboration with Google's Creative Lab. *The Oracles* engaged local primary school children over a period of several weeks in a story world via a tablet game that told the story of a village that was under a spell. Later, their teachers guided the children to the physical village of Fallow Cross, which they entered through the village school, which existed in both the digital and the physical storyworld. The game-world village was modelled on the physical village of Fallow Cross, and the children were transported between the two via the school building. Once inside, they were met by actors who guided them through to the reveal, a window through which the children could suddenly see the whole game-world, made real with a change in the lighting.

The Oracles integrates large scale physical world-building with game technology and blended realities; a formula that Punchdrunk began working with in *Goldwell* (2012), which was an early blended reality R&D project over three weeks in collaboration with Rose Bruford College. In *Goldwell*, which was inspired by the story of Bluebeard's Castle, participants entered the storyworld through a simple game for smartphones with multiple levels. They crossed over into the physical storyworld as they progressed through the game via actors and experiences embedded within the college and its grounds. Those who persevered with the game were given clues to find characters that seemingly worked at the college, and as the play unfolded, they proceeded towards the finale in the college grounds.[16] *Goldwell* was an early example of game-world initiation in preparation for the encounter with the physical storyworld, and shares the points gathering formula within a game script around searching and persevering with later productions that are introduced by phone or tablet games, for example, *Silverpoint* (2015) and *The Oracles* (2017). While the virtual and physical scenographies of *The Oracles* mirrored each other, *Silverpoint* combined the structure of *Goldwell* with the use of city spaces that was later developed with *Kabeiroi* (2017), bridging the two approaches.

From theatre craft to blended and cross-reality experience design, Punchdrunk's work reflects the opportunities and the tensions of scenography in the two first decades of the twenty-first century. They work methodically across physical and blended storyworlds with a unique and functional vision of what immersive experience is, and what it might become, for diverse audiences and technologies. Beginning in 2019, their R&D activities in Tottenham Hale are focused on exploring new approaches in the Audience of the Future programme, supported by AHRC. In tandem they are developing Punchdrunk International, a company created to oversee international productions with local collaborators to ensure the integrity of Punchdrunk's aesthetic vision. The relationship between Punchdrunk Enrichment and Punchdrunk International is designed to ensure that the ongoing evolution of their work remains grounded in a coherent vision, based on practice. Their role in the UKRI Audience of the Future programme will further Punchdrunk's development in the direction of experience design as distinct from pure theatre, but also challenge the coherence of their artistic legacy and vision. Collaboration with other organisations to develop new ways of thinking and designing for audiences positions the company as world-leading innovators beyond the realm of theatre as the influence of their methodologies for embodied dramaturgical and scenographic experience are expanded to other platforms and experiences. Premiering in May 2020, *The Third Day* is a collaboration between Punchdrunk and Felix Barratt, Dennis Kelly, Plan B (Brad Pitt's production company), Sky and HBO to create the world's first immersive drama series spanning live action, web and TV. Starring Jude Law and Naomi Harris, the cross-platform drama *The Third Day* takes the company's work out of designed shadows, bringing their approach to questions of representation to wider audiences. As explored in this book, how participation is conceptualised is critical to conditions of possibility and Punchdrunk's way of thinking their audiences will now span networked screens and live events.

Notes

1. The Audience of the Future programme is a major funding and acceleration initiative by UK Research and Innovation (UKRI) to bring creative practitioners, researchers and technology experts together with a focus on creating innovative immersive experiences for entertainment, arts, sports and the third sector and position the United Kingdom as a world leader in immersive media.
2. See Chapter 1 for a discussion and analysis of *The Séance*.
3. COM4; see Chapter 3 for a closer discussion of *Silverpoint*.
4. See Chapter 1 for the analysis and an outline of the methods in the Appendix.
5. See Chapters 3–5.

6 With the exception of particular scenes, for example, the banquet and finale in *Sleep No More*, the finale in *The Drowned Man,* and specific moments that receive additional focus through lighting, the overarching scenography incorporates auditorium and stage, with shared lighting conditions.
7 AUD1, AUD2, AUD4, AUD5.
8 AUD1.
9 AUD1.
10 COM3.
11 This intimate, durational performance format has been explored since 2001 by Odyssey Works (2019).
12 COM4.
13 COM3.
14 Technical and contextual information from a conversation with Adam Grint at The Mill 15 March 2019.
15 Technical and contextual information from a conversation with Adam Grint at The Mill 15 March 2019.
16 COM4.

Appendix

Analysis of interview data

This ethnography of the experience of making and participating in Punchdrunk productions was carried out as a participant study, with field observations and extensive interviews with company members and audiences. These were recorded and transcribed, fully anonymised and analysed in NVivo according to two distinct approaches to modelling the data. The first analysis, which is discussed in Chapter 3, was performed within a framework based on de Certeau's theory of space and place. The second analysis was informed by Deleuze and critical posthumanist theory with a focus on perceptions and processes in relation to the experience as described by participants and is discussed in Chapters 4 and 5.

In the first analysis, de Certeau's theory of space and place was used to investigate the relationship between extended agency and its regulation within the company, and the embodied practices that mediated spatial operations between the two. This included descriptions by company members and audiences in relation to their experience of licence and control. An additional category of descriptions concerned *metis* or tactical intervention and adaptation in the service of the narrative, that is, situated emergent negotiation. References to the experience and extension of space and licence were assigned to the category of 'space', and descriptions of order, mapping and scheduling, either as practices or experiences, were assigned to the category 'place'. Descriptions of how transitions were managed were coded to 'narrative regulation – spatial operations', and adaptive responses to changing circumstances were coded to 'changing tactics' (Table A.1).

The prevalence of each in interviews with audience versus company members was calculated from queries of the data set using NVivo, compared in relation to the total to arrive at a ratio. As can be seen in Table A.2, the spatial tactics of audience members only converged weakly. Only the third level of analysis showed convergence.

The first two levels of audience references to spatial tactics were scattered across all four categories, with the third level of analysis yielding a convergence of Narrative Regulation – Spatial Operations, suggesting awareness of the ongoing, moment-by-moment negotiation of social contract/s in response to

Table A.1 Categories (nodes) for discourse analysis using de Certeau's theory of space and place

Node	Type of reference
Space	Interview references describing practices that extend licence and/or experience potential, and the experience thereof.
Place	References to practices that schedule, order or map the performance space, time and in-system behaviours of participating audience members.
Narrative Regulation – Spatial Operations	References to practices that regulate or manage transitions between the extension of licence within the interactive environment and order or alignment with the design.
Changing Tactics	Descriptions of adaptive responses to changing circumstances.

Table A.2 The prevalence of audience references coded to nodes Changing Tactics (CT), Space (Sp), Place (Pl) and Narrative Regulation – Spatial Operations (NR-SO)

Interview	Dominant node	Secondary node	Tertiary node
AUD6	CT	NR-SO	NR-SO
AUD1	CT	Pl	NR-SO
AUD2	Sp	CT	Pl/NR-SO
AUD4	Pl	Sp	NR-SO
AUD5	NR-SO	Sp	CT
AUD3	Pl/NR-SO	Pl/NR-SO	Sp
Audience totals	-	-	NR-SO (4:6)

Dominant and secondary nodes were spread across all categories, indicating that none of the spatial approaches dominated clearly in audience interviews. Only the tertiary node revealed a convergence of references mapping to NR-SO.

the performance environment, actors and Black Masks (Table A.2). In contrast, the references to spatial tactics made by company members showed a strong and consistent convergence pattern, with Narrative Regulations – Spatial Operations again dominating, but now at the top level, and with a more defined convergence (Table A.3).

The second analysis focused on textural and experiential descriptions of experience and actions, 'descriptors' and 'actions', respectively. The most common thousand words at least three characters long were listed, common

Table A.3 The prevalence of company member references coded to nodes Changing Tactics (CT), Space (Sp), Place (Pl) and Narrative Regulation – Spatial Operations (NR-SO)

Interview	Dominant node	Secondary node	Tertiary node
COM3	NR-SO	Pl	Sp
COM5	Pl	NR-SO	CT
COM2	NR-SO	Sp	Pl
COM4	NR-SO	Sp	Pl
COM6	NR-SO	Sp/Pl	Sp/Pl
COM1	NR-SO	Sp	Pl
Company totals	NR-SO (5:6)	Sp (4:6)	Pl (4:6)

Spatial approaches mapping to NR-SO has a clear predominance in the interviews where company members describe their work, with five out of six company members referring most commonly to spatial operations that regulate the interactive narrative, and to practices that serve to manage transitions between extensive/emergent behaviours and experiences. The second most common type of reference, used by four out of six interviewees, indicated practices associated with facilitating extension of audience agency and emergent behaviours. The third most common reference (four of six) fell under the ordering/scheduling/mapping category. CT was the least predominant approach.

figures of speech, for example, 'fine' and 'right', were removed from the descriptor sample, as were descriptors specific to features of the performance, for example, 'black' referring to Black Masks rather than participant responses to low lighting, or 'bloody' referring to paint or stage blood. The same process was applied to verbs and actions, with verbs used in generic additions to other verbs such as 'do', 'be', 'take', 'make', 'keep', 'come' and generic activities such as 'stand' or 'sit' removed. Descriptors and actions were then grouped according to their meaning in context. The predominance of each was calculated as the percentage of the total number of descriptors included in the sample. This yielded sets of experience and action categories describing embodied meaning-making by company members and audience participants within the story world or interactive system. Finally, the two sets (experience descriptors and actions) were mapped against each other in order of prevalence.

The largest category of descriptors concerned sensory deprivation and disorientation, and included a relatively broad range of words, for example, 'crazy', 'mad', 'bizarre', 'curious', 'weird', 'strange', 'cryptic', 'tricky', 'confused', 'baffling', 'unknown', 'lost', 'deprived', 'random', 'accidental' and 'chaotic'. Alternative descriptors based on the same words were also included, for example, 'weirdness'. Interviews revealed a rich and varied range of words describing bewilderment and confusion, which, as an aside, suggests that this may be an important field of human experience, that we do not assign sufficient attention to, particularly for interaction design. This group comprised 11.8 per cent of the total number of descriptors in the sample. Other descriptor groups with a strong presence in the interview data were 'love', 'enjoy' and similar, at 10.0 per cent, 'different', 'original' etc. at 7.6 per cent, 'interesting' at 6.4 per cent, and 'impressive', 'magnificent' etc. at 6.4 per cent (Table A.4). The largest group of action descriptors, comprising 18.3 per cent of the sample, were those associated with 'figuring out' and grasping ideas or phenomena, for example, 'understand', 'know', 'realise', 'learn', 'figure', 'discover', 'notice', 'find' and related forms (Table A.5). These came from interviews with people who all enjoyed the experience to a considerable degree, suggesting that active 'figuring out' in response to confounding circumstances, that is, a form of embodied problem-solving, was framed in a very positive light. The second

Table A.4

Descriptor/s of experience	Prevalence (%)
Bizarre, curious, strange, cryptic, confusing, chaotic, lost, deprived, random, etc.	11.8
Love, enjoy, [it was] good, nice, appreciate	10.0
Different, new, original	7.6
Interesting	6.4
Impressive, awesome, incredible, magnificent, unique, extraordinary, etc.	5.7
Big, huge, massive, large	5.3
Open, accessible, allowed, free	4.7
Real, authentic	2.9
Hard, difficult, uncomfortable	2.8
Direct, straight, linear	2.6
Powerful, intense, bold, strong, passion	2.4
Interactive	2.3
Immersive, full, experiential	2.2
[In a] dream, dreaming, dreamlike	1.8
Live, alive	1.7

The prevalence of the fifteen most common descriptor subsets listed above is described as the percentage of the total number of descriptors that were used to qualify the experiences of participants, extracted from a sample of the most frequently used thousand words (at least three letters long) in participant interviews that were undertaken in the course of this research.

Table A.5

Action words	Prevalence (%)
Understand, know, realise, learn, figure [out], discover, notice, catch, find, hold	18.3
Think, believe, suppose, guess	13.5
Go, walk, move, leave, wander, head, follow, lead, run, charge	12.0
See, look, gaze, focus, view, watch	8.8
Talk, say, tell, speak, describe, explain, articulate, mean	7.2
Feel, sense, experience	5.9
Work, try, engage, challenge, fight	5.9
Want, need, wish, hope, expect	5.6
Act, dance, pretend, play, game [as activity]	3.6
Create, recreate, build, form, devise, design, develop, craft	2.2
Choreograph, arrange, train, control, manipulate	1.5
Change, adapt, shift	1.0
Decide, choose, pick	0.9
Question, ask, doubt	0.8
Contact, approach, meet	0.7

The prevalence of the fifteen most common action word subsets listed above is described as the percentage of the total number of words signifying the actions of participants, extracted from a sample of the most frequently used thousand words (at least three letters long) in participant interviews that were undertaken in the course of this research.

largest group of action descriptors was closely associated with the first, and included more speculative and prospecting types of cognition, for example, 'think', 'believe', 'suppose' and 'guess'. These comprised 13.5 per cent of the total sample, and if the two largest groups of action descriptors (describing figuring out/grasping cognitive activities and more prospecting ones) were combined, they would comprise 31.8 per cent of the sample. As the first analysis was performed against the background of de Certeau's theory, I chose to keep the open-ended and prospective cognitive action descriptors separate from the 'figuring out'/grasping ones, as they can be regarded to be associated with space and place, respectively. Further action descriptor categories, as detailed below (Table A.5) described cognitive and embodied processes that broadly retain the characteristics of spatial operations, with attention to their specific texture.

Social media data

The social media fandom discourse was gathered and analysed manually. The language used in the posts is rich in metaphors, which made manual analysis the most productive method. The fandom community for *The Drowned Man* on Facebook ran the 'Spoiler' group during and after the end of the performance run. Due to the very large number of posts, I selected the sample from posts made between July 2014 and May 2015, from the final period of the production run until the group was closed for further contributions, and the community moved over to a broader interest group called *Punchdrunk Lovers*.

The sample was based on direct references to *The Drowned Man* and *Sleep No More*, including references to symbols, storylines, or memories from these productions as well as games and other forms of artwork developed on the basis of such content, or to the meta-narrative of Punchdrunk as a company. Based on these criteria, the size of the sample I selected from the period was $n = 1,196$. The objective was to seek a measure of topics and a top-level engagement metric for these topics that distinguished between approval and participation. I recorded the number of comments the posts in the sample received but not the content of those comments (although I made notes when the comment thread was of particular interest).

Discourse analysis of the Facebook 'Spoiler' posts revealed a pseudo-religious register within which the majority of fan activities and reflections fell. Within this, five nodes were identified for coding; references to ritualistic practices relating to the communal, references to sacrifice either in the form of symbolic blood rites or offerings in homage to the object of worship, references to omens in the form of the storyworld pervading on the real world, references to ephemerality and loss inspiring obsessive or worshipful behaviour, and references to the collection or acquisition of 'relics' (items from the production in question) (Table A.6). Some posts contained references to more than one of the categories listed below, which is why the total percentage exceeds 100 per cent. Community-building activities of a patterned nature, including assistance extended to other fans wanting to participate in the activities around which the community was formed, fell under the category

Table A.6 Breakdown of references to pseudo-religious practices in the Facebook 'Spoiler' fan community for *The Drowned Man*

Ritual	Sacrifice	Omen	Ephemerality	Relics
31.6%	23.2%	10.6%	21.8%	21.8%

The given percentage number shows the proportion of posts of the sample with references to the categories listed.

'Ritual', while offerings of personal time and effort, as well as fan activities related to blood and body modification, were coded to the category 'Sacrifice'. The 'Omen' category concerns posts referring to perceived incursions of the story world on real life in the form of signs and omens, as well as descriptions of dreams and premonitions. Wistful and nostalgic expressions of longing and loss, often associated with fragrance memories, were coded to the 'Ephemerality' category, and references to articles bought or otherwise obtained from the production, as well as the building of personal 'altars' were coded to the 'Relics' category.

Additional research data, including anonymised interview transcripts and social media data, is available at BORDaR (https://bordar.bournemouth.ac.uk).

References

Aherne, J. (1995) *Michel de Certeau: Interpretation and Its Other*. Stanford, CA: Stanford University Press.

Alston, A. (2013) 'Audience Participation and Neoliberal Value: Risk, Agency and Responsibility in Immersive Theatre'. *Performance Research*. Vol. 18, No. 2, pp. 128–38.

Alston, A. (2016) *Beyond Immersive Theatre: Aesthetics, Politics and Productive Participation*. Houndsmills, Basingstoke, Hampshire: Palgrave Macmillan.

Andersen, U. and Pold, S. B. (2018) *The Metainterface*. Cambridge, MA: MIT Press.

Anderson, L. (2018) 'Chalkroom'. *LaurieAnderson*. Available at: http://www.laurieanderson.com/?portfolio=chalkroom (Accessed 27 January 2019).

Apollinaire, G. (1918) 'L'Esprit nouveau et les Poetes'. *Mercure de France*. No. 491, 1 December, Tome CXXX, pp. 385–96.

Apperley, T. (2015) 'Glitch Sorting: Minecraft, Curation and the Postdigital'. In: D. Berry and M. Dieter (eds.) *Postdigital Aesthetics: Art, Computation and Design*. Houndsmills, Basingstoke, Hampshire: Palgrave Macmillan, pp. 232–44.

Aronson, A. (2018) *The History and Theory of Environmental Scenography*. London: Bloomsbury Methuen Drama.

Artaud, A. (1958) *The Theatre and Its Double*. New York: Grove Press.

Artaud, A. (1976) *Antonin Artaud, Selected Writings*. 1st ed. New York: Farrar, Straus and Giroux.

Axner, J. (2012) 'What Is Nordic LARP?' *NordicLARP*. Available at: https://nordiclarp.org/what-is-nordic-larp/ (Accessed 4 February 2019).

Bachelard, G. (1994) *The Poetics of Space*. Boston: Beacon Press.

Bailes, S. J. (2011) *Performance Theatre and the Poetics of Failure: Forced Entertainment, Goat Island, Elevator Repair Service*. London: Routledge.

Baird, S. (2008) 'Red Death Lates'. *Time Out*. Available at: http://www.timeout.com (Accessed 17 October 2013).

Bakhtin, M. M. (1984) *Rabelais and His World*. Bloomington: Indiana University Press.

Bamford, K. (2012) *Lyotard and the 'Figural' in Performance, Art and Writing*. London: Bloomsbury.

Banes, S. (1993) *Greenwich Village 1963*. 1st ed. Durham, NC: Duke University Press.

Bassett, C. (2007) *The Arc and the Machine: Narrative and New Media*. Manchester: Manchester University Press.

Belcen, A. (2015) 'AnOther Luminary: Sophie Taeuber-Arp'. *AnOther*. Available at: http://www.anothermag.com/fashion-beauty/7828/another-luminary-sophie-taeuber-arp. (Accessed 3 February 2019).

Benyon, D., Innocent, P. and Murray, D. (2014) 'System Adaptivity and the Modelling of Stereotypes'. In: H.-J. Bullinger and B. Schackel (eds.) *Proceedings of the Second IFIP Conference on Human-Computer Interaction*. University of Stuttgart, Germany. Elsevier, pp. 245–53.

Berry, D. (2014a) 'The Postdigital'. *Stunlaw*. Available at: http://stunlaw.blogspot.co.uk/2014/01/the-postdigital.html (Accessed 26 April 2014).

Berry, D. (2014b) 'Digital/postdigital'. *Stunlaw*. Available at: http://stunlaw.blogspot.co.uk/2014/02/digitalpostdigital.html (Accessed 26 April 2014).

Bignall, S., Bowden, S. and Patton, P. (2014) *Deleuze and Pragmatism*. New York: Routledge.

Billington, M. (2013) 'The Drowned Man: A Hollywood Fable – Review'. *The Guardian*, 17 July. Available at: https://www.theguardian.com/stage/2013/jul/17/drowned-man-hollywood-fable-review (Accessed 16 September 2016).

Bishop, C. (2006) *Participation*. 1st ed. London: Whitechapel Gallery Ventures.

Bishop, C. (2012) *Artificial Hells: Participatory Art and the Politics of Spectatorship*. 1st ed. London: Verso Books.

Blast Theory (2015) 'Blast Theory'. *Blast Theory*. Available at: http://www.blasttheory.co.uk (Accessed 22 August 2015).

Blau, H. (1992) *To All Appearances: Ideology and Performance*. New York: Routledge.

Bleeker, M. (2008) *Visuality in the Theatre*. London: Palgrave Macmillan.

Bogost, I. (2007) *Persuasive Games*. Cambridge, MA: MIT Press.

Bogost, I. (2012) 'Persuasive Games: Process Intensity and Social Experimentation'. *Gamasutra*. Available at: http://www.gamasutra.com/view/feature/170806/persuasive_games_process_.php (Accessed 10 January 2016).

Bogost, I. (2015) 'Video Games Are Better Without Characters'. *The Atlantic*, March. Available at: https://www.theatlantic.com/technology/archive/2015/03/video-games-are-better-without-characters/387556/ (Accessed 17 February 2016).

Boltanski, L. and Chiapello, E. (2005) *The New Spirit of Capitalism*. London: Verso.

Bonta, M. and Protevi, J. (2004) *Deleuze and Geophilosophy: A Guide and Glossary*. Edinburgh: Edinburgh University Press.

Bourdieu, P. (1984) *Distinction: A Social Critique of the Judgement of Taste*. London: Routledge.

Bowness, A. (1972) *Modern European Art*. 1st ed. New York: Harcourt, Brace, Jovanovich.

Bradshaw, P. (2019) 'The Great Hack Review – Searing Exposé of the Cambridge Analytica Scandal'. *The Guardian*, 23 July. Available at: https://www.theguardian.com/film/2019/jul/23/the-great-hack-review-cambridge-analytica-facebook-carole-cadwalladr-arron-banks (Accessed 31 July 2019).

Brandon, R. (1999) *Surreal Lives: The Surrealists 1917–1945*. New York: Grove Press.

Braidotti, R. (2013) *The Posthuman*. London: Polity.

Braidotti, R. (2016) 'Posthuman Critical Theory'. In: D. Banerji and M. R. Paranjape (eds.) *Critical Posthumanism and Plantetary Futures*. Berlin: Springer, pp. 13–32.

Cadwalladr, C. (2017) 'Robert Mercer: The Big Data Billionaire Waging War on Mainstream Media'. *The Guardian*, 26 February. Available at: https://www.

theguardian.com/politics/2017/feb/26/robert-mercer-breitbart-war-on-media-steve-bannon-donald-trump-nigel-farage (Accessed 14 April 2017).

Caillois, R. (1961) *Man, Play, and Games*. 1st ed. New York: Free Press of Glencoe.

Certeau, M. de (1988) *The Practice of Everyday Life*. Berkeley: University of California Press.

Chiesa, L. (2009) 'A Theatre of Subtractive Extinction: Bene without Deleuze'. In: L. Cull (ed.) *Deleuze and Performance*. Edinburgh: Edinburgh University Press.

Chow, R. (2012) *Entanglements, or Transmedial Thinking about Capture*. Durham, NC: Duke University Press.

Chun, W. (2011) *Programmed Visions*. Cambridge, MA: MIT Press.

Clarke, B. (2008) *Posthuman Metamorphosis: Narrative and Systems*. New York: Fordham University Press.

Couldry, N. (2012) *Media, Society, World*. Cambridge: Polity.

Cull, L. (2009) 'Introduction'. In: L. Cull (ed.) *Deleuze and Performance*. Edinburgh: Edinburgh University Press.

Cull, L. (2012) *Theatres of Immanence*. Houndsmills, Basingstoke, Hampshire: Palgrave Macmillan.

Davies, C. (2012) 'Char Davies: Immerscence'. *Immersence*. Available at: www.immersence.com/osmose/ (Accessed 29 August 2015).

Deleuze, G. (1970) *Spinoza*. Paris: Presses univeritaires de France.

Deleuze, G. (1979) 'One Manifesto Less'. In: C. V. Boundas (ed.) *The Deleuze Reader*, translated by A. Orenstein. New York: Columbia University Press, pp. 204–22.

Deleuze, G. (2014) *Difference and Repetition*. London: Bloomsbury.

Deleuze, G. and Guattari, F. (2004) *A Thousand Plateaus*. London: Continuum.

Derrida, J. (2001) 'Structure, Sign and Play in the Discourse of the Human Sciences'. In: J. Derrida (ed.) *Writing and Difference*. 2nd ed. London: Routledge, pp. 351–70.

Dixon, D., Rogers, J. and Eggleston, P. (2012) 'Between Worlds: Report for NESTA on MIT/Punchdrunk Theatre Sleep No More Digital R&D Project'. *Arts Council*. Available at: http://artsdigitalrnd.org.uk/features/overview-of-the-rd-pilot-projects/ (Accessed 25 May 2016).

Dolan, J. (2005) *Utopia in Performance: Finding Hope at the Theatre*. Ann Arbor: University of Michigan Press.

Dow, S., Mehta, M., Harmon, E., MacIntyre, B. and Mateas, M. (2007) 'Presence and Engagement in an Interactive Drama'. In: *Proceedings of the SIGCHI Conference on Human Factors in Computing Systems*. San Jose, 30 April–3 May 2007. ACM, pp. 1475–84.

Doyle, M. (2006) 'Maxine Doyle in Discussion with Josephine Machon'. *Maxine Doyle*. Available at: http://maxinedoyle.com (Accessed 3 February 2019).

Drew, D. (2013) 'The Borough'. *Exeunt Magazine*. Available at: http://exeuntmagazine.com/features/the-borough/ (Accessed 21 October 2013).

Dubbelboer, M. (2012) *The Subversive Poetics of Alfred Jarry*. 1st ed. London: Legenda.

Eyre, H. (2011) 'How Punchdrunk Theatre Troupe Is Taking over the World'. *Evening Standard*. Available at: http://www.standard.co.uk (Accessed 17 October 2013).

Favret, M. A. (2009) *War at a Distance: Romanticism and the Making of Modern Wartime*. Princeton, New Jersey: Princeton University Press.

Fazi, B. (2018) *Contingent Computation: Abstraction, Experience, and Indeterminacy in Computational Aesthetics*. London: Rowman & Littlefield.

Fischer-Lichte, E. (2008) *The Transformative Power of Performance: A New Aesthetics*. London: Routledge.

Forced Entertainment (2015) 'Forced Entertainment'. *Forced Entertainment*. Available at: http://www.forcedentertainment.com (Accessed 22 August 2015).

Fuller, M. and Goffey, A. (2009) Towards an Evil Media Studies. In: J. Parikka & T. D. Sampson (eds.) *The Spam Book: On Viruses, Porn, and Other Anomalies from the Dark Side of Digital Culture*. Cresskill, NJ: Hampton Press, pp. 141–59.

Galloway, A. (2004) *Protocol: How Control Exists after Decentralization*. Cambridge, MA: MIT Press.

Galloway, A. (2012) *The Interface Effect*. Cambridge: Polity.

Gardner, L. (2013) 'Does Punchdrunk's the Drowned Man Live Up to the Hype?' *The Guardian*, 19 July. Available at: https://www.theguardian.com/stage/theatreblog/2013/jul/19/punchrunk-hype-drowned-man-lyn-gardner (Accessed 16 September 2016).

Gjefsen, R. (2012) *Det Nye Regiteatret: I ljos av samspelet mellom norsk og tysk tradisjon*. Masters thesis. University of Bergen, Norway. Available at: https://docplayer.me/12194000-Masteroppgave-i-teatervitskap-det-nye-regiteatret-i-ljos-av-samspelet-mellom-norsk-og-tysk-tradisjon.html (Accessed 16 January 2016).

Goldberg, R. (2011) *Performance Art*. 1st ed. London: Thames & Hudson.

Goulish, M. and Cull, L. (2009) 'Sub Specie Durationis'. In: L. Cull (ed.) *Deleuze and Performance*. Edinburgh: Edinburgh University Press.

Grosz, E. (2011) *Becoming Undone: Darwinian Reflections on Life, Politics, and Art*. Durham and London: Duke University Press.

Gumble, D. (2019) '"A World Led by Sound": Saatchi Gallery Multimedia Show Boosted by d&b Soundscape'. *PSN Europe*. Available at: https://www.psneurope.com/installation/a-world-led-by-sound-saatchi-gallery-multimedia-show-boosted-by-db-soundscape. (Accessed 2 September 2019).

Harvie, J. (2013) *Fair Play – Art, Performance and Neoliberalism*. Houndsmills, Basingstoke, Hampshire: Palgrave McMillan.

Hayles, K. (2002) 'Flesh and Metal: Reconfiguring the Mindbody in Virtual Environments'. *Configurations*. Vol. 2, No. 2, pp. 297–320.

Hayles, K. (2017) *Unthought: The Power of the Cognitive Nonconscious*. Chicago, IL: University of Chicago Press.

Hess-Luttich, E., Muller, J. and Zoest, A. (1998) *Signs and Space*. 1st ed. Tubingen: Narr.

Hicks, M. (2017) *Programmed Inequality: How Britain Discarded Women Technologists and Lost Its Edge in Computing*. Cambridge, MA: MIT Press.

Hoggard, L. (2013) 'Felix Barrett: The Visionary Who Reinvented Theatre'. *The Guardian*, 14 July. Available at: http://www.theguardian.com/theobserver/2013/jul/14/felix-barrett-punchdrunk-theatre-stage (Accessed 17 October 2013).

Holmqvist, K. and Pluciennik, J. (2002) 'A Short Guide to the Theory of the Sublime'. *Style*. Vol. 36, No. 4, pp. 718–37.

Huizinga, J. (1955) *Homo Ludens: A Study of the Play Element in Culture*. Boston, MA: Beacon Press.

Ito, J. (2018) 'Resisting Reduction: A Manifesto'. *MIT Press Journal of Design and Science*. No. 3.

Jakob-Hoff, T. (2014) 'Interview with the Dust Wizard'. *A Gold Bug Variation*. Available at: http://classicgoldbug.Tumblr.com/post/85123828608/interview-with-the-dust-wizard (Accessed 30 December 2015).

Jamieson, L. (2007) *Antonin Artaud: From Theory to Practice*. London: Greenwich Exchange.

Judge, A. (2019) '"Playable Shows Are the Future": What Punchdrunk Theatre Learned from Games'. *The Guardian*, 8 February. Available at: https://www.theguardian.com/games/2019/feb/08/playable-shows-are-the-future-what-punchdrunk-theatre-learned-from-video-games (Accessed 13 March 2019).

Kant, T. (2020) *Making It Personal: Algorithmic Personalization, Identity and Everyday Life*. Oxford: Oxford University Press.

Kaufman, S. (2011) '"Sleep No More": A "Macbeth" Full of Sound and Fury – and Fear'. *Washington Post*, 18 April. Available at: https://www.washingtonpost.com/entertainment/theater-dance/sleep-no-more-a-macbeth-full-of-sound-and-fury--and-fear/2011/04/18/AFGndVPE_story.html (Accessed 16 September 2016).

Kittler, F. (1999) *Gramophone, Film, Typewriter*. Stanford, CA: Stanford University Press.

Klich, R. and Sheer, E. (2012) *Multimedia Performance*. Houndsmills, Basingstoke, Hampshire: Palgrave Macmillan.

Klossowski, P. (2017) *Living Currency*. London: Bloomsbury.

Knowlson, J. (1996) *Damned to Fame: The Life of Samuel Beckett*. London: Bloomsbury.

Kobsa, A. (2001) 'Generic User Modeling Systems'. *User Modeling and User-Adapted Interaction*. Vol. 11, No. 1, pp. 49–63.

Latour, B. (1993) *We Have Never Been Modern*. Cambridge, MA: Harvard University Press.

Lawton, A. (ed.) (1998) *Russian Futurism Through its Manifestoes, 1912–1928*. Ithaka and London: Cornell University Press.

Lehmann, H.-T. (2006) *Postdramatic Theatre*. Abingdon: Routledge.

Libeskind, D. (2011) *Jewish Museum: Berlin*. Madrid: Ediciones Poligrafa.

Lovinck, G. (2016) *Social Media Abyss*. Cambridge: Polity.

Lütticken, S. (2017) 'The Powers of the False'. *Texte Zur Kunst*. No. 105, pp. 72–92.

Lyotard, J.-F. (1984) *The Postmodern Condition: A Report on Knowledge*. Minneapolis: University of Minnesota Press.

Lyotard, J.-F. (1991) *The Inhuman: Reflections on Time*. Cambridge: Polity.

Machon, J. (2013) *Immersive Theatres: Intimacy and Immediacy in Contemporary Performance*. Houndsmills, Basingstoke, Hampshire: Palgrave Macmillan.

Machon, J. (2019) *Punchdrunk: The Encyclopaedia*. London: Routledge.

Mackay, R. and Avanessian, A. (2014) *#Accelerate#*. Falmouth: Urbanomic.

McKinney, J. and Palmer, S. (eds.) (2017) *Scenography Expanded: An Introduction to Performance Design*. London: Bloomsbury Methuen Drama.

McMullan, T. (2014) 'The Immersed Audience: How Theatre Is Taking Its Cue from Video Games'. *The Guardian*, 20 May. Available at: http://www.theguardian.com/technology/2014/may/20/how-theatre-is-taking-its-cue-from-video-games (Accessed 26 October 2014).

Meyrowitz, J. (1985) *No Sense of Place*. New York: Oxford University Press.
Montola, M., Stenros, J. and Waern, A. (2009) *Pervasive Games: Theory and Design*. Burlington, MA: Morgan Kaufmann.
Motherboard (2016) '"_9MOTHER9HORSE9EYES9" Is Reddit's New, Terrifying Mystery'. *Motherboard*. Available at: http://motherboard.vice.com/read/9mother9horse9eyes9-is-reddits-new-terrifying-mystery (Accessed 8 May 2016).
Mueller, R. (1994) *Valie Export: Fragments of the Imagination*. Bloomington: Indiana University Press.
Nietzsche, F. (1993) *The Birth of Tragedy Out of the Spirit of Music*. 1st ed. London: Penguin.
Odyssey Works (2019) 'Odyssey Works'. Available at: http://www.odysseyworks.org/ (Accessed 2 September 2019).
O'Grady, A. (2017) 'Risky Aesthetics, Critical Vulnerabilities, and Edgeplay: Tactical Performances of the Unknown'. In: A. O'Grady (ed.) *Risk, Participation and Performance Practice: Critical Vulnerabilities in a Precarious World*. Cham, Switzerland: Palgrave Macmillan.
O'Grady, K. A. (2013) 'Exploring Radical Openness: A Porous Model for Relational Festival Performance'. *Studies in Theatre and Performance*. Vol. 33, No. 2, pp. 133–51.
Pain, B. (1901) *Stories in the Dark*. Paris: Olympia Press.
Palmer, S. (2017) 'Harnessing Shadows: A Historical Perspective on the Role of Darkness in the Theatre'. In: A. Alston and M. Welton (eds.) *Theatre in the Dark: Shadow, Gloom and Blackout*. London: Bloomsbury Methuen Drama.
Parikka, J. (2011) 'Operative Media Archaeology: Wolfgang Ernst's Materialist Media Diagrammatics'. *Theory, Culture & Society*. Vol. 28, No. 5, pp. 52–74.
Parikka, J. (2012a) *What Is Media Archaeology?* Cambridge: Polity.
Parikka, J. (2012b) 'New Materialism as Media Theory: Medianatures and Dirty Matter'. *Communication and Critical/Cultural Studies*. Vol. 9, No. 1, March, pp. 95–100.
Phelan, P. (1996) *Unmarked: The Politics of Performance*. 1st ed. London: Routledge.
Posada Trobo, I., Díaz, V. G., Espada, J. P., Crespo, R. G. and Moreno-Ger, P. (2019) 'Rapid Modeling of Human-Defined AI Behavior Patterns in Games'. *Journal of Ambient Intelligence and Humanized Computing*. Vol. 10, pp. 2683–92.
Rancière, J. (2004) 'The Sublime from Lyotard to Schiller: Two Readings of Kant and Their Political Significance'. *Radical Philosophy*. No. 126, July/August, pp. 2–15.
Rancière, J. (2009) *The Emancipated Spectator*. London: Verso.
Reddit.com (2016) 'Index – 9M9H9E9'. *Reddit*. Available at: https://www.reddit.com/r/9M9H9E9/wiki/index (Accessed 8 May 2016).
Roose-Evans, J. (1996) *Experimental Theatre: From Stanislavsky to Peter Brook*. 1st ed. London: Routledge.
Sauvagnargues, A. (2013) *Deleuze and Art*. London: Bloomsbury.
Schechner, R. (1993) *The Future of Ritual*. London: Routledge.
Schechner, R. (2013) *Performance Studies: An Introduction*. 3rd ed. New York: Routledge.
Shaw, J. et al. (2000) 'Staged Mixed Reality Performance "Desert Rain" by Blast Theory'. CID-181, eRENA ESPRIT Project 25379 Report. Stockholm: KTH.

Silverstone, R. (1999) *Why Study the Media?* London: Sage.
Sloan, C. (2018) 'Understanding Spaces of Potentiality in Applied Theatre'. *Research in Drama Education: The Journal of Applied Theatre and Performance.* Vol. 23, No. 4, pp. 582–97.
Smithies, J. (2017) *The Digital Humanities and the Digital Modern.* Houndsmills, Basingstoke, Hampshire: Palgrave Macmillan.
Sterne, J. (2006) 'Communication as Techne'. In: G. J. Shepherd, Jeffrey J. St. John and T. Striphas (eds.), *Communication as ...: Perspectives on Theory.* Thousand Oaks, CA: Sage, pp. 2–6.
Sutton-Smith, B. (2001) *The Ambiguity of Play.* Cambridge, MA: Harvard University Press.
Templeton, F. and Nelson, S. (1990) 'You – The City' vs. 'Nelson – The Critic'. *TDR.* No. 2, pp. 12–17.
The Great Hack (2019) [Documentary] Directed by K. Amer and J. Noujaim. Netflix.
The NSA Files (2018) 'The NSA Files'. *The Guardian.* Available at: https://www.theguardian.com/us-news/the-nsa-files/all (Accessed 31 August 2019).
Tomlin, L. (2014) *British Theatre Companies 1995–2014.* London: Bloomsbury.
Trimingham, M. (2010) *The Theatre of the Bauhaus: The Modern and Postmodern Stage of Oskar Schlemmer.* London: Routledge.
TripAdvisor (2015a) 'Sleep No More'. *Trip Advisor.* Available at: http://www.tripadvisor.co.uk/Attraction_Review-g60763-d2631104-Reviews-Sleep_No_More-New:York_City_New:York.html (Accessed 4 April 2015).
TripAdvisor (2015b) 'The Drowned Man: A Hollywood Fable'. *Trip Advisor.* Available at: http://www.tripadvisor.co.uk/Attraction_Review-g186338-d4579588-Reviews-The_Drowned_Man_A_Hollywood_Fable-London_England.html#REVIEWS (Accessed 4 April 2015).
Turner, L. (2011) 'Metamodernist // Manifesto'. *Metamodernism.* Available at: http://www.metamodernism.org/ (Accessed 28 December 2015).
Turner, L. (2015) 'Everything You Always Wanted to Know about Metamodernism'. *Berfrois.* Available at: http://www.berfrois.com/2015/01/everything-always-wanted-know-metamodernism/ (Accessed 28 December 2015).
Turner, V. (2017) *The Ritual Process: Structure and Anti-structure.* London: Routledge.
Vermeulen, T. and van den Akker, R. (2015) 'Utopia, Sort Of: A Case Study in Metamodernism'. *Studia Neophilologica.* Vol. 87, pp. 55–67.
Wardrip-Fruin, N. and Montfort, N. (2009) *The New Media Reader.* Cambridge, MA: MIT Press.
Willett, J. (1979) *Theatre of Erwin Piscator: Half a Century of Politics in the Theatre.* 1st ed. London: Bloomsbury.
Wolf, G. and Mahaffey, N. (2016) 'Designing Difference: Co-Production of Spaces of Potentiality'. *Urban Planning.* Vol. 1, No. 1, pp. 59–67.
Worthen, W. B. (2012) 'The Written Troubles of the Brain: Sleep No More and the Space of Character'. *Theatre Journal.* Vol. 64, pp. 79–97.
Wrights & Sites (2019) 'Wrights & Sites'. Available at: mis-guide.com (Accessed 4 February 2019).
Zima, P. V. (2010) *Modern/Postmodern: Society, Philosophy, Literature.* London: Bloomsbury.

Index

1789   58
6 x 9   175
9MOTHER9HORSE9EYES9   177–8

absurdism   49, 53, 57, 61
accelerationism   7, 171
acting   3, 15, 41, 51, 54, 56, 65, 74, 79, 81, 83, 85, 98, 106, 108, 111, 115, 130, 132, 142, 151
aesthetics of failure   168
Against Captain's Orders   179
agency   2, 6, 11, 22, 25, 35, 37, 39, 45, 47, 57, 59, 63, 70, 73, 75, 81, 85, 88, 91, 98, 100, 116, 119, 122, 124, 127, 129, 133, 135, 138, 141, 144, 151, 153, 156, 159, 169, 180, 183, 185
Agency of Coney   47
algorithm   92, 119, 121
ambiguity   11, 15, 37, 40, 86, 115, 122, 126, 130, 149, 152, 155
Anderson, Laurie   167
Apollinaire, Guillaume   49
Apollonian   56
Artaud, Antoine   2, 13, 28, 43, 47, 53, 57, 87, 156, 159, 166
artificial hells   47, 53, 85, 119
artificial intelligence (AI)   153, 173
Art Informel   57, 61
augmented reality (AR)   1, 20, 26, 66, 74, 141, 166

Bachelard, Gaston   93, 103
Bakhtin, Mikhail   91, 139, 146, 155
Barrett, Felix   18, 38, 51, 67, 74, 83, 126, 147, 162, 178
Bauhaus   47, 56
becoming-other   116, 127
Beyond the Road   78
big data   10, 35, 147, 173
Bishop, Claire   2, 14, 46, 52, 57, 59, 64, 86, 119, 121, 137, 148, 156

Black Masks   41, 80, 85, 88, 92, 114, 127, 129, 134, 138, 152, 156, 168, 174, 177, 184
Blast Theory   47, 49, 51, 65, 148, 168, 178
blended reality (XR)   1, 3, 47, 57, 62, 68, 90, 137, 163, 177, 179
Bloody Thirsty   61
Boal, Augusto   59, 65
Borough, The   77
boundary/bounded   1, 4, 6, 14, 16, 22, 25, 28, 35, 40, 51, 60, 64, 73, 79, 82, 85, 87, 104, 111, 114, 116, 122, 124, 130, 133, 145, 148, 153, 155, 167, 169, 175
Braidotti, Rosi   29, 98, 106, 116, 127, 129, 136, 150, 157, 162
Brecht, Bertolt   2, 55, 148, 155
Breton, André   53, 124

Caillois, Roger   74, 86, 146, 155
capture   2, 6, 11, 14, 65, 73, 75, 98, 149, 154, 177
carnival/carnivalesque   18, 35, 51, 91, 93, 131, 144, 146, 155
Cartesian   38, 45, 57, 130, 157, 165
Certeau, Michel de   3, 8, 24, 35, 38, 41, 60, 74, 82, 86, 91, 93, 120, 124, 133, 138, 144, 152, 155, 159, 163, 166, 177, 183, 187
Chair   69
Chalkroom, The   167
Chinese Room   23, 166, 170
choreography   17, 31, 52, 61, 64, 69, 79, 81, 88, 94, 98, 104, 106, 112, 117, 132
Chow, Rey   2, 14, 47, 60, 64, 73, 88, 92, 94, 101, 120, 149, 155
chronos   87, 91
Cogito   38
communitas   27, 131, 151
complicity   1, 11, 22, 46, 57, 59, 75, 88, 90, 120, 124, 131, 148, 168

INDEX

composition 22, 26, 30, 54, 65, 88, 108, 116, 131, 151, 170
coup 38, 153
Craig, Edward Gordon 74
cross-platform 159, 180
Cull, Laura 7, 45, 61, 98, 110, 125, 130, 141, 144, 156, 173

Dada, Dadaism 46, 48, 51, 55, 62, 74, 171
dance 16, 51, 56, 61, 67, 79, 108
data harvesting 92, 129, 135, 147, 150, 153, 161
data modelling 120, 129, 135, 147, 150, 153, 161, 173, 183, 186
Davies, Char 23, 64, 167
Dear Esther 166, 170
Deleuze, Gilles 2, 13, 22, 28, 39, 45, 60, 65, 74, 88, 98, 100, 108, 120, 124, 130, 133, 136, 143, 147, 149, 151, 163, 170, 173, 183
delinquency 8, 24, 41, 130, 134, 138, 145, 151, 157, 159, 163
demassification 137, 157, 162, 165, 170
dérive 61
Derrida, Jacques 45, 53, 62, 74, 82, 86, 94, 149, 155, 162, 165, 170
Desert Rain 65, 167
détournement 174
difference (concept) 2, 13, 28, 32, 37, 40, 45, 62, 65, 70, 79, 100, 109, 130, 133, 143, 146, 149, 163, 173
Dionysian 56
discourse analysis 184, 188
disorientation 16, 22, 38, 60, 74, 81, 89, 94, 119, 121, 124, 137, 142, 149, 157, 168, 185
dissensus, scenes of 143, 148, 151, 154, 156, 160
Dobbie, Stephen 78, 151
Doyle, Maxine 14, 51, 69, 106
Drowned Man, The 8, 16, 19, 28, 31, 33, 48, 70, 74, 84, 87, 97, 99, 101, 104, 108, 114, 116, 120, 125, 129, 132, 168, 178, 188
Duchess of Malfi, The 69, 75

effectiveness (vis-à-vis efficiency) 138, 151, 178
efficiency (vis-à-vis effectiveness) 24, 41, 62, 134, 138, 143, 150, 157, 159, 162, 166, 168, 175
Elevator Repair Company 168

embodiment 1, 15, 22, 37, 45, 91, 109, 136, 144, 162
emergence 5, 10, 13, 15, 21, 28, 35, 38, 40, 45, 56, 60, 62, 79, 81, 85, 91, 94, 109, 115, 117, 119, 129, 131, 135, 138, 142, 145, 151, 156, 159, 165, 170, 183, 185
encounter 3, 11, 13, 16, 19, 60, 65, 75, 81, 85, 88, 105, 123, 125, 127, 131, 147, 155, 170, 175, 179
English National Orchestra (ENO) 69, 75
Ephémère 64
Epic Theatre 55, 57, 60
Everybody's Gone to the Rapture 23, 166, 170
expanded cinema 58
EXPORT, Valie 58

Façade 66, 88
Fallow Cross 178
fandom 19, 23, 28, 31, 34, 63, 70, 97, 123, 188
fas (ritual) 83, 153, 177
Faust 55, 69, 75, 114, 138
Firebird Ball, The 69, 75
Fluxus 61
Forced Entertainment 61, 68, 168
framing 1, 5, 10, 13, 18, 21, 31, 53, 74, 81, 85, 89, 92, 98, 105, 114, 117, 119, 122, 125, 128, 130, 137, 141, 144, 146, 153, 157, 159, 166, 169, 173, 177
freeplay 11, 45, 82, 86, 162
Futurism 46, 50, 171

Galloway, Alexander 8, 35, 39, 44, 47, 74, 135, 143, 148, 151, 153, 155, 158, 170
Gallow Green 52, 77, 104
games 18, 27, 29, 33, 44, 53, 61, 63, 69, 74, 82, 88, 90, 112, 125, 141, 148, 153, 166, 170, 178, 187
gaze 5, 13, 22, 27, 37, 40, 45, 58, 85, 87, 111, 129, 134, 141, 146, 150, 156
Gesamtkunstwerk 47, 54, 64, 74, 79
Goldwell 90, 163, 179
gravity 2, 15, 21, 23, 36, 39, 50, 91, 125, 131, 159, 168
Grosz, Elisabeth 1, 7, 13, 23, 165, 174

INDEX

happenings 47, 56, 62, 79
Hayles, Katherine 82, 103, 122, 144, 149, 162, 172
Higgin, Peter 14, 67, 75, 179
Hofesh Shechter Company 75, 90
Homo Ludens 155
House of Oedipus, The 69, 75
House Where Winter Lives, The 19, 102
Huizinga, Johan 74, 86, 155

immanence 1, 4, 8, 10, 11, 23, 26, 29, 32, 35, 38, 44, 47, 62, 65, 87, 90, 98, 110, 114, 120, 122, 130, 133, 138, 143, 147, 152, 154, 157, 163, 166, 170, 174
infrastructure 3, 6, 10, 33, 34, 44, 65, 74, 79, 86, 94, 137, 141, 145, 149, 151, 154, 162, 171, 178
Interface Series, The 177
It Felt Like a Kiss 75

Jarry, Alfred 49, 51, 57
Johnny Formidable 69

Kabakov, Ilya 64
Kabeiroi 29, 73, 178
kairos 87, 91, 131
Kant, Immanuel 4, 22, 87, 154, 168
Kaprow, Allan 56, 79
Karen 66
Kittler, Friedrich 36, 156, 159
Klossowski, Pierre 3, 46, 65, 150, 165

Laterna Magika 58
Lazaretto 78
lighting, theatre 7, 17, 54, 56, 64, 67, 74, 80, 88, 97, 101, 112, 115, 124, 127, 129, 131, 139, 156, 169, 179, 185
liminality 27, 30, 86
Living Currency 3, 65, 165
Lost Lending Library, The 179
ludus 86, 155
Lyotard, Jean-François 4, 22, 29, 40, 87, 89, 116, 138, 149, 151, 154, 157, 166, 169

machine learning 35
A Machine to See With 66
McKittrick Hotel 77, 104
Marinetti, Filippo Tommaso 50
masks 5, 6, 18, 26, 29, 59, 88, 109, 113, 116, 125, 130, 144, 146, 167

Masque of the Red Death 69, 84
metainterface 44, 142, 162
metamodernism 32
metamorphosis 94, 144, 177
metaphor 11, 15, 37, 45, 60, 65, 67, 92, 94, 101, 152, 162, 171, 178
metaphorai 145, 152, 159
metis 7, 11, 39, 152, 175, 183
A Midsummer Night's Dream 69
The Mill 175
Minns, Beatrice 83, 97
mise-en-abîme 3
Mixed Reality Lab 65, 167
Mnouchkine, Ariane 57, 60
modernism 32, 46
Moon Slave, The 68, 75, 77

National Theatre 69, 75
New Games movement 61
Nietzsche, Friedrich 56
Nightingale, Colin 14, 69, 78, 113

one-to-one (performance) 15, 17, 20, 31, 48, 60, 68, 77, 79, 81, 89, 104, 111, 113, 126, 157, 178
Ontroerend Goed 49, 148
Operation Black Antler 66
Oracles, The 166, 170, 179
Orlando Furioso 59
Osmose 23, 64, 167
ou-topia 137, 143

paidia 86, 91, 155
Parade 48, 50
Paraiso Secreto 176
personalisation 39, 135, 153, 163, 165, 175
Phelan, Peggy 6, 38, 61, 135, 144, 150, 156, 170
Ping Pong 58
Piscator, Erwin 47, 55, 60
place (vis-à-vis space) 3, 35, 41, 74, 82, 84, 86, 93, 103, 111, 120, 131, 143, 148, 154, 155, 158, 163, 166, 171, 178, 183, 187
play space 67, 87, 146, 159
play theory 157
postdigital 2, 11, 25, 40, 148, 150, 154, 158, 162, 169, 173
post-dramatic theatre 150
posthumanism 3, 98, 103, 122, 129, 144, 162, 177, 183

postmodernism   22, 32, 40, 47, 61, 64, 168
proscenium   13, 54, 57, 75, 93, 168
prosumption   15
Punchdrunk Enrichment   179

Rancière, Jacques   2, 4, 10, 22, 143, 150, 160, 166, 169
Red Death Lates   69
Reinhardt, Max   47, 54
repetition (concept)   2, 13, 23, 28, 45, 49, 65, 70, 80, 100, 109, 133, 147, 149, 163, 174
rhetoric, procedural   148, 151, 153
rhizomatic   136
Rider Spoke   66
ritual   18, 27, 32, 47, 60, 83, 86, 126, 151, 153, 177, 189
Ronconi, Luca   57, 59

Schechner, Richard   27, 57, 146, 151
Schlemmer, Oskar   43, 56
Séance, The   19, 25, 31, 38, 86, 90, 163
Secret Cinema   58
self-abduction   63, 73, 88, 101, 105, 125
self-exploitation   14, 46, 61, 119, 148, 156
Silverpoint   90, 163, 166, 179
Situationist International   47, 57, 60, 62, 68
Sleep No More   8, 16, 19, 25, 29, 33, 48, 51, 70, 76, 79, 103, 108, 121, 126, 163, 188
social turn, the   47, 60
sound (design)   24, 50, 53, 64, 68, 74, 77, 86, 90, 129, 175, 178
space (vis-à-vis place)   3, 11, 35, 38, 41, 61, 64, 82, 84, 86, 100, 103, 110, 120, 124, 143, 148, 151, 163, 169, 171, 178, 183, 187
spect-actors   59, 158
storytelling   25, 37, 74, 137, 147, 149, 152, 159
subject position   2, 13, 18, 21, 27, 37, 41, 43, 52, 55, 57, 61, 67, 75, 87, 89, 120, 122, 124, 131, 137, 141, 144, 147, 162, 166, 170, 175
sublime, the   4, 11, 18, 22, 28, 33, 40, 48, 59, 64, 87, 93, 105, 114, 119, 130, 138, 142, 148, 154, 157, 166, 168, 173, 177

superfans   31, 97, 164
Surrealism   44, 48, 53, 56, 62, 74, 124, 136, 171
Sutton-Smith, Brian   86, 146, 155
Svoboda, Josef   58, 67
Symbolism   44, 46, 48, 51, 53, 74

Tempest, The   69
Temple Pictures   17, 33, 77, 80, 104, 108, 168
Theatre du Soleil   58
theatre machine   3, 7, 10, 14, 18, 24, 38, 46, 55, 60, 79, 83, 85, 88, 91, 100, 106, 112, 119, 129, 139, 145, 162
theatre of actions   39, 83, 177
Theatre of Cruelty   2, 23, 43, 45, 54, 56, 67, 149
Theatre of the Absurd   56, 62
Theatre of the Oppressed   59, 158
Third Day, The   180
Touch Cinema   58
transcendent   2, 4, 11, 27, 29, 32, 35, 38, 44, 56, 60, 62, 87, 98, 110, 120, 134, 143, 147, 156, 159, 163, 166, 169, 172
Tunnel 228   70

Ubu Roi   49
uncertainty   14, 23, 60, 73, 85, 88, 91, 101, 120, 125, 131, 148
Under the Eiderdown   179
Unmarked   6, 38, 135, 144, 150, 156, 170
user modelling   153
utopia   60, 137, 143, 171

Vaughan, Livi   83, 97
Verfremdungseffekt   2, 55, 67, 131
vertigo   4, 11, 22, 40, 59, 63, 65, 73, 82, 88, 114, 116, 123, 127, 130, 149, 154, 156, 169, 175
virtual reality (VR)   1, 3, 64, 137, 164, 167, 175

white masks   88, 109, 126, 129
Wilson, Robert   43, 56, 67
Woyzeck   17, 68, 75, 80, 126

XX   59

Yellow Wallpaper, The   69

www.ingramcontent.com/pod-product-compliance
Ingram Content Group UK Ltd.
Pitfield, Milton Keynes, MK11 3LW, UK
UKHW021908220326
469204UK00008B/255